# THE METHOD OF HENRY JAMES

# The Method of
# HENRY JAMES

*By Joseph Warren Beach*

PHILADELPHIA
ALBERT SAIFER: PUBLISHER
1954

# CONTENTS

PAGE

# THE METHOD OF HENRY JAMES

# ACKNOWLEDGEMENTS

Acknowledgement is made to the following authors and publishers for permission to quote brief passages from the works named: Quentin Anderson, editor, Introduction to "Henry James: Selected Short Stories," Rinehart and Co. Inc., New York, c.1950; Van Wyck Brooks, "The Pilgrimage of Henry James," Dutton, New York, 1925; Anna Robeson Burr, editor, Introduction to "Alice James: her Journal, her Brothers," Dodd, Mead and Co., New York, 1935; Henry Seidel Canby, "Turn West, Turn East: Mark Twain and Henry James," Houghton, Mifflin and Co., Boston, 1951; Leon Edel, editor, Introductory essay to "The Complete Plays of Henry James," J. B. Lippincott Co., Philadelphia and New York, 1951; Francis Fergusson, "Drama in *The Golden Bowl*," in *Hound and Horn*, April-May, 1934; C. Hartley Grattan, "The Three James, a Family of Minds," Longmans, Green and Co., London and New York, 1952; F. R. Leavis, "The Great Tradition: George Eliot, Henry James, Joseph Conrad," George W. Stewart, New York, 1948; Ezra Pound, essay on Henry James in "Instigations," Boni and Liveright, New York, c.1920; Edwin Marion Snell, "The Modern Fables of Henry James," Harvard University Press, Cambridge, Mass., 1935; Stephen Spender, "The Destructive Element," Jonathan Cape, London, 1935 (Albert Saifer: Publisher, Philadelphia, 1953); Rebecca West, "Henry James," Henry Holt and Co., New York, 1916; Edmund Wilson, "The Triple Thinkers: Ten Essays on Literature," Harcourt Brace and Co., New York, c.1938 (revised, Oxford University Press, New York).

## INTRODUCTION: 1954

This volume is a reissue of "The Method of Henry James" published by the Yale University Press in 1918, two years after the death of James. The text is identical with that of the original book with the correction of a few misprints. It has been out of print since the time of the Second World War. Whether it is of sufficient interest to call for a reprint is something others will be able to judge better than the author. But there has been a steady small demand for the book since it was not to be had, and many people of good judgment have assured me that it has, in the flood of James literature, its own distinctive merits which make it desirable that it should be made accessible to scholars and serious readers of fiction. And it has the historical interest of being for James "fans" a pioneer work in the field.

It was suggested by the publishers that, considering the large amount of important material, critical and biographical, that has appeared in print since its first publication, what I should offer is a *revision* of the original work. But that I do not see my way to doing. Any serious revision would involve me in a book quite different in scope, in which my account of James's story-telling technique would be fortified and *nourri* (as James might say) by consideration of a thousand matters of biographical and psychological interest which have come to light since 1918, and in which advantage might be taken of the insights of several dozen distinguished critics and a review made of the controversies that have raged since the book was published. This would be a very long and arduous task, as any one knows who is at all acquainted with the literature. It would require a largeness of leisure that I do not have at my command. And it might involve the loss of such elements of form and order, of strict and relevant organization, as the original work possesses.

I have decided, accordingly, to use this medium of an Introduction to make a brief review of the James literature since 1918, to argue a few points with critics with whom I do not agree, and to develop other points where my own opinions have altered or taken larger dimensions during twenty-five years of reading. I am also supplying a 1954 Supplement to the bibliographical note, and a few Supplementary Notes to particular passages (at the end of the book) where later information or maturer thought calls for some addition to, or qualification of, the statement in the text.

It should be noted that "The Method of Henry James" is rather strictly limited to the subject of James's story-telling techniques, and that mainly in his longer narratives. There was no attempt to present the man Henry James, to place him in his background of family, habitat and period. And as for the other major topics of interest—his subject-matter, his philosophy of life, even his style—these are all rigorously subordinated to the one subject, his methods as a novelist.

I would not have it thought for a moment that, in any form of literature, it is the author's techniques that in themselves most appeal to me and make me wish to spend my days and nights turning his pages. In poetry it was perhaps Tennyson that first seized on my imagination and rang in my ears, at a time when I had not the remotest notion of what it is, in craftsmanship, that gives a poet his importance. It was "A Dream of Fair Women," "The Lady of Shalott," it was "Mariana of the Moated Grange" that bespelled me and made the landscape and atmosphere of Tennyson's Lincolnshire as much my native country as the daisy-and-buttercup fields of Fulton County, New York, or the flowing March gutters of our own Main Street. In fiction it was, I think, the droll characters of Dickens that made me first aware of what a novel is. It was Mr. Micawber, Mr. Pecksniff, Mr. Alfred Jingle, it was Sammy Weller and Betsy Trotwood and Sairey Gamp. In a later time, when I had become a grave university scholar, and after I had come out from my graduate immersion in Chaucer and Dante, the romances and the ballads, in Werner's Law and Middle English final e's, and had begun to look round me upon the modern scene, it was George Meredith who occupied my days and nights, and that, quite simply, because he was the writer of all times who seemed to offer me the most guidance and inspiration in forming a philosophy of life. His fiction and poetry were about on a par in interest and promise; but if the poetry gave me Nature herself and the religious philosophy of a Darwinian and a positivist, it was the novels that gave me a picture of men and women living, or not living, according to Nature, meeting their ordeals of snobbery and sentimentalism, and working through, if they were fortunate, to a good way of life. The one aspect of style or "technique" that most attached me to Meredith—and here it was Chaucer and Rabelais and Molière who had prepared me to appreciate him—was the comic spirit that showed him the way in his story-telling and enabled him to distinguish between the true and the false in motive and sentiment.

So far as I can remember, James first "swum into my ken," first positively captured my imagination, during the course of the year 1903, when the successive installments of "The Ambassadors" were appearing in the North American Review. Once a month, after I had finished reading Freshmen themes, I used to mount the steps and pass through the pillared portico of the Old Library— a Greek temple on the banks of the Mississippi—and lose myself for an hour in the glamorous underseas world of Lambert Strether's Paris. I had myself made the briefest of visits to the Ville Lumière and saw no reason to question the rightness of his rendering of its atmosphere. I had lived all my life in something equivalent to Woollett, Mass. I had no difficulty, in spite of my age, in identifying myself with Strether, or for that matter, in spite of everything, with Chad. I knew people who could very well serve as models for Mrs. Newsome and Jim Pocock. Above all, I had among my friends women who could be figured as Maria Gostrey and Mme. de Vionnet, with only a little help from Henry James. It was a glamorous underseas world all the same, and when I emerged from swimming under water and holding my breath, and found myself in the full brightness of University Avenue, the enchantment of the underseas remained with me for the following week. It was a strange world, but it was also more right than that of every day in the sun, better ordered, making more sense and a more refined and coherent music. It was then that the James virus definitely entered into my blood, and I was never after to be free from it.

But it was a long time before I was allowed to indulge my passion. There came the years of Old English metrics and medieval folklore. Then came the years of Meredith and living according to Nature. But since Meredith was, after all, a novelist, I was led into the the consideration of the novel as an art form, and I was launched on the great seas of Tolstoy and Flaubert, of Fielding and Thackeray and Hardy and Zola. This was all so much "life" for me. It was seeing the world, getting acquainted with human nature, acquiring wisdom and refining the sensibilities. I was a teacher, and I might have been content, I suppose, with giving my students an "impressionistic" account of my travels through books. But I was a conscientious teacher, and I wanted to give them something that would hold together, that would not be mere disconnected entertainment or a mere course in assorted philosophies of life. I had been trained in the rigorous Kittredge school of precision. Kittredge could spend a semester over two plays of Shakespeare, giving the exact contemporary meaning of every word, with parallels from other Elizabethan writers, and the exact force of each word in the context of the play. He could spend a full semester tracing the origins of "Gawain and the Green Knight" in a reconstructed genealogy of lost and hypothetical, but scientifically determinable, romances. He had nothing to say about anything so modern as novels. But I had the impulse to apply the same precision of method in dealing with them. The current writing about fiction in magazines and reviews, and generally in books too, was as scattering and invertebrate, as "impressionistic," as the writing about music or pictorial art.

The only notable exception to this was the "new humanism" of Irving Babbitt and Paul Elmer More, which consisted in judging all literature by the standards of a highly provincial puritanism seasoned with a dash of Indian or Platonic philosophy. And that, while I respected it for its seriousness and coherence, repelled me by its reduction of the most complex operations of the human spirit to a naive Spoon River Sunday School formula, not to speak of the almost complete insensitiveness of these men to esthetic and imaginative effects. Their rivals in the field of criticism were often less rewarding, since they offered so little in the way of systematic thought, and were so brash in passing off their accidental likes and dislikes as critical pronouncements. What it most often came to was that they liked or disliked— found pleasant or "unpleasant"—the subject-matter which the author had chosen to treat.

In music, at least, there were writers of program notes who would analyze the thematic material of a symphony or sonata, trace the several themes through each movement, separately and in combination, note the key of each movement and change of key where it occurred, and in short do justice to a piece of music as a formal exercise in the use of the medium. And since that time it has become a matter of course in the plastic arts to treat a painting or piece of sculpture in a similar way, with due regard for the peculiarities of the medium and the composition of the several elements. It struck me that something of the same sort might be done for the art of the novel. And by this time I had found, in Henry

James, the novelist who, in actual practice and in critical comment on his own and others' work, had shown himself most thoroughly aware of the elements involved in the composition of a piece of fiction. Here seemed to be the case that would be the most rewarding in a study of story-telling techniques.

I never imagined for a moment that the primary appeal of any first-rate novelist, his value and importance, could be reduced to mere questions of technical procedure. I knew that what we most prize in a novelist is the inherent interest of his subject-matter (as he sees it), his knowledge of the world (or his chosen part of the world) his eye for the salient in character and situation, his imagination, his philosophy, his spiritual insights; and that very much in his appeal depends on his way of dealing with words, his "style," as distinguished from his deliberately chosen devices for assembling his material, lighting it, "focussing," "dramatizing," creating suspense, and the like. I also realized that, after all these things are taken care of, there still remains that indefinable residuum of personal quality that draws us to individual authors as it does to individual men. And I knew of course that all technical devices justify themselves in the end by their usefulness in enabling the artist to realize his non-technical "intentions."

But in an author who himself puts so high a valuation on technical craftsmanship, and who has told us in such detail what he considers to be the most important items in fictional craft, I thought it would be worth while to see how far one might isolate this one factor—though without losing sight of its functional character by reference to his ultimate intentions—and attempt to estimate the degree to which his mere techniques might be held responsible for his peculiarities and his effectiveness within the limitations of his special genre. Such was my intent in "The Method of Henry James." In later years, I was more impressed with his importance in the general development of what I called the "well-made novel," and more particularly what I called the "dramatic" novel; and in "The Twentieth-Century Novel" (1932) I featured him, along with Dostoevski, as the classic example of these ideals in fiction. In the meantime, Percy Lubbock, in his notable study of fictional art, "The Craft of Fiction" (1921), had made many enlightening suggestions in regard to James's art. But he did not seem to me to have carried as far as it could go the analysis of what we may call the *mechanics* of technique, whether in James or Tolstoy or any of the writers he considered.

I use the word "mechanics," as I realize, with great danger of being misunderstood. But the reader of "The Method" will soon see that what I have in mind is nothing suggestive of the machine age, though it is meant to suggest something like scientific precision in the use of terms for designating methods and scientific scrupulousness in determining whether or not such and such a method is actually used in a particular case. When I use the term "point of view" in a discussion of technique, I do not mean anything so broad as the general outlook of the author, as Mr. Lubbock sometimes uses it, and with entire justification within the framework of his discussion. I use the term "point of view" to designate what is sometimes called the "angle of vision" from which the scene is surveyed in a given chapter of a book,—whether that of an omniscient author ready to enter into the minds of all the characters at once as well as to describe them objectively, or, on the contrary, that of some person in the story who sees whatever is to be seen by him, and interprets all that he sees by the light of his own mind and vision. The limitation of the point of view to the vision of one person is thus a "mechanical" device for securing certain sorts of effects sought by the author.

Of the three books on James in print in 1918, there was only one that paid the slightest attention to such technical considerations. Elizabeth Luther Cary, in "The Novels of Henry James" (New York, 1905), makes the flat statement: "The questions of method, style, and theory, so deeply important to the artist himself, are only secondarily interesting to the critic." Her main discussions are on subjects like American Character. Her chapter on Imagination is largely devoted to James's figures of speech. Ford Madox Ford, on the other hand, in "Henry James: a Critical Study" (London, 1915), considers that method is the all-important subject of criticism, whereas, he says, "I can't myself, for the life of me, see that a writer's subjects concern any soul but himself. They have nothing more to do with criticism than eggs with aeroplanes." But unfortunately, as Mr. Ford admits with disarming candor, he has allowed himself to take up more than four-fifths of his book with "irrelevant matters" (Subjects, Temperaments) and has left himself only twenty pages for Methods. And what he has to say about James's methods is virtually limited to this, that "James has carried the power of selection so far that he can create an impression with nothing at all"; that James held that "a subject from the life was the merest suggestion. Once the suggestion was taken hold of, it should be turned over and over in the mind until the last drop of suggestion that could come from the original suggestion was squeezed out of it."

By far the best written and most challenging of the early books on James is Rebecca West's "Henry James" (New York, 1916). But Miss West's longest and meatiest chapter is on The International Situation; and throughout she is almost exclusively taken up with James's attitudes towards Europe and America, the past and the present, towards politics, women, sex. Writing so soon after James's death, she felt bound to express admiration for the American writer who had become a British citizen and received the Order of Merit. But she had been irritated by his anti-feminism, his "nagging hostility to political effort." She asserts that "he could not grasp a complicated abstraction, was teased by the implications of a great cause, and angered by an idea that could be understood only by a synthesis of many references." She can be very tart in her account of the behavior of people in James's later novels, not to be reconciled with the high opinion which James evidently had of them. The nearest she comes to commenting on his methods as such is in the following sentences: "It was peculiarly unfortunate that, while his subjects grew flimsier and his settings more impressive, his style became more and more elaborate. With sentences vast as the granite blocks of the Pyramids and a scene that would have made a site for a capital he set about constructing a story the size of a hen-house."

## II

It seems clear that in 1918 there was room for a book dealing with James's formal techniques in the light of his extensive account of his theory and practice in the Prefaces to the New York Edition. It is equally clear that there was room for what has appeared in such abundance in the years that followed: first, biographical studies showing us the man himself, with circumstantial accounts of his training and background and his career as a writer; and then, second, of critical work in which a relation is established between the character of his art and the personality of the man as it appears in his biography; and finally and of, presumably, the greatest importance, purely critical studies of his work in an effort to evaluate it esthetically and distinguish degrees of excellence among his productions. There was also room, we might admit, for more comprehensively informative writing about him, which might serve as an introduction to him for beginning readers, including detailed accounts of the subjects and qualities of the several novels and tales.

To this last category we might assign the early "Henry James, Man and Author," by Pelham Edgar (Boston and New York, 1927), a well-written and sensitively appreciative study, which suffers only by comparison with later productions in which the dominant critical attitudes come out in sharper relief. Mr. Edgar had the benefit of James's autobiographical accounts of childhood, youth and early manhood in "A Small Boy and Others" (1913), "Notes of a Son and Brother" (1914), and "The Middle Years" (1917), and of James's Letters (selected and edited by Percy Lubbock, 1920). But he concludes, rather prematurely, that "when the circle that claimed his friendship have disappeared, these biographical records and the letters must be the only material from which the future may reconstruct his merely human identity." And he is perhaps too ready to dismiss merely biographical data as irrelevant to his subject. "My concern in the pages that follow will not be to re-establish Henry James in his habit as he lived; gossip and anecdote will not be invoked for aid; and such stray wisps of biographical fact as drift into the record will serve only to indicate the conditions under which his work was produced."

As a matter of fact, Mr. Edgar was on the threshold of a period in which our knowledge of James as a person was destined to be very greatly enlarged and copious material supplied to such critics as wished to find in his history and psychology the determining causes of his quality as a writer. Mr. Lubbock's selection from his letters left many things about his personality and character unillumined. Further data are supplied by "The Letters of William James," published in the same year (1920) by his son Henry James, and in unpublished letters made available in "The Thought and Character of William James" (ed. Ralph Barton Perry, 2 vols., 1935) and elsewhere. Much light is thrown on the personality of James by the diary of his sister (Anna Robeson Burr, ed., "Alice James: her Journal, her Brothers", 1935). Leon Edel opens up a whole new chapter of the literary career of James in "Henry James: the Dramatic Years," which serves as introduction to his edition of "The Complete Plays of Henry James" (Philadelphia and New York, 1949). (This essay is an enlargement of Mr. Edel's Sorbonne doctor's thesis, "Henry James: les Années dramatiques", Paris, 1931.) As a social and intellectual phenomenon, James takes on higher color and more discriminated character from his association in the family group with his brilliant and venerable father, his illustrious brother, his gifted and fascinating sister, not to mention his vivid unfortunate younger brothers, Robertson and Wilkinson, and the shadowy band of uncles and aunts, whose leisured and "wild" and generally wasted lives seem to have loomed large for the novelist as examples of what was wrong with American society. The general treatment of the James family was begun by Hartley Grattan in "The Three Jameses, a Family of Minds" (London and New York, 1932). It was brought to its most brilliant culmination in F. O. Matthiessen's "The James Family," in 1947. Worthy of mention, in the same connection, are special studies of James's father in Austin Warren's "The Elder Henry James" (New York, 1934) and Frederick Harold Young's "The Philosophy of Henry James Sr." (Bookman Associates, 1951).

Other aspects of James which are partly biographical and partly literary are featured in Theodora Bosanquet, "Henry James at Work" (1924), in which his secretary describes his methods of composition in the later days at Lamb House, when he had taken to dictating his stories as well as his outlines or "scenarios" for projected stories; in Elizabeth Robins, "Theatre and Friendship: Some Henry James Letters, with a Commentary" (London, Jonathan Cape, 1932); and in Janet Adam Smith, "Henry James and Robert Louis Stevenson: a Record of Friendship and Criticism" (London, 1948).

As for "gossip and anecdote," one realizes at once how inadequate these slurring words are to the lively record of James's opinions and manner of speech as recorded in books like Edith Wharton's "A Backward Glance" (New York, 1924) or Simon Nowell-Smith's "The Legend of the Master" (1948). How he talked, as recorded by George Moore, James Barrie, A. C. Benson, J. E. Blanche, how his speech-impediment affected his style in conversation, how indifferent he was to the peasant style of "Ethan Frome," how he translated "M'-Andrew's Hymn" into vigorous idiomatic French on the spur of the moment while standing by the fire at Bourget's home, how eloquently for Edith Wharton he read aloud "When Lilacs Last in the Dooryard Bloom'd" and "Out of the Cradle Endlessly Rocking"—these intimate touches of his personality are not without relevance to his style as a writer or even to his theory and practice of the art of story-telling.

Altogether our knowledge of James's life and our understanding of his character and personality have come flooding in in great tidal waves since Mr. Edel opined that, with the Lubbock letters and James's autobiographical sketches, the returns were all in on the subject of his private life. And only last year the whole crowded picture was made available in judicious perspective by F. W. Dupee in his definitive and critical biography (Sloane).

Apart from work throwing light on the life and personality of James, the last thirty years have produced a number of books of great value for the understanding of his theory and practice of fiction. In 1934, under the editorship of R. P. Blackmur, James's Prefaces were published in a single volume entitled "The Art of Fiction." And in 1947 was published "The Notebooks of Henry James," edited by F. O. Matthiessen and Kenneth B. Murdock, containing James's priceless original notations of hints and suggestions for a large number of his novels and tales and longer written projects for several of the novels. Altogether, with the "scenarios" for "The

Ivory Tower" and "The Sense of the Past", we have now the largest body of material ever made available in the case of any writer for the study of the imaginative process by which the first dim hint of a story is elaborated, modified, and carried through infinite readjustments in detail to its triumphant objectification in the finished work. Among other scholarly helps to the understanding of James's work are Morris Roberts's "Henry James's Literary Criticism" (Cambridge, 1929) and Cornelia Pulsifer Kelley's "The Early Development of Henry James" (Urbana, 1930).

When it comes to critical and interpretative studies of James's fiction, it is most convenient to distinguish between work which is purely critical and that in which evaluation of his work is bound up with some theory of how it is related to his psychological make-up as determined by the circumstances of his life and training. And we might distinguish also the type of criticism that is dominated by some attitude toward James's political or social "ideology"; but this we may be able to lump together with criticism having a biographical slant, since James's ideology is so invariably associated with his being a member and a creature of what is called the leisure class.

When I speak of "pure" criticism, I have in mind such essays as those of Ezra Pound (published in his "Instigations," New York, 1920, and also in "Make It New: Essays by Ezra Pound", New Haven, 1935), of Herbert Read (published in his "The Sense of Glory," New York, 1930), of Edmund Wilson, on "The Ambiguity of Henry James", and Francis Fergusson, on "Drama in *The Golden Bowl*," (both appearing in the

April-June 1934 number of Hound and Horn, and Wilson's again in his volume, "The Triple Thinkers," New York, c.1938), of Francis Fergusson on "James's Idea of Dramatic Form" and R. P. Blackmur, "In the Country of the Blue" (both in the Autumn 1943 Kenyon Review); as well as the more extended consideration of James by Percy Lubbock in "The Craft of Fiction" (London, 1921) and F. R. Leavis in "The Great Tradition" (New York, 1948); and the following entire volumes devoted to James: Edwin Marion Snell, "The Modern Fables of Henry James" (Cambridge, Mass., 1935), F. O. Matthiessen, "Henry James: the Major Phase" (1944), F. W. Dupee, "The Question of Henry James: a Collection of Critical Essays" (New York, 1945), and Elizabeth Stevenson, "The Crooked Corridor: a Study of Henry James" (New York, 1949). I might also list here what I have published on James since "The Method": my chapter on James in the "Cambridge History of American Literature" (New York, 1921); chapters on him in my volume, "The Twentieth-Century Novel: Studies in Technique" (New York, 1932); my essay on "The Witness of the Notebooks," in William Van O'Connor's "Forms of Modern Fiction" (Minneapolis, 1948); and my Introduction to "The American" (in the Rinehart Editions, New York, 1949).

In the group of books dominated by the biographical or ideological bias, the notable items are Van Wyck Brooks, "The Pilgrimage of Henry James" (New York, 1925); C. Hartley Grattan, "The Three Jameses," already mentioned; Stephen Spender, "The Destructive Element" (London, 1935; Philadephia, 1953), though this comes very near the line of "pure" criticism; and Henry

Seidel Canby, "Turn West, Turn East: Mark Twain and Henry James" (Boston, 1951).

### III

In the brief review of this body of critical work which follows, I shall have in general less to say of the "pure" critics than of the biographical-ideological ones, and this for the rather queer though natural reason that the formers' approach is so much more like my own and this gives less opening to objection and is less of a challenge to me to state my own views and, so to speak, set things right. If I begin with Ezra Pound, it is not merely that he comes early in time, but that, with so many good things to say, Pound's well-known capriciousness gives me the first strong clue to what it is puts so many more responsible critics off the track. Pound considers James to be "the greatest writer of our time and own particular language." He is of supreme importance as having spent a lifetime "in trying to make two continents understand each other, in trying....to make three nations intelligible to one another." If people had listened to James, they might have prevented the first World War! And he is of equal importance for his defence of the individual against the mass tyranny, "against all the sordid petty personal oppression, the domination of modern life."

The bulk of Pound's essay is devoted to detailed comment on James's stories in illustration of his strengths and weaknesses in rendering the "feel" of life and the distinguishing qualities of people and places. He makes a detailed outline of the technical points involved in James's notes to "The Ivory Tower," which, he says, gives us "the measure of this author's superiority, as conscious artist, over the 'normal' British novelist."

What most challenges me to objection in Pound's essay is his reference to the "cobwebby" texture of "The Wings of the Dove" and "The Golden Bowl," and his assertion, in this connection, that "Henry James is certainly not a model for narrative novelists, for young writers of fiction." Not that I do not consider this statement literally true. James is probably not, in any period of his writing, a model for young writers of fiction, if one has in mind the slavish imitation of the master's effects. And indeed what great novelist is? What I object to is the implication that James is not a good model for other writers because, while he was very great as a conscious artist, he had very little natural command of narrative skill, and that such as he had was less in evidence in his later novels than in his earlier. It is just at this point that Pound betrays the fact that he never did really "get" James, to use a typical phrase of his own. (James never really did "get" Flaubert or Baudelaire.) For the point I shall most want to make in this Introduction, if I have not sufficiently made it in the book that follows, is that James was a master of story-telling, and that the system of story-telling that he was aiming at through-out his career is that best exemplified in the three novels of his "major phase," as Matthiessen calls it.

Well, there are many kinds of story-telling, Scott's and Balzac's and Dickens's and Hardy's and Flaubert's and Dostoevski's and Dumas', and any one is free to choose the kind of story-telling he prefers. But the mistake that Pound falls into, like so many good men before and after him, is not to see that what he objects to in the latest novels of James is just his peculiar kind and method of story-telling.

Many people frankly dislike all of the later James. Some think it is his style that is to blame for his falling off in the later work. And that is indeed the best reason to assign for their dislike. But others like to think that the trouble is rooted deeper in something in his conception of life which they can blame as amounting to a defect in art. Mr. Brooks likes to think it was James's "deracination"—his cutting himself off from his American roots—that impoverished his imagination and made his later work thin and windy. Mr. Leavis likes to think it was both over-"doing" technically and "a loss of sureness in his moral touch." And others think it was a growing limitation of his sense of life through his confinement to the leisure class. Mr. Brooks, as it seems to me, does not really "get" James, perhaps not at any period of his writing. Mr. Leavis does not "get" him except in the period of his "New England Puritanism" when his characters were seen pretty much in black and white. And most of the biographical-ideological writers and some of the "pure" critics are so much taken up with the sociological or the ethical implications of his writing that they do not stop to consider that he was first and last primarily a story-teller.

I do not mean to suggest that what he was psychologically and what he was as a product of his class did not affect his style of writing and even the way he conceived and told his stories. And I do not feel that we need at all blink the peculiarities and limitations of his personal character. We may well grant that these limitations and peculiarities have much to do with his choice

of subject-matter, with his idiosyncrasies of style in conversation and writing, with his philosophy, the type of
story that he liked to tell, and with the technical devices
by which the narrative was carried forward in this type
of story-telling.   But no such admissions necessarily prevent us from thinking that his subject-matter was well
chosen for interest and significance within the limits of his
temperament and experience, or that his style was suited
to the effects he aimed at.   We are not obliged to think
that his philosophy is shallow because it was the product
of his special approach to life, or that his type of story-
telling can have no appeal to readers like ourselves who
are so different from him in psychological make-up.   The
history of all the arts is full of examples of creative minds
who turned their personal disabilities into assets in the
way of depth of penetration and originality of method.

And the history of criticism in our time is particularly
full of brilliant writers in whom it is very easy to see
how their "ideological" bias colors their statement of the
facts in regard to works of art and even renders them
incapable of taking pleasure in the work of men whose
temperament is too unlike their own.   Thus Van Wyck
Brooks and Rebecca West, in a period of social reform-
ism and hopeful progressive political activity, were obviously impatient with James for his "passivity" in the
face of the spectacle of life and the public movements of
the time.   Of some statement of James's in his autobiographical picture of childhood days, Mr. Brooks remarks:
"He means that the passive role, the role of the spectator
of life, had suddenly been endowed in his eyes with a
certain high legitimacy; he had 'worked out,' as Miss
Rebecca West puts it, 'a scheme of existence....in which

one who stood aside and felt rather than acted acquired thereby a mystic value, a spiritual supremacy, which.... would be rubbed off by participation in action'." And Mr. Brooks goes farther and finds in the personality of "an embarrassed man", unsuccessfully trying to make himself at home in the alien society of England, the clue to the eccentricities of his style from the nineties on. He speaks of the "extraordinary metaphors like tropical air-plants." And then he continues: "For other things had passed into his style—the evasiveness, the hesitancy, the scrupulosity of an habitually embarrassed man. The caution, the ceremoniousness, the baffled curiosity, the nervousness and constant self-communion, the fear of committing himself—these traits of the self-conscious guest in the house where he had never been at home had fashioned with time the texture of his personality."

Mr. Van Wyck Brooks is certainly a rarely accomplished writer. I don't know anyone who has hit off with deadlier aim the fussy and eccentric manner of Henry James in his personal talk as later recorded by many admiring friends in the pages of Nowell-Smith. For those who do not like James's stories, or do not like his later stories, Brooks has furnished all the sharp weapons they need for defending themselves (in a period when it is modish to like him) and convicting him of being a vicious stylist and a bore. What Brooks quite fails to explain is why so many of his associates found his talk fascinating and instructive, amusing and even eloquent. He does not mention the droll humor and fulgurant irony that regularly lighted all he said in private talk and were a sparkling overtone in such books as "The Awkward Age" and "The Ambassadors".

Mr. Leavis, whose strong point as a critic is certainly not his humor, is shocked by the way James in his later novels "counts on our taking towards his main persons attitudes that we cannot take without forgetting our finer moral sense." He cites as an example the reminder by James that the high-minded Adam Verver and his daughter Maggie, in "The Golden Bowl," 'collect' the Prince "in much the same spirit as that in which they collect their other 'pieces'." Mr. Leavis admits that James is "explicit about it," and quotes the author himself: "Nothing perhaps might strike us as queerer than this application of the same measure of value to such different pieces of property as old Persian carpets, say, and new human acquisitions; all the more, indeed, that the amiable man was not without an inkling that he was, as a taster of life, economically constructed. He put into his own little glass everything that he raised to his lips." Well, Mr. Leavis grants, James can be ironic in regard to the inconsistencies of human nature, but "our attitude towards the Ververs isn't meant to be ironical. We are to feel for and with them." And so, I suppose, towards our own personal friends, whom we love and admire for their sterling virtues, we are not to be allowed to be a little amused at the mixture in them of noble traits with vanities from which, of course, we are personally free. Mr. Leavis clearly prefers work of James where character is presented more in black and white than that in which it appears in the lively complexity and ambivalence of "real life."

As for James's ceremoniousness, that must indeed have been a trifle quaint, and betrayed the provincial in him in a way that we trust he didn't suspect. As for "the evasiveness, the hesitancy, the scrupulosity" of his manner, I have no doubt these were in part the effect of the family situation as indicated by many of his biographers. But they were also, it is more important to note, the social and verbal accompaniment of his aim at precision, at comprehensiveness, and at depth of penetration. And these latter were the means by which, in characterizing people and situations, he secured that nuanced "solidity of specification" at which he aimed and which gave to his people and situations their highly discriminated quality and vibrant liveness of effect. And above all, they were the means by which he kept the story in that state of slow and constant and just sensible progress from phase to phase which is the essence of his narrative method. That his sentences are unnecessarily long and unnecessarily loaded with qualifications, almost all readers will grant, as all must grant that James was a man "as nervous as he could live." But the reader who has once been really caught by the interest of the story will readily take these things in his stride, and at the worst concede that all these things are the *défaults de ses qualités*.

Going back to the psychological origins of his character, we find that the most deadly and penetrating of his analysts are Anna Robeson Burr and Leon Edel. Mrs. Burr speaks of a "timidity about facts" in the young Henry James "which he was later to develop into a literary manner." She lays great stress on the "neuroticism" which more or less characterized his father as well as his sister and all three of his brothers.

"Such intensities of feeling" as were manifested by his father "take their toll of nervous resistance and thus the writer's gifted children strive for self-protection according to their several natures. Therefore Alice, as her brother tells, 'jeered' at sympathy and refused to accept the horizon of invalidism. William met the foe with the weapons of science, dragging him from the recesses of self-consciousness into the light of study, by means of a book as penetrating as it is human. Bob's inner turmoil demanded incessant change and the novelist brother found in the slower rhythm of his English life a protection from nervous fatigue and a means of avoiding those demands on his sympathies which he felt interfered with his art."

Every one recognises that William was the active leader in the brothers' life together, and that Henry was the "passive spectator."

"Deep-seated shyness, twin-born with as deep an egotism, sensitiveness, dread of responsibility and the stumbling-block of a slight impediment of speech, made up an equipment the antithesis of his brother's.... Fear, fear for the talent he adored, for the privacy that fostered it, for his independence threatened with responsibility—these seem the motives which took this sensitive, easily upset person as far as possible from America that he regarded as the seat of all disturbance."

Mrs. Burr considers that his inability to go to the war along with his younger brothers was a source of great humiliation to Henry. "The injury which kept him from joining the Army was a humiliation in more senses than one. It was hard to be kept from serving one's country but worse to be forced to see one's younger brothers in the limelight, with the banners and bands. This disappointment echoes through his autobiographical writings."

Mrs. Burr does not, I think, make the point recently made by Mr. Canby that financial insecurity began to worry the young Jameses from the time that their father began to worry about it, probably as a result of the panic of 1857. But she does find, like Mr. Edel, that money considerations were a prominent factor in his desperate effort through many years to make a success as a playwright. After William's visits to him in England, she suggests, "an outburst of latent Americanism would make him feel that he was a failure because his books had not made him enormously rich. Insistence on material success was one of his paradoxical, most American qualities; it led him to the theatre, for which his art was not fitted; it filled his books with vast estates, and vast fortunes and all the things his father told him were 'vulgar,' but which somehow did not appear so when they occurred in England."

Whatever one may think of the general tone of her discussion, one must listen to what Mrs. Burr has to say. But while she does not concern herself directly with James's literary art, one has the feeling that she has no great liking for it, and that her picture of the man is a bit colored by a feeling of partisanship for his sister. I find it possible myself to be an intense admirer of Alice and William James without losing anything of my appreciation for Henry; and certainly from Alice's journal one gets the impression that Alice and Henry were very dear friends and unqualified admirers of one another.

Mr. Edel moves on a higher level of discrimination, but the picture he gives of Henry James is essentially the same as Mrs. Burr's. He shows how, in regard to the drama as a literary form, to the stage as it existed in his time in England, and his own ambition to write plays, James oscillated between two extremes, now speaking of the drama as of all literary forms the noblest, being the form that most required "a masterly structure," and assuring his friends that in the drama he had found his *"real* form;" now writing of it as "a most unholy trade," and of himself as "overcome by the vulgarity, the brutality, the baseness of the condition of the English-speaking theatre today," and yet persisting in his attempt to produce plays for purely financial reasons. This financial motive Mr. Edel regards as, in large part, a rationalization of deeper motives. He represents James as, in these years, in a perpetual state of inner conflict, in which fiction and drama stand for two opposed ways of living, the one congenial to his shy and (shall we say) introverted nature, the other suggesting the image of himself as a man in the world of men.

> "The reticent, secretive aloof literary alchemist of Bolton St. and De Vere Gardens, a fêted London 'lion' moving in the world as a conscious observer and recorder, rebelled at the very things which are the life of the stage.... For him.... the theatre became the focus of anxiety, fear, insecurity, conflicting emotions which caused him to approach it with faltering footsteps. A work of fiction might receive adverse reviews and fall flat in the market and still remain an honorable performance; it did not nvolve the public *exposure..* that went with a play."

Mr. Edel sees this opposition of fiction and drama as one form of an emotional conflict which had raged within him all along. "A choice between Boston (home, art, the study) and Europe (the world) had imposed itself and he had made it, although in reality without resolution of the inner conflict. So his original choice of letters (home, the study) instead of law (the world). Thus (in "The Tragic Muse") Nick Dormer's conflict, Parliament (the world), the palette (art) and Miriam Rooth's—the art of the stage (world) and marriage (home)." James was driven to the stage by the poor success of his books in the period of "The Bostonians" and "The Princess Casamassima." And immediately after the failure of "Guy Domville" on the stage, we find him in his stories of artists dreaming self-consolatory dreams, seeking "compensations and solutions." His final solution was the conviction that, in his practice of the art of play-writing, he had mastered the "dramatic" principle as it applies to novel and tale, so that "what I call the divine principle (of the Scenario)..is a key that, working in the same *general* way, fits the complicated chambers of both the dramatic and the narrative lock," so that "my infinite little loss is converted into an almost infinite little gain."

Well, whether James, in his later stories, had secured this almost infinite little literary gain, or was a victim of self-delusion, is the chief moot point of most criticism dealing with him.

The man thus characterized by the biographers has been made the subject of a psychiatric study by Dr. Saul Rosenzweig in an article appearing in the Partisan Review (Fall, 1944). The most comprehensive and judicious of James's biographers, Mr. Dupee, testifies that "although I have dealt with the topic in no more than a very general way, what I do say about it implies an agreement with Dr. Rosenzweig's findings." It is argued by Dr. Rosenzweig that James's accident in youth was for his psychology but the culmination of a long series of circumstances, largely having to do with the personal prestige of his father and his elder brother, contributing in him to the development of a "castration complex," or to the psychological "death" which corresponds to the actual death of characters in a considerable number of his stories.

Mr. Canby does not refer to Dr. Rosenzweig, but he may be adverting impatiently to his interpretation of James's psychology when he says: "James found it difficult to marry, by which I mean no nonsense about congenital or accidental impotence." And he states that, in the matter of the accident sustained by James at the age of nineteen, as "the story was told me by his nephew," it was a question of his "falling over a fence," and straining his back, with perhaps the displacement of a vertebra or injury to the sacroiliac. I am not well enough acquainted with psychological theory to know the precise implications of the term "impotence" (whether psychological or physiological); but Mr. Canby's account of James sounds very much like what I suppose this term to imply.

"Of course," Mr. Canby says, "there may well have been *something physiological or psychological* (my italics) in the boy or man. He was presumably of the median sexual type, like Thoreau, the kind of man who gets along most easily with men, or--as with James, and his father—with attractive older women, usually married.... With so many close female friends, there is no known record of Henry having ever been passionately in love.... He expressly denied it of Minny Temple.... What he got afterward were rare and even exciting affections, unclouded by sexual desire. Pain, according to my thinking, had deprived him in his youth....of the first steps toward a normal sexual life; and later the urge was not strong enough, the deep involvements in art, intensely emotional as we shall see, satisfied a nature always most responsive to the esthetic and the intellectual."

Psychological problems of this sort are, I suppose, beyond the competence of any but scientific experts; and many thoughtful people have less confidence in the pronouncements of the experts in psychology than in physics or biology. For my own literary approach to the problem of James's psychology, I will borrow a few sentences from an essay entitled "The Witness of the Notebooks," which may be found in O'Connor's "Forms of Modern Fiction."

"Whatever we may think of this particular formula (of Rosenzweig's) we cannot but be impressed with the essential loneliness of James, his comparative want of commitment to intimate personal relations of the kind that require an absolute surrender of one's self to the demands of "life."....No one touched life at more points, but he seems to have touched it with the imagination, at a distance, with a steady maintenance of esthetic detachment. Perhaps this makes him the artist in essence, but we have few records anywhere of the artist so reduced to essence and uninvolved with the urgencies and appetites of the man. There is something pathetic in James's references to his own intensities of "living" in the seclusion of his workshop—living, that is, in the passionate reconstruction of the lives of imaginary beings....James's intense concern with very special and esoteric "relations", relations with a *difference,* might be seen as an effort at compensation for what he had missed in the way of the old standard shopworn relations into which the ordinary man plunges so recklessly and with so little thought of making them special. The ideal (or sentimental) *essence* of living experience which he so steadily pursued would be, in this view, a substitute for the gross stuff of experience which he may have felt obscurely as having passed him by. One special gain that he had made in passing from the gross substance to the refined essence of human experience was his vastly greater freedom in invention and manipulation of the elements of story."

## IV

What we may call the ideological approach to James's art is perhaps best represented by Miss West in the 1910's, by Mr. Brooks in the 1920's, and by Mr. Grattan and Mr. Spender in the 1930's. And they are all concerned to show the reasons for the very limited appeal of James's work especially from the 90's on. Mr. Grattan's formula is much the simplest. He regards James as primarily an exponent of the ideals of the leisure class which is soon to go out of existence with the passing of capitalism.

"In direct contrast to the world of his brother William, he believed in the fixed and the permanent. His world was a static world, a closed universe.... Far from being a defender of civilization against barbarism as a distinguished and cultured critic has recently celebrated him for being, or the proponent of cosmopolitanism against provincialism as he frequently envisaged himself, he was the supreme representative of the leisure class advanced to the stage of selectivity admitting the moneyed middle class to a part in the life on sufferance, but not to the stage of seeing that the whole structure was in acute danger of collapsing and disappearing at the demand of the onward marching proletarians."

But though James was so blind to the historical forces that produced him, Mr. Grattan acknowledges that he was a powerful writer if only for the convincingness of his portrayal of this deluded society, and he ends on a rather droll note of concession by giving him a more exalted niche in his historical museum than even his clear-seeing brother. He thinks indeed that "the next period of fiction will be characterized by the social novel, the prewar development of which Henry James so thoroughly ignored." But "whatever happens it seems correct to believe that, long after William James's ideas have been so thoroughly assimilated in the cultural stream that his name is no longer associated with them, long after Henry James, Sr., has ceased to be interesting as an unregarded protagonist of supernaturalism, Henry James's novels will be studied as the most brilliant projections of leisure class society under the capitalistic regime." We trust that Soviet authorities will take notice and for all young proletarians make required reading of "The Awkward Age" and "What Maisie Knew."

Miss West's slant is somewhat different. After quoting the enthusiastic terms in which James refers to old England in "The Passionate Pilgrim," she says:

> "There you have the first statement of the persistent illusion, to which he was helped by his odd lack of the historic sense and which confused his estimate of modern life, that the past would have been a happier home for those who like himself loved fastidious living.... He never perceived that life is always a little painful at the moment, not only at this moment but at all moments; that the wine of experience always makes a raw draught when it has just been trodden out from the bruised grapes by the pitiless feet of men, that it must be subject to time before it acquires suavity."

There is indeed a general truth that cannot be denied, and few will deny that James, like Walter Scott, did have a strong tendency to idealize the past. What one cannot understand is why, when James had seen through the fair mask of traditional English society, to which he was drawn as preserving the beauty of the past, when even aristocracy and good society were found to be a whited sepulchre, Miss West is even less well pleased with the "melancholy series" of fictions in which all his major characters "are in some way or other trying to preserve some decency from engulfment in the common lot of nastiness." In short, as he grows more critical of traditional English society, and gives up the illusions which rouse her gentle scorn, he is even less acceptable to this critic than during the time when he so persistently cherished them.

This paradox of taste comes into even higher relief in Mr. Brooks's interpretation of James. With him it is England that is idealized by James beyond all recognition, America being for him "the dark country, the sinister country, where the earth was a quicksand, where amiable uncles ended in disaster, where men were turned into machines, where genius was subject to all sorts of inscrutable catastrophes." England was for James a fairer world than ours. And his England was indeed "a fairer world than England's, a fairer world than ever existed outside the pages of a romance." This being so, James's task as a writer was to saturate himself in the actual world of English society and make that his special subject as Balzac had made an earlier French society his. But James was not Balzac. Unfortunately he was an outsider and English society really inaccessible to him. In time he became discouraged, his material ran thin and his inspiration flagged. He found that he had fought a losing battle "against that superstitious valuation of the Old World."

And here we run into that same curious inconsistency that puzzled us in Miss West's interpretation. Mr. Brooks acknowledges that James had lost his illusions about English society, but he seems to like him no better for that. He even quotes from James's letter to Norton in 1886 referring to the English upper class: "The condition of that body seems to me to be in many ways very much the same rotten and collapsible one as that of the French aristocracy before the revolution—minus cleverness and conversation; or perhaps it's more like the heavy, congested and depraved Roman world upon which the barbarians came down." Mr. Brooks then goes on to outline the plots of many of the later stories, including "The Spoils of Poynton," "What Maisie Knew," "The Awkward Age," "The Turn of the Screw," "The Wings of the Dove" and "The Golden Bowl," and notes how frequently the theme is "the victimization of some innocent cat's-paw at the hands of conspirators or of a negligent, insensible, malevolent and callous world."

At this stage in his argument, it is sometimes rather difficult to make out the direction of his thought and determine whether he is half-heartedly praising James for his growing realism or commiserating with him on the progressive weakening of his mental powers. But his thesis requires him to weight the scales in favor of the latter view. "It is true perhaps," he concedes, "that in this world the 'low sneaks' have it all their own way, true that the subtle are always the prey of the gross, that the pure in heart are always at the mercy of those that work iniquity." And he then goes on to inquire "why did the predicament of the innocent victim possess for James such an irresistible fascination?" To this question he gives no clear answer, or none that is relevant to his argument. And he certainly fails to make clear why, when James had shed his illusions about England and about aristocratic society—as Marcel in Proust's series shed his about the Guermantes—why, when he has taken on some measure of realism in his treatment of the social scene, he, the social-minded critic, should like him less well than when he was a pure deluded romantic.

Moreover, his characterization of James's theme as "the victimization of some innocent cat's-paw at the hands of conspirators," etc., must seem to the careful and sympathetic reader of many of the novels in question a quite misleading account of both the moral and the material facts of the case. Neither Fleda Vetch, nor Maisie, nor Nanda Brookenham, nor Milly Theale, nor Maggie Verver, was strictly speaking or in the end a cat's-paw, though there were plenty of unscrupulous people ready to use them as such. And none of them was, essentially, a victim of other people, or a victim of anything except their own sometimes exaggerated idealism. Maggie was certainly not in the end the victim of Charlotte Stant, but vice versa. In "The Wings of the Dove" it was Milly that won out against Kate Croy, even in death, and prevented her marriage to Merton. Maisie was certainly a poor waif and badly abused by her callous parents and step-parents; but at least she made her moral profit and came out of the whole sordid business with a character and a mature sense of values. What Brooks fails to recognise is that every one of these innocent women does, in some sense, triumph over the conspirators, and does indeed "preserve some decency from engulfment in the common lot of nastiness". He fails to recognize that, along withthe new note of realism, James's accent is in all these books more on the positive than on the negative in the scale of ethical values.

Stephen Spender, writing on James in 1935, in the full flood of Marxian hopefulness, was frankly writing "in defence of a political subject." But something in his poetical make-up saved him from weighting the scales against the artist who was notoriously free from any taint of Marxist or even utilitarian intention. It is probable that Spender gave James credit for a larger and more penetrating view of social issues and the significance of the historical moment than James actually possessed. But in doing so, he gave him a fairer hearing than the others in this group. He underlined James's conviction that European society was decadent, but made it a credit to him that he was "imposing on a decadent aristocracy the greater tradition of the past." Spender grants that this notion of the greater tradition of the past is a legend, but as a poet he recognises that the creation of a suitable legend is one of the finer devices of the poetic imagination for giving body to its ideal insights. "Take James, then, as the greatest of a line who owe more to an un-English (a Celtic and a Continental) tradition than to the purely Anglo-Saxon one: Joyce, Yeats, Ezra Pound and Eliot. These writers have all fortified their works by creating some legend, or by consciously going back into a tradition that seemed or seems to be dying."

Not having the socialistic or communal view, James has no recourse but to be an extreme individualist.

"Since James condemns society and yet is no revolutionary, it follows that for him the individualist is the only person who is free to do good or evil. For that reason his virtuous characters, Milly, Strether and Maggie Verver, are essentially all isolated and cut off from their surroundings. They lead a life which is morally conscious, but which is cut off from the main stream of contemporary life and which borders very close to death, so many of them die. Yet they die to avoid

the living death of people who are alive, but dead to all consciousness of moral values. The evil of society is that it is
dead to those values."

This Marxian determinism shows itself more strikingly in Spender's charitable treatment of the "bad" characters. Their badness "lies primarily in their situation.
Once the situation is provided, the characters cannot be-
have otherwise. Their only compensation is that by the
use of their intelligence, by their ability to understand, to
love, and to suffer, they may to some extent atone for the
evil which is simply the evil of the modern world. It is
these considerations that make his later books parables of
Western civilization." It is by virtue of this queer Marxian indulgence that Spender was able to do better justice
to many of James's characters than Leavis can do with his
stricter moralism. It is so that the true Churchman can
look with more indulgence on men's frailities (we are all
miserable offenders!) than the Puritan for whom black
is black and white is white, and who considers that to
give absolution, or even to "understand" the sinner, is to
condone the sin. Of course the virtues of James's people
are "bourgeois" virtues, but Spender does not give the
impression of having been thoroughly weaned from bourgeois sentiment in things ethical, and is able to say without condescension: "Civilization, tradition, high intelligence, the ability to love and to suffer, are the chief moral
values which one finds in James's work."

Still, great as James was as an artist, he would of
course have been better if he had been less individualistic
—in short, if the truth had made him free. That is Spender's conclusion. Each critic admits that James is "diffi-

cult" reading, and each one has his own theory to account for this. For Spender it is James's inveterate individualism, with its attendant evils, that makes him a difficult writer.

## V

Mr. Leavis I do not include among the "ideological" critics of James, for it is an ethical system or bias instead of a political one that forms the ground from which he delivers his critical judgments. Or rather, it is not perhaps his ethical system, which is highly refined and readily applicable to works of literary art, but a certain want of imagination he occasionally shows in applying it. James belongs to the "great tradition" in the English novel, as I understand it, because his criticism of life is conducted from the vantage point of a truly moral and humane ideal, consciously held and responsibly directed. "His registration of sophisticated human consciousness is one of the great classical achievements: it added something as only genius can. And when he is at his best, that something is seen as of great human significance. He creates an ideal civilized sensibility; a humanity capable of communicating the finest shades of inflection and implication: a nuance may engage a whole complex moral economy and the perspective response be the index of a major valuation or choice."

Leavis has no quarrel with James for the choice of Europe as his main field of observation, and he is not tempted to call James an "esthete" because of his concern with matters of taste, or a snob because of his fondness for the ritual of leisure-class society. (Spender acquits

James of the charge of snobbishness on the grounds that "if he is a snob," it is simply "that he is imposing on a decadent atristocracy the greater tradition of the past.") Leavis does not, I think, even raise the question of snobbishness, for he finds that with James the art of social intercourse is simply the port of embarkation for a voyage into the regions of ideal moral refinement. What he admires in James is "his evident glimpse of a possible 'civilization' in which the manners belonging to a ripe art of social intercourse shall be the index of a moral refinement of the best American kind and a seriousness which shall entail a maturity of humane culture." One is here strongly reminded of the connection regularly made by Matthew Arnold between outward manners and the "kingdom of Heaven" that is "within you." Leavis quotes from "The Golden Bowl" a passage in which the word "taste" is used in a sense suggestive of Arnold's "criticism" of life: "....the whole growth of one's 'taste'; a blessed comprehensive name for many of the things deepest in us. The 'taste' of the poet is, at bottom and so far as the poet in him prevails over everything else, his active sense of life: in accordance with which truth to keep one's hand on it is to hold the silver clue to the whole labyrinth of his consciousness."

This active sense of life Leavis finds working finely and surely in all the early period of James's writing, but not in the later period. "It is certainly true," he says, "that James's development was towards over-subtlety, and that with this development we must associate a loss of sureness in his moral touch, an unsatisfactoriness that in some of the more ambitious later works leads us to question his implicit valuations."

There are a number of points one would like to raise in this connection. Suppose it to be a simple case of the moral valuations placed by James as author and teacher upon the characters he presents, isn't it a good deal to expect that they should always be just right according to some absolute standard? There have doubtless been authors whose implicit moral valuations were in pretty complete accord with those of the age in which they lived or the class of readers they addressed. Perhaps this was the case with Shakespeare, though I imagine that passages might be taken from "King Lear" which would bring this in doubt for certain of his contemporaries. (We know that Socrates sharply questioned the morality of Homer.) Perhaps it was the case with Walter Scott, or with George Eliot. But is it not possible that an author might be on the whole and in his main drive "sound" according to the standard of the age and class he represents and yet here and there deviate from that standard because of some peculiarity of his temperament or small defect of understanding? Or may there not be situations in a complicated social order, cases of conscience, in which an expert casuist might have to struggle long indeed with the diverse aspects of the case before making a pronouncement, and in which in the end his pronouncement would be larded with whereases and provisos? Is there any standard of moral judgment known to our English critic that does not to some extent share the *relativity* of other systems of valuation?

But according to Mr Leavis James's moral touch was sure enough in the plain-spoken earlier work, in "The Bostonians" and "The Portrait of a Lady", and progressively less sure until its uncertainty reaches its climax in the three ambitious works which—and he thinks it is to be deplored—are generally recommended as his masterpieces.

The examples he gives of this unsureness are not always of the most convincing. In the case of Milly Theale, one feels that he has allowed himself to be swayed in some unaccountable way by a sentiment of national loyalty which the case does not call for. In general he approves of James's way of handling the "international situation" and his use of his innocent Americans to underline his moral idealism. But when it comes to Milly Theale, something has crept in, one supposes, from his "unconscious" to confuse the issues. He speaks of the "long series of works in which James may be said to offer his native country its revenge for *Martin Chuzzlewit!*" But, he goes on,

> "The attempt to isolate and exalt the distinctively and uniquely American is—on the showing of the consequences in James's art—misconceived..... The Americanism results ultimately (to consider now James's women) in a feebleness and in a perversity of valuation we may figure by Milly Theale in *The Wings of the Dove.* An American heiress, merely because she is an American heiress, is a Princess, and such a princess as, just for being one, is to be conceived as a supreme moral value: that is what it amounts to. And, in bearing this significance, Milly Theale has, in the Jamesian *oeuvre*, a sufficient company of other examples."

Well, yes, and the best of the other examples is Isabel Archer in "The Portrait of a Lady," in whom Mr. Leavis finds no "perversity of valuation." The parallelism between the two women is very marked all along the line. Isabel too is an American heiress in full romantic panoply, and accordingly treated by every one as a Princess. There can be no denying that Milly's fortune made her a Princess, a society queen, in the eyes of Mrs. Lowder and Lord Mark and Kate Croy, all English judges, as Isabel's made her one in the judgment of Lord Warburton and Gilbert Osmond and Madame Merle. And the role assigned her Milly was able to sustain not by any queenly pretensions but by her simplicity and wit, her unaffected style, her innocence and candor and social tact. Certainly picturesqueness and glamour are lent to her **figure** by the Venetian palace where, in accordance with many American precedents, she chose to live out her short life. To Merton Densher Milly appeals by her radiance, her pluck, her obstinate refusal to allow any reference to her fatal illness. The circumstances of her life as an invalid in the dim splendor of her palace, her seclusiveness and rare appearances, do indeed give her the air, as James suggests, of a fairy princess or *Princess Lointaine*. Her pathos and pluck are important factors in this poetic buildup. But what puts the final seal upon her royalty is her never abusing her more than royal power and her capacity for showing the utmost magnanimity towards those who come beneath her sway.

Such magnanimity, such a combination of innocence and intelligence, are indeed frequently found in James's women. It is perhaps their naiveté together with their zest for life that gives them their distinctively American accent; but innocence, intelligence and magnanimity were not in James the monopoly of American women—one has but to think of Fleda Vetch and Nanda Brookenham, not to speak of little Maisie. James was certainly ready as an artist to take what advantage he could of American fortunes and the American zest for life as colors in his palette. But one hardly knows what Mr. Leavis can mean by James's "attempt to isolate and exalt the distinctively and uniquely American." This is the very opposite to the charge more often made against James of gushing over the distinctively European.

It is a different, and perhaps this time a more positively moralistic, bias that Leavis betrays in his remarks about "The Ambassadors." "*The Ambassadors, too,* which he seems to have thought his greatest success, produces an effect of disproportionate 'doing'—of a technique the subtleties and elaborations of which are not sufficiently controlled by a feeling for value and significance in living. What, we ask, is this, symbolized by Paris, that Strether feels himself to have missed in his own life? Is it anything adequately realized?"

One is quite at a loss to understand how this enlightened critic should so resolutely decline to read what is written in capitals on every page of this book. Does James need to tell us in so many words that Paris is, for Strether, as it has been for many generations of Americans, and Englishmen too—the *Ville Lumière*, the place where ideas are everywhere in circulation, and subject to free and animated discussion—and that in this respect it is the absolute antithesis to Woollett, Mass., where Strether had been spending his starved life? Does he need to tell us—but this he does plainly—that it is physically and socially a seat of great amenity, where one can exercise and communicate with "an ideal civilized sensibility; a humanity capable of the finest shades of inflection and implication," where "a nuance may engage a whole complex moral economy and the perceptive response be the index of a major

valuation or choice"? Is it not clear that what Paris gives
to Strether, under the helpful direction of Maria Gostrey,
is a "glimpse of a possible 'civilization' in which the manners belonging to a ripe social intercourse shall be the
index of a moral refinement"—well, if not "of the best
American kind" as conceived in Woollett, at least of the
kind that was implicit in every turn of James's father's
ethical philosophy? For the elder James was determined
to cultivate the spirit and substance of the moral life, and
was highly scornful of the "flagrant moralism" which he
found so often taking the place of true ethical judgment.
And so Strether.

He went to Paris to fetch back Chad Newsome, so
that the young man might go into the business and further augment the family fortune; and he was expected to
pry him loose from some low sexual involvement. It took
some time to determine just what this involvement was,
but it soon became evident that it was not so low but what
it had made a thoroughly "civilized" man of Chad. To
Strether it was clear that Chad owed something to a relationship so serious and of such long standing, which involved so genuine and deep a love on the part of the
woman, and in the end he is greatly disappointed with
Chad for his willingness to ditch his love so irresponsibly,
so that he can return to Woollett and go into the advertis-
ing end of the business.

In the course of the series of occasions necessary to
bring about these successive changes of view in regard to
Chad, Strether has had an opportunity to revise his opinion of Mrs. Newsome and to take a good dose of the Woollett tone in the persons of the Pococks, sent over to keep
him in line. None of this is too subtle for any interested

reader to take in, but it does take a good deal of "doing." For it involves nothing less than the formal opposition of a commercial, utilitarian and narrowly puritan way of living and thinking to that "possible 'civilization' in which the manners, etc., shall be the index, etc." That is, for Strether it involves his instinct to judge moral situations from the inside by their quality and substance rather than by the labels attached to them by conventional opinion from the outside.

Perhaps the unsureness of James's moral touch is betrayed, for Mr. Leavis, by the fact that, when Strether is thoroughly persuaded of the rightness of Chad's attachment to Mme. de Vionnet, and of the obligation to loyalty which it entails for Chad, he is scarcely perturbed by his accidental discovery that their relation is a "guilty" one. But that can hardly be what troubles a critic like Mr. Leavis, who prefers genuine though "guilty" love relations to sentimental platonic ones such as those involving Adam Verver and his daughter in "The Golden Bowl"— a critic who can say, of the characters in that novel, "if our sympathies are anywhere, they are with Charlotte and (a little) the Prince, who represent what, against the general moral background of the book, can only strike us as a decent passion; in a stale, sickly and oppressive atmosphere they represent life."

Or perhaps the unsureness of touch is shown in the several changes of attitude undergone by Strether between the first page and the last. It is here that we may have come to the heart of the matter. For the great peculiarity of James's later narratives is that we do not arrive at his final valuations without going through a long course of "visions and revisions." And while it may seem to some of us that this is the very way that, in actual life, we do win through to our valuations, and that indeed such is the true essence of a live and working ethical experience, it may appear to others to be the sign of a radical unsureness of touch in author and character, and a fertile source of obscurity and obfuscation for the reader.

Another case in point is that of "The Golden Bowl," and here we do come on something in the temperament of Henry James that has given pause to more critics than Leavis. Mr. Leavis cannot get over the fact that Mr. Verver secured the Prince for his daughter somewhat as the collector of *objets d'art* secures a new "piece" for his collection, and he wonders how, in view of that, either of them can legitimately be supposed to have fine sentiments for their mates. This should not be so difficult to conceive when one considers that something analogous happens whenever a marriage is arranged with any view to social position and financial competence. We can hardly suppose that, throughout the Christian world, it is impossible for genuine love to manifest itself in any union that is entered into with some view to social convenience."

## VI

But there are other things here that give some color to Leavis's characterization of the atmosphere of this book as "stale, sickly and oppressive." They are what lead one critic to call the people of this novel "sexually mad", and Mr. Spender to accuse James of "vulgarity" because of his gingerly treatment of the subject of sex. Mr. Spender dilates on the deep conflict here "between the two kinds of marriage, the spiritual and the platonic. Maggie will not abandon her father: the injury done to the *sposi* is that the marriages have been arranged— Maggie's in part, Mr. Verver's entirely—simply in order to improve the relationship of the daughter and father.. Moreover, the platonic relationship of the daughter and father not only competes with the relationship of Charlotte and Amerigo, it also affects a third concurrent relationship, which is the sexual life of each party with his or her marriage partner. The platonicism of the father and daughter creeps into their marriages."

Now, that is a pretty sober reminder of something in James's treatment of human nature that we cannot ignore. James first and last is much concerned with sex relations, and not infrequently they appear in situations which must have been shocking to the American and even to the English public of his time. He takes sexual passion for granted, but often he does not seem to make sufficient allowance for it as a dominant force in human behavior. And one cannot help speculating on the effect his personal "psychology" as described by his biographers may have had on his imagination as an artist.

And there is more involved here than the question of his "moral touch." There is, as Mr. Leavis points out, the question of our attitudes towards the characters that he commends to our interest and sympathy. The most penetrating study of this subject was made by Edmund Wilson in his essay on "The Ambiguity of Henry James." Beginning with the famous ghost story, "The Turn of the Screw," Mr. Wilson suggests that we are left in doubt by James whether the children in that story were actually subject to the visitation of ghosts that corrupted them, or whether the ghosts were the product of the imagination of the governess, a sex-starved woman. No one can say with certainty whether James actually had in mind these two alternatives and which one of them he would have embraced. In this case it does not greatly matter, since it is obvious from all he has had to say about this story that his primary, perhaps his sole, concern was the production and maintenance of a certain eerie tone. But Mr. Wilson goes on to "The Sacred Fount" and "The Awkward Age" and many of James's short stories, indicating how often the central characters are persons with whom it is hard for us to maintain full sympathy. He points out how often these are the type of the "American bourgeois," somewhat the equivalent of the type satirized by Flaubert in the person of Frédéric Moreau in *"L'Education Sentimentale."*

"These men turn their back on business; they attempt to enrich their experience through the society and art of Europe. But they bring to it the bourgeois qualities of timidity, prudence, primness, the habits of mind of a narrow morality which, even when they wish to be open-minded, cause them to be easily shocked. They wince alike at the brutalities of the aristocracy and at the vulgarities of the working class; they shrink most from the "commonness" of the less cultivated bourgeoisie, who, having acquired their incomes more recently, are not so far advanced in self-improvement. The women have the corresponding qualities: they are innocent, conventional and rather cold—sometimes they suffer from immaturity or Freudian complexes, sometimes they are neglected or cruelly cheated by the men to whom they have given their hearts."

It must be obvious that Mr. Wilson does not allow his admiration for James's art to interfere with the cold objectivity with which he looks upon his characters—like, say, a sociologist and psychologist from some remote planet. He writes as if the historian of Hecate County were not affected himself by his personal involvement in any particular social or cultural order. He goes much farther than Leavis in his recognition of James's uncertainties of attitude towards the people of his stories. "In Henry James's mind," he says, "there disputed all his life the European and the American points of view; and their debate, I believe, is closely connected with his inability to be clear as to what he thinks of a certain sort of person."

The most admirable thing about Wilson as a critic is that this extreme objectivity in his view of the psychological and cultural types featured by James does not prevent him from thoroughly appreciating James's *comédie humaine* and especially those later novels in which "the Americans come back into the picture."

"With James, except in his most morbid phases, the absurdities, the artificialities, the trivialities are all on the surface: beneath, the grasp on reality is firm, the intelligence profound. Others have done the American character with greater brilliance or dramatic vitality; none has shown it so successfully as James has done it in relation to the rest of the world. Narrowly specialized in certain ways though his Americans may seem to be, they stand as a record of significant realities. All that was human, magnanimous, reviving in the new American spirit as it was still preserved in Henry James's time by the American leisure class is caught in the Milly Theales, the Lambert Strethers, the Adam Ververs of James's latest novels; and also all that was frustrated, sterile, excessively refined, depressing—all that they had in common with Frédéric Moreau and with the daughters of poor English parsons.

There they are with their ideals and their blights."[1]

And so in the upshot Wilson shows how James made profit out of his disabilities and limitations, by virtue of his scrupulous truth-telling; and, so to speak, in his novels provided a diagnosis, almost a therapy, for the ills from which he suffered as a member of his class. "He was one of the coolest-headed of novelists, one of the least capable of faking. And the very phases of ambiguity I have noted, blurring the focus of a mind of the first order, avow the dilemmas by which it is taxed, the maladies of which they are symptoms."

## VII

It must be evident that Wilson, while maintaining his admiration for James's art, has made the extremest concessions to those readers who complain that James confuses them by commending to their sympathy characters whom they cannot find altogether "sympathetic" or even admirable. And his emphasis, like theirs, is strongly on the later work of James as the flourishing ground of his ambiguity. But now that Mr. Wilson has given us this finely provocative term "ambiguity," we might as well take full advantage of it, and note that James's ambiguity, or variation of attitude towards certain types of character, is very frequently something quite other than a betrayal of positive uncertainty as to what is admirable in human nature. It is much more evidence of the fine discrimina-

---

[1] These sentences I have ventured to quote, for convenience, in the condensed form as they appear in *Hound and Horn* rather than in the more elaborated form of the essay printed in "The Triple Thinkers."

tion with which he ponders the problem of the ideal in human nature, taking into account the several elements that enter into the ideal character and the delicate balance of these elements, and exhibiting, as Matthew Arnold would say, the *excess* and the *defect* of each several element as it results in throwing the character out of balance.

And while there is in the later stories a much greater subtlety in this discrimination, and the unbalance of character is there more elaborately dramatized, the same process of discrimination was going on actively in the earlier work, as even Mr. Leavis recognizes and illustrates from "The Bostonians" and "The Europeans" for example. The simple fact is that there are traits of character that James can unaffectedly admire in an Isabel Archer or a Lambert Strether and yet quite gaily and pointedly hold up to ridicule in a Louis Leverett or a Miss Miranda Hope. The reader of "A Bundle of Letters" will recognize these latter as personages in that hilarious and very early tale, which is devoted to the humors and oddities of a French boarding house for foreigners seeking culture in Paris.

There is here no drama, and no question of the "moral touch"; for what we have here is simply an exhibition of national traits on the "cultural" level. James is, in Pound's words earlier quoted, "trying to make two continents understand each other....trying....to make three nations intelligible one to another." Or rather, *four* nations; for the most screamingly funny of these nine letters is that of Dr. Rudolph Staub to another German "doctor" in Göttingen, in which the quaintest of Teutonic philosophical method is brought to bear on the problem of national traits, and the German writer is so sure (in 1879!) that the French are incapable of *revanche* ("the French nature is too shallow for that large and powerful plant to bloom in it"), and equally sure (again in 1879!) that the Americans in the boarding house are types of the already manifest national decadence.

> "What strikes one (in the Boston character) is that it is a phenomenon to the best of my knowledge....unprecedented and unique in the history of mankind; the arrival of a nation at an ultimate stage of evolution without having passed through the mediate one; the passage of the fruit, in other words, from crudity to rottenness, without the interposition of a period of useful (and ornamental) ripeness. With the Americans indeed the crudity and the rottenness are identical and simultaneous."

Of these Americans, Britishers, Frenchmen and Germans, women and men, every one is a caricature of a recognizable type. And the pertinent point for us in the present discussion is that several of these types are such as, with a slight change of emphasis, James is capable of wholeheartedly admiring. The earnestness of Louis and Miranda in self-improvement, their determination to get the most for themselves out of European culture, and to "see something of *real French life,*" are traits to be found in the best of James's Americans abroad, as they were dominant traits in James himself. Even Miranda's dismay over the complacency with which the English accept and revel in their caste system corresponds to something that, with a slight variation of accent, may often be found in James's letters and stories and is a recurring note in the journal of his sister Alice. It is their abysmal naiveté that makes these young Americans so funny; it is the Bangor bumptiousness of Miranda, her brassy innocence and self-confidence, her gullibility, and the strenuous, mechanical way she goes about to gather the fruits of ages in the shortest possible time; it is the mild and flabby Boston estheticism of Louis Leverett, his Pateresque impressionism. As the English girl says, he's "always sitting over the fire and talking about the colour of the sky. I don't believe he ever saw the sky except through the window-pane."

This "Bundle of Letters," by the way, is our assurance that James, whose sentence-structure often reminds us so much of Pater's, had actually been reading Pater, had more or less assimilated him, but had never quite succumbed to the tyranny of the Pater cult; as it also assures us, in Dr. Staub's letter, that James had been reading Arnold's "Friendship's Garland."

Now, this "dreadful little man," Louis Leverett, is in several ways a caricature of Henry James. In Auden's poem, "At the Grave of Henry James," he manages to make use of half a dozen French phrases; he is obliquely paying tribute to the master in the act of "taking off" one of his eccentricities. Louis Leverett, writing to his friend Harvard Tremont in Boston, manages to use a dozen French phrases in less than half dozen pages, and in each case followed by the English phrase, "as they say here." "There are times, my dear Harvard, when I feel as if I were really capable of everything—*capable de tout*, as they say here—of the greatest excesses as well as the greatest heroism. Oh to be able to say that one has lived—*qu'on a vécu*, as they say here—that idea exercises an indefinable attraction for me." This young Harvard man is, like Henry James, a great admirer of Balzac, "whose almost *lurid* pictures of Parisian life have often haunted me in my wanderings through the old wicked-looking streets on the other side of the river." He likes to think of his boarding house as a pension bourgeoise like the Maison Vauquer of *Le Père Goriot*. Like James, Leverett feels there is something lacking to the American character. "We're *thin*—that I should have to say it!—we're pale, we're poor, we're flat. There's something meagre about us; our line is wanting in roundness, our composition in richness. We lack temperament; we don't know how to live; *nous ne savons pas vivre,* as they say here." This insistence on the importance of *living* reminds us of Lambert Strether in Gloriani's garden; it reminds us of James confiding his deepest feelings to his note-book. The young man has, to be sure, his own strenuous tone, a sort of amalgam of "The Psalm of Life" with Pater's "hard gem-like flame." "The great thing is to *live,* you know, to feel, to be conscious of one's possibilities; not to pass through life mechanically and insensibly, even as a letter through the post-office."

What is there in Louis Leverett except the accent, the emphasis, that differentiates him from Henry James? One knows what an ambiguous word is this word, to *live*. How to live....*bon viveur*....to have life and to have it more abundantly. If we are hunting ambiguities, we have them first of all in James's attitude towards himself, this "dreadful little man....who's always sitting by the fire and talking about the colour of the sky"; who is forever using French phrases, and phrases from the studio, and doting on Balzac and the wicked-looking streets of the Rive Gauche; who is so sure that "the great thing is to *live*." If that is not James, or what he was conscious of being at the time of writing, it is what he *had* been, what he was afraid of being, what he hoped he was not. It was one side of him; it was an aspect of his nature that he hoped he had toned down or adequately supported by qualities more substantial. So he was making fun of himself? and is it not confusing for the reader to have fun made of the character who, of all others, should enlist his sympathy and confidence—that of the author himself?

Or there is the American character, there is the English character. In this story fun is made impartially of both the American and the English character, not to mention the glib, shallow Frenchman and the solemn, arrogant German. Is there not here an unsureness in the "moral touch"? Whom or what are we to admire, and to what are we to pin our loyalty? The answer is of course simple enough. What we are to admire is the *ideal* in character wherever it is found; but to fix the ideal there is required a vigilant awareness, a critical spirit that at its simplest is hardly more than the sense of the ridiculous, but that, in James's more serious work, where the characters are shown at grips with test-problems of conduct, demands a deeper probing and a subtler balance of contending forces. There were certain things in the American character that James deeply admired, and it is these that furnished the substance of his most famous heroes and heroines.

Again, there were certain refinements in the art of living that he found best exemplified in European society, and he never gave up the notion that Americans had much to learn from European manners. Moreover, as an artist in human nature, he was drawn to the European scene as a most rewarding subject because as a social order or complex it was so much more colorful and picturesque than what he had seen in Albany and New York, Newport and Boston. This is what fascinated him in Balzac, and late in life he wrote: "What we on our side in a thousand places gratefully feel is that (Balzac) cares for his monarchical and hierarchical and ecclesiastical society because it rounds itself for his mind into the most congruous and capacious theatre for the repertory of his innumerable comedians. It has, above all, for a painter abhorrent of the superficial, the inestimable benefit of the accumulated, of strong marks and fine shades, contrasts and complications."

James believed that any literary artist must make himself master of, "saturate" himself with, some special subject-matter, some social order and milieu; and after many trials he fixed upon the English scene as the most appealing to his imagination. The bulk of his work in his middle period of the eighties and nineties features English people in English settings. And while Mr. Brooks considers that England was essentially impenetrable to this American, and that he suffered from a sense of not being qualified to write of English manners with freedom and intimacy, the sturdily English Leavis holds, on the contrary, that "he knew English manners too well; he had penetrated too thoroughly." At the turn of the century James returned to Americans as his central and most admired characters; but the scene is still Europe, still mainly England, and his admirable but unschooled Americans are engaged in desperate battles with forces representative of European society, such as Kate Croy and Lord Mark in "The Wings of the Dove," the Widmores in "The Sense of the Past," and Prince Amerigo in "The Golden Bowl."

And here again the figure of the stage-setting appears in James's own account of his work. In his fine essay on "The Drama in *The Golden Bowl*," Mr. Francis Fergusson describes the work of James as a special type of romance, a type of romance more specifically characterized by T. S. Eliot as "metaphysical." And Fergusson has this to say of the part played by Europe in his work as it reaches its final phase:

"It was of course Europe that started James on his romantic way. But he soon distinguished the Europeans, and the Europe, which every traveller sees, from what he learned through an experience of Europe. And when his own vision is thoroughly developed he uses Europe quite craftily and without 'illusion' to provide functional settings for his characters' growth in awareness: 'Europe so constantly in requisition as the more salient American stage or more effective *repoussoir,* and yet with any action on this scene depending on one of my outland characters'."

## VIII

*His characters' growth in awareness*—that is a phrase to set off and ponder, for it puts in a nutshell what is most characteristic of James's later work, both in substance and in method. It looks in two directions at once, towards James as a revealer of ethical truth and James as a manipulator of the art of revelation. In all that has gone before, since we began to discuss the subject of his "ambiguity," we have been concerned with James as a revealer or truth-teller. It still remains to consider him as a story-teller—which, after all, is not a secondary issue in the case of any one whose chosen art is fiction. It is perhaps, in recent criticism, Mr. Fergusson, Mr. Snell and Miss Stevenson who most confirm me in my own views on this subject. And the beauty of it is that, taking James as a story-teller helps to clear up much of the confusion connected with the question of his "moral touch." For it is an almost total misapprehension of the nature of the story that leads so brilliant a writer as Mr. Brooks, and even sometimes so penetrating a critic as Mr. Leavis, into their curiously undiscerning judgments on the reality and the ethical implications of the work.

Perhaps the extremest obliquity to which an intelligent reader may be led by neglecting the story appears in the following blanket statement of Brooks in regard to all the later fiction of James:

> "No, the behavior of his characters bears no just relation to the motives that are imputed to them. They are 'great,' they are 'fine,' they are 'noble'—and they surrender their lovers and their convictions for a piece of property. They are 'eminent'—and their sole passion is inquisitiveness. Magnificent pretensions, petty performances!—the fruits of an irresponsible imagination, of a deranged sense of values, of a mind working in the void, uncorrected by any clear consciousness of human cause and effect."

There are three main misapprehensions here. The first is that the epithets applied to the characters in James's stories are applied by him as the author and are to be taken as his judgment on them. The second is that these epithets, whether of commendation or disapproval, are terms of absolute value and universal application, on all levels of reference, social, esthetic and moral. And the third misapprehension is that the valuation placed on any character at the beginning of the story is identical with that placed upon him at the end. The fact is that, in his later work, in all that has to do with characterization, whether of people or situations, James very seldom shows his own hand. The characterization is almost invariably rendered in terms of the impressions formed by the several persons of one another. The terms used are such as the people use in conversation or such as occur to them in their private ruminations. All readers of James are acquainted with the special type of adjective, often vague and extravagant in praise, lavished on one another by his "society" people—their behavior is beautiful, extraordinary, sublime; they show themselves magnificent, prodigious, stupendous. The simplest of such terms of commendation is *clever;* the most metaphysical is *real.* And the poles between which the people move, in the estimation of one another, is that of the *vulgar* and the *civilised.*

All of these words, as it happens, are taken from "The Wings of the Dove,"; but they, and others of a similar sort, will come to mind for readers of "The Awkward Age," "The Golden Bowl," "The Ivory Tower.' Taken all together the reader will distinguish in them a "Jamesian" quality. But the alert reader soon becomes aware that these are not *his* words but those of his characters. They are not ordinary dictionary words with fixed denotation and connotation. They are more or less the jargon of social cliques, carrying esoteric meanings, and meanings, too, that shift as the same word is used by different people and on different levels of reference. *Stupendous* is several times applied by Kate Croy and Merton Densher to the magnanimous behavior of Milly Theale. But there is always the sense that Kate is thinking more of the bigness of the sum bequeathed by Milly, the greatness of the act as measured by figures, whereas Merton is more conscious of the moral fineness of the act; and one feels that, though he never speaks out, he is conscious of the inadequacy of Kate's term in her own mouth.

Again, these words have different shades of meaning as they are applied *to* different persons. *Prodigious* is used of Kate and Milly in quite different senses. Kate says of Milly that she's prodigious (or magnificent) in the way she handled her interview with Merton. Merton replies: "So are you, my dear. But so it is; and there we are." The application of the same word to the two such different women brings out the irony. Both women were capable of taking the high line; but in one case it was the high line of a guardian angel (the dove), in the other it was simply that of a woman bold in her candor, her intelligence and unscrupulousness, but certainly not angelic in her spirit.

*Sublime* is used of Susan Stringham and of Kate: but the application gives it a different sense in each case. Susan lies to Milly. " 'I'm not worrying, Milly.' And poor Susie's face registered the sublimity of her lie." Much more ambiguity attaches to Merton's application of the word to Kate. We are conscious of his sense of Milly's innocence, of all she doesn't know; we are aware of his scruples and his sense of guilt. "So he felt all the parts of the case together, while Kate showed, admirably, as feeling none of them. Of course, however, when hadn't it to be his last word?—Kate was always sublime." Well, Kate's sublimity—shown precisely in seeming to ignore the complications of the case, its final effect on Milly, and so its ethical bearings—was a very different thing from the sublimity of Susan, whose every effort was to protect Milly and secure for her such happiness as could be found in her situation.

But, we are told, James asks us to admire people who are not admirable. "Kate showed, *admirably,* as feeling none of them" (the complications of the case). James throws in the guiding adverb *admirably*. But no, but no, this is not James but Merton. It is the loyal lover of Kate, clinging to the last to whatever can be said in her favor. And besides, it is Merton ignoring for the nonce the ethical aspect of Kate's diplomacy, and thinking of it only in terms of its social amenity. The ambiguity here, as so generally in these books, grows out of the fact that the same term which applies on the strictly social level proves in the end not applicable on the higher, the ultimate, level of the moral. One of the main conditions of James's theatre is that people should talk and act in a civilized manner. In the complications and awkwardnesses of social intercourse, it is being civilized that keeps things running smoothly, enables one to avoid awkward situations, to set one's conduct in a good light, to avoid the display of mean jealousies and suspicions. When Milly encounters Kate and Merton in the National Gallery it is potentially a very awkward moment, considering the fact that neither of these women has confessed the degree of her intimacy with this man. "That he was at the end of three minutes, without the least complicated reference, so smoothly 'their' friend was just the effect of their all being sublimely civilized." This is what Milly thinks. And she goes on to wonder what they had actually said to bring about this effect. "Whatever were the facts, their perfect manners, all round, saw them through."

Enormous stress is thus laid on good manners, and a careless reader might at times think that this element of civilization is for James the last word. But it never is. And this so-called civilization can be a rather silly affair, as Merton later reflects in regard to the freakish and ac-

cidental success of Milly and Susan in London society—
so much like the "booming" of a new book, cheap or good,
simply because a dull season calls for it. Merton realizes
how much there is of bogus and factitious in the whims
of "society." "He had supposed himself civilised; but if
this was civilization.....! One could smoke one's pipe
outside when twaddle was within."[2]

Emphasis is laid on "cleverness" and "intelligence"
as qualities that save a social situation and help maintain
difficult relationships; and in the early half of the book
these are the peculiar virtues of both Kate and Lord Mark.

---

[2]For anyone who likes to trace back images in fine poetry to
their possible sources in the "deep well of the unconscious," it
is interesting to note that T. S. Eliot also finds in the tobacco-
pipe a symbol for this same protest against social sophistication
and pseudo-"civilization." In "The Love Song of J. Alfred Prufrock," where

> "In the room the women come and go
> Talking of Michelangelo,"

but where the protagonist says he

> "..should have been a pair of ragged claws
> Scuttling across the floors of silent seas,"

Prufrock also remarks, after describing a typical disillusioning
social occasion,

> "Shall I say, I have gone at dusk through narrow streets
> And watched the smoke that rises from the pipes
> Of lonely men in shirt-sleeves, leaning out of windows?"

He welcomes wth relief the sight of something so natural and so
free from suggestion of the sentimentalities of "cultured" people.
And again. in the poem that takes its title from James's novel,
"The Portrait of a Lady." the man of the poem finds it necessary
to get away from the sentimental refinements of an over-civilized
woman, engage in various banal occupations, and

Every one agrees at the beginning that Mark is enormously clever. But opinions are constantly changing on the degree of his cleverness, until in the end he becomes no better than a "blundering weathercock," and a "horrid little beast." The great point in this shift is that, while he *is* clever on a certain level, where deep and tragic feelings do not intrude, he proves incapable of dignity and sensitiveness in dealing with situations that call for imaginative insight and deep human feeling. And the "European" *sophistication,* which seems to bear the premium in the early part of the story, yields place to the American *"imagination",* or social values to what we may call *spiritual values,* though James refrains from using that more pretentious term.

But it is Kate Croy who, in "The Wings of the Dove," bears the "most questionable shape." It is in reference to her that the shifting of opinion is going on most constantly and with the subtlest shades of differentiation. The story, or drama, is perhaps best defined as the process by which Merton, first, falls under her spell, and then, by very gradual degrees, is weaned away from her by the more powerful spell worked on his imagination by the image of Milly. This drama is made up of a succession of intimate situations, or "playlets", as Mr. Fergusson

> "....take the air in a tobacco trance."

These poems were written at a time when James was fresh in his mind. Is it too fanciful to suppose that Eliot's imagination had been sharply struck by this image of James's, wittily phrased as it is in words that fall, by exception in his writing, into a perfectly metrical pattern?

> "One could smoke one's pipe outside
>      When twaddle was within."

calls them, and it is, as he says of "The Golden Bowl," "through the successive illuminations of these playlets, these groping and scrupulous situations, that we are led to see what is really happening." The main thing that is happening is, of course, what is happening in people's minds in regard to Kate's unspeakable scheme and in regard to her character. But—is it necessary again to remind the reader?—it is in the minds of the dramatis personae that these things are happening; and in this case not in the minds of one but of several characters in succession.

Of all the leading characters, Kate is the most ambiguous. How finally to characterize her, what to think of her, remains in doubt up to the end—if not for us the readers, then at least for Merton. The determining question of all the later chapters is how Merton feels about her. How he will act determines the outcome of the plot; and, to some extent at least, how she will act is a factor in how he will. It is of the very essence of the plot and theme to determine how we (and Merton) shall finally judge Kate; it is of the essence of the plot, therefore, that she shall remain ambiguous up to the end—the final judgment on her brings on the solution of the intrigue and the declaration of the author's ethical attitude as embodied in Merton. But it all has to be done through Merton, and his point of view must dominate the second volume.

However, Kate's character is involved in her predicament. She is, in a sense, the victim, or at least the product, of her situation. And the situation in which Merton finds himself involved is of her invention. She spins the web. We must therefore be shown her situation as she only can see it. We must see her in action in the family situation which determines her later action. We must see this not merely for the sake of the plot; we must see it for the sake of her character. It is essential to the whole intrigue, to Merton's predicament, to his being bewitched, that Kate should be shown so far as possible in a sympathetic light. Whatever we think of her in the end— however we may judge the ethics of her behavior—we must realize how strong a character she is, how free from minor vulgarities, how capable of taking the "high line." And so Kate is first shown us, in the masterly opening chapters, as she is seen by herself in the desperate situation created by her father's turning her out to retrieve the family fortunes.

Note in passing that James's limitation of the point of view, in a given scene, to that of a certain character, does not necessarily mean that we see everything in the heart and mind of that character. It is a means of focussing on whatever it is in the particular situation that the author wishes to show us, for a particular purpose, through the "camera-eye" (to use Dos Passos' phrase) of the chosen character. James has infinite powers of reserving and keeping back what at the moment he does not care to reveal—leaving it for us to work out the interpretation as we go along, or leaving it to some other character to make the interpretation at the point where it will be most effective, after all the returns are in.

What we learn in these early chapters is how Kate feels about the situation in which she finds herself. We also learn, by indirect means, that she is handsome, intelligent, a social asset; that she would be willing to sacrifice much to the interests of her father and sister; that she is revolted as much by their shiftiness and meanness of character as she is by the material shabbiness and messiness of their surroundings. The build-up of her personality is continued through the succeeding chapters, indeed through the whole novel; but it is a significant fact that there is not another chapter in the whole book given over to her point of view. From now on, though she is very much present, the impression of her is registered, apart from what she says and does, from the point of view of Merton, then Milly and Susan, and then again, through the second volume, of Merton.

In the fourth book, the character of Kate is developed through the realization, by Milly and Susan, of how queer it is that Kate should never mention Merton Densher. They realize that they are moving in a labyrinth. Milly and Kate are now very intimate friends. "Yet it now came over (Milly) in a clear cold way that there was a possible account of their relations in which the quantity of what her new friend had told her might have figured as small, as smallest, beside the quantity she hadn't." Here the careful reader, well acquainted with James's system, would take warning. Milly, in her generous American unsophistication, wants to think only good of her friend, and deliberately rules out the hypothesis of double-dealing on the part of Kate. The ordinary reader will accept Milly's interpretation....as James wants him to. It is going to be necessary not merely for Milly, but still more for Merton, to put the best possible construction on Kate's motives. We too are puzzled by her never mentioning Merton, but like Milly we are willing to be put off. However, the word *duplicity* has been sounded, and it will serve to prepare the reader's mind for a later reading of Kate's character.

In the sixth book, there is a series of five chapters (xvii-xxi) all from the point of view of Merton. These were for James the crucial chapters of the book, and must have required the greatest finesse on his part to bring off. For they record the process by which Merton is brought within the silken net, brought to a line of action which he must instinctively have felt to be dishonest, involving as it did the deception of Milly in regard to his sentiments for Kate. Merton is too much taken up at this time with his own problem to be passing a conscious judgment on Kate, but in the end it is his realization of what her scheme amounts to that enables him to make this judgment. For the moment we are almost more aware of the light it throws on his own character. Through the process of his thought in regard to the trap he is being drawn into we are being shown that, fine as he is, he is also weak. This is surely not what James wants to underline; it just can't be avoided in the end; what James wants us to feel is how much harder it is for Merton to be dishonest—how it goes against the grain with him. Emphasis is laid on the sides of his nature that make him peculiarly subject to the spell: he is in love with Kate ("spirit and flesh"); he feels his obligation not to betray the woman he loves, to assume the best in her; in their relation to Aunt Maud he had already put himself under her guidance. And then, at the point where he positively turns the corner, it is his tenderness and consideration for Milly that make it impossible for him to let her down by telling her the truth.

Meantime, it is not Kate alone who is weaving the web. Aunt Maud and Susan are, each for her own reasons, in the conspiracy to make him deceive Milly. It is not till three or four weeks later (two books later), in

Venice, that Kate's scheme is baldly put into words by Merton: "Since she's to die I'm to marry her?.... So that when her death has taken place I shall in the natural course have money." Many characteristic features of James's art are to be noted. Until this point there has never been any outright statement, either in dialogue or in any one's recorded thoughts, of just what line of positive action is expected of Merton, apart from saying nothing to undeceive Milly or Aunt Maud. An intrigue of Jacobean crudeness and ugliness is here involved; but where the Jacobean dramatist would have used all his rhetoric to bring out its ugliness in high relief, it is here for the most part kept on a plane of genteel vagueness and elevation. There is a sort of piquancy in the baldness with which, in the end, at some critical moment, the terms are stated after so much polite evasion.

One's first feeling might be that after all the characters are sheer sentimentalists, speaking always in the most "beautiful" terms of acts and situations that are plain ugly. One even wonders for a time whether James himself is in the conspiracy of sentimentalism, rating good manners and delicate evasions above all else. It is the final turn that, in each case, convinces us that he is not really taken in by fine words—that it is rather we that, by his finesse, are temporarily taken in or left guessing.

The question of Merton's own character has now become a pressing one. In the end he proves himself of a fineness and a straightness: but through all this part of the story, the only virtue he unmistakably shows is his reluctance to lend himself to these deceptions. He is undoubtedly engaged in an ugly business; but there are for him two extenuating circumstances: his infatuation with

Kate, and the impossibility of undeceiving Milly without "killing her." It is not possible to deny that Merton is a weak character. He shows plenty of strength in the end —a sort of passive moral strength, involving a capacity to sacrifice every material good to a scrupulous sense of honor. But he is weak in action in the heat of action. And so, imaginatively, he is a weak character for fiction. The situation makes him so—The *donnée* of the plot; and while James exercises enormous ingenuity in masking this, the fact remains. For ordinary imaginative fictional interest we have to fall back on the characters of Kate Croy and Milly Theale.

In the final books it is mainly the contrast between Kate and Milly, constantly present to the mind and feelings of Merton, that makes the drama, completes the interpretation of Kate's character, and determines the final action of Merton. The contrast between the two women first comes to a head in the great *scène a faire* in Book X Chapter xxxiii, where Merton reports to Kate on his final interview with Milly in Venice. It is here that we have the first strong cold breath of an intimation that Milly, by her fineness of quality, has come between him and Kate. For here every word is loaded, and whatever Kate says serves the more to give her away—to give away the ruthless crudity of her attitudes. The author nowhere says so, nor does Merton explicitly think so. But it becomes steadily clearer in the chapters that follow that, while still loyal to Kate, still in love with her, and in need of her love, he is being forced to give her up by the logic of his feeling about their scheme and about Milly's "magnificence" in the face of it. In this chapter xxxiii, this is *everywhere implicit in the dramatic interchange. Kate* refers to Milly's magnificence; Merton says she *doesn't know* how magnificent she was. He explains it was Mark's visit that killed her, his blunt statement that Kate and Merton were in love. Kate wants to know if Merton couldn't have denied the truth of Mark's information. Merton replies: "We are, my dear child, I suppose, still engaged." The implication is double: to have denied Mark's word would have been to lie; it would also have been to repudiate his love for Kate. Kate replies: "But to save her life—" No comment; but somehow by now we feel the falseness of this; Kate is thinking of this argument merely as an argument and a means of securing her own ends. Merton says he didn't even seriously think of a denial to her face. Milly was dying. "If I had denied you," Densher said with his eyes on her, "I would have stuck to it." We realize now that his honesty is such, and his notion of honor such, that their scheme had really been impossible from the first for a person like him. Not so for Kate. For her the thought is that what Milly wanted (woman-like) was not the truth but Merton. What she is mainly interested in now is not Milly's "magnificence", or the hope of "saving her life," but the evidence that she was not alienated, so that Merton need not be afraid of not coming into money!

While in all this Kate had managed miraculously to maintain the *right tone,* verbally, the proof of her "magnificence," her line reveals in all its nakedness the selfishness, the insensibility, and the consciencelessness of her character. What follows is a dotting of the i's and crossing of the t's for Merton.

It is not altogether clear in the end whether Kate was right in assuming that Merton had fallen in love with

Milly. Perhaps that is a woman's over-personal interpretation. What is more clear is that, in comparison with the
stainless magnanimity of Milly, Kate's ruthless scheming
proves too horrid for Merton. At any rate, for him the
need for honorable conduct, together with his feeling for
Milly's situation, makes it impossible for him to reap the
fruits of Kate's, and his, nefarious scheme. Perhaps we
might say that neither James nor Merton passes ethical
judgment on Kate, but they do dramatically represent the
contrast between two systems of value, of which one is
felt to be horrid and impossible by persons who stand for
the other.

## IX

There are two reasons for my dwelling so long on
"The Wings of the Dove." One is that in my "Method
of Henry James" I did scant justice to this book in comparison with the other works of his "full prime," even
suggesting that it was not so "steadily and singly conceived as its companion works." The other is that, with later
reading, this novel has come to seem to me perhaps the
best example of his ultimate story-telling method. And
the consideration of it as a story is just what is needed
to do away with much of the confusion attaching to
James's "ambiguity." The suspicion of unsureness of
"moral touch" in this case completely vanishes with an
alert reading of the story. It was not James but his characters here who were uncertain in their moral touch, who
were, indeed, simply feeling their way, as we all do in
life, through long, ill-lighted corridors. This is, as Mr.
Fergusson keenly says, implicit in his technique of situa-

tions. For "the important point about his technique of situations is that it is based in a fundamental truth : people do find their way, when they find it at all, by fumbling about in immediate dealings with other people."

Mr. Fergusson is discussing more specifically the drama in "The Golden Bowl," and his statement of how this system works in that novel is the best answer I know to the objections of Spender and Leavis to the moral tone of that book.

> "The main action is carried by Maggie Verver and her father, those over-delicate American souls who have from the beginning 'the superstition of not hurting'; have 'others on their minds.' 'I don't think we lead, as regards other people, any life at all,' says Maggie when she begins to understand herself; 'Free as air—great if we act on it. Not if we don't.' The spirit had grown sleepy and squeamish through starvation and *acedia,* an excellent picture of a familiar plight. But the drama which follows is grandiose : the spirit coming to life through realizing the possibilities Europe reveals; seeing its nourishment and deciding to take its responsibility for getting it: acknowledging evil and trying to deal with it; coming down to earth from the distractions and abstractions of money—you may say the belated but for once triumphant American variation on the Empire theme, the setting explored and realized at last."

But the point I wish to lay my stress on here is not the ethical but the dramatic aspect of James's story-telling, above all in this period of "full prime." For that is the main subject of all my concern in "The Method." And curiously enough, I must here endeavor to correct the impression derived by one highly discerning reader of that volume, none less than Mr. Fergusson himself. In his essay on "James's Idea of Dramatic Form," while he gives a highly understanding digest of several things I have said about James's method in the later novels, he seems to have got the impression that I do not find this method "dramatic", and that, moreover, I think "the narrative movement is lost in these later novels." I have no doubt there are phrases and emphases in my book which may well have given rise to these misapprehensions. In the case of the narrative movement, the misapprehension doubtless rests on my noting how often it is not the overt action of the characters that is being given but their discovery of where they are, or, to use Mr. Fergusson's phrase, the process by which they "find their way." But I never meant to suggest that they were not finding their way, and that at every point what they were finding was not with the character a matter of exciting suspense, so that there is always plentifully present what Miss Stevenson calls "the basic narrative pull that makes a reader want to know what is going to happen next"—even if what happens may not be in the form of revolver shots or telephone calls but in that of new discoveries in regard to themselves and the situation in which they are involved.

When it comes to "drama," the misapprehension to which I gave rise was largely due to my wish to distinguish clearly between the peculiarly Jamesian drama, which takes place largely in the characters' minds, and the more theatrical type of drama that so largely held and holds the boards. But I fear it is also true that I have been guilty, at different times, of using the word "drama" in two quite different senses. In my chapter on "Drama" in "The Method," I was using the word in reference particularly to the sort of scene in which the participants are clearly ranged against one another as antagonists, instead of being, as so often in Jamesian dialogues, "confederates" working something out together between them. And in that chapter I do classify several of James's best novels as being more or less dramatic according to the degree of this overt antagonism between the characters. I still find this to be a not insignificant distinction. But I also see most clearly, at this distance, that I overlooked one highly important consideration: that sometimes a seeming confederate may be, in effect, a deadly antagonist. And that is perhaps why I failed to do better justice to "The Wings of the Dove"; I failed to see, apparently, that Merton's struggle with Kate has the tension and agony of a genuinely dramatic antagonism, and that through all that succession of outwardly decorous scenes, Merton was simply fighting for his life.

In my later book, "The Twentieth-Century Novel," James is definitely presented as a chief exemplar of dramatic method; and there the word dramatic is used rather in James's sense of "scenical," and his novels considered as, precisely, that succession of "playlets" to which Mr. Fergusson refers, representing particular intimate situations, or, in James's phrase, "discriminated occasions."

This is the sense of the word dramatic that has mainly interested me during many decades of thinking and writing about James, since it is this type of dramatic structure that sharply distinguishes his work from that of authors like Thackeray, or Balzac, say, or H. G. Wells, who are always *telling* the reader what happened instead of showing them the scene, telling them what to think of the characters rather than letting the reader judge for himself or letting the characters do the telling about one another. I like to distinguish between novelists that *tell* and those that *show;* and when I say that James was a dramatic story-teller, I mean that he was one of those that show through *scenes.* In "The Twentieth-Century Novel," I find the essence of the dramatic, in fiction, in the confinement of the story, like a stage-play, to the "here and now," that is to the particular place and time in which the dialogue is occurring or the characters' ruminations are being carried on.

Now, many great writers of fiction have been anything but consistently or consciously dramatic in this sense. They have thought of themselves as historians, philosophers, social scientists, and have indulged ad lib. in description, in historical summaries, in explanations and philosophical commentary. And they have been read with interest because the world is interested in all these things. It is probably true that all live writers of fiction tend instinctively to make the most of vivid dramatic moments. But relatively few novelists have so consciously conceived of the novel in terms of "scene," have tried so resolutely to keep themselves out and let the characters themselves conduct the narrative. And very few indeed have so made their stories out of the process of the characters' finding their way in regard to issues that need to be clarified. At this point, I cannot do better than quote from Mr. Snell's Harvard thesis in English, in which he dwells on one special feature of James's dramatic method:

"Dealing with subject as measured by the characters involved, (James) used their measure not as a static or a merely contributory element, but as a process and as a primary force itself constituting the real action. The great technical problem, involving a host of lesser ones, was this: the reader's degree of enlightenment must always be just enough greater than that possessed by any of the characters, to allow him to grasp the immediate significance of the difference between what each of them does know and what he does not know; yet it must never become great enough to destroy his interest in the clarification of issues going on before him. For that reason he must *see* what is happening; it must never (in theory) be outlined or explained—hence James's extension, into the smallest detail, of the technique of the dramatist."

And again, some pages later:

"If James, in accordance with the tradition of English fiction, had only appeared in these novels himself, as the omniscient and critical author, they would have been not only easier to read, but less disquieting. But he was resolved to be only the showman, presenting his actions without comment, letting the reader see for himself, as the story progresses, the abyss between what the characters know at first and what they learn, between what they know and what they do not, and above all, between cultivated appearances and the corresponding reality."

When Mr. Snell speaks of a type of novel that is "easier to read," I don't imagine he is suggesting that James is hard to read, or still less inviting, to a certain sort of reader; but simply that he is hard to read for those who have mistaken the kind of story he tells or cannot get the hang of it. When he speaks of James novels as "disquieting" to the reader I suppose he has in mind particularly stories like "The Sacred Fount" or "The Awkward Age," in which Mr. Wilson finds so much of his ambiguity, and of which readers like Brooks and Leavis complain that he asks us to admire characters who are simply not admirable. For he goes on to ask: "Why must James's readers, seeing the vacuity of life he described ('highly modern and "actual",' as he said) incautiously deny that he saw it, disregard his ironic detachment, read him into all his characters, make him plead for them? This is to ignore the significance of his technique." But of course Mr. Snell may be thinking of people like Kate Croy and Aunt Maud in "The Wings of the Dove," or the Newport set in "The Ivory Tower," of whom one of them says himself, "But we're all unspeakably corrupt," or of the Midmore set in "The Sense of the Past," English people a century earlier who drove Ralph Pendrel back in revulsion from the past he fondly idealized into the future to which he belonged. Or he may be thinking of people like Charlotte and the Prince in "The Golden Bowl," when Maggie at length realizes "the horror of finding evil seated all at its ease where she had only dreamed of good." We have it from more than one source that Henry James was of a deeply melancholy nature and that he did not think too highly of our life or of the world. And it was certainly not an ideal world which formed the stuff out of which his later heroes and heroines had to fashion their lives, the setting against which they were made to play their idealistic parts.

One might say that the same thing holds for early stories like "The American" and "The Portrait of a Lady," if one thinks of the Marquise de Bellegarde in the one, or of Gilbert Osmond and Madame Merle in the other. But the "evil" in these stories is figured by circumstances more melodramatic and seeming less typical of the real world. And there is no hint of ambiguity in the treatment. So they are less disquieting for readers who prefer books that make them feel good about the world. But after all, most serious people know that the *world* is corrupt, and that we must pin our hopes to the "saving remnant" of individuals who are free from corruption. And it does not take exceptionally tough-minded people to find some hope for humanity in a world which includes a Milly Theale and (in the end a Merton Densher), or a Maggie Verver and (in the end) a Prince Amerigo, or a young man like Gray in "The Ivory Tower" "who doesn't want to act in fear of anything or anyone whatever", and a millionaire Betterman, who will leave his millions only to a man who has had no slightest commerce with Mammon.

But here I am anticipating the topic of my next and, I earnestly hope, my final section of this introduction. And I still have something further to say on the subject of drama in James's novels. In confining itself to the here-and-now, or "dramatic present," as I call it, in dealing with particular intimate occasions, and with psychological issues whose clarification or resolution defines the very action of the story, the Jamesian novel, in its "major phase," lends itself to other characteristic features of drama, and reminds us, in its own medium, of the dramatic ideal embodied in the old formula of the three unities. It tends to be highly selective in the subject-matter chosen for presentation. It takes up the story in the middle, at the point where the issues have begun to define themselves. It limits itself to the comparatively small number of occasions in which the issues work themselves out. It thus tends to cover a relatively small extent of time; and the successive "scenes" follow close upon one another, one growing out of another in strict logical sequence, thus producing an effect analogous to the classical *"laison des scènes."* Here we have evidently the fruits of James's long and devoted study of the French "well-made play." Here we have, too, a close analogy between the novels of James and the social dramas of Ibsen; and we understand why, in spite of features in the Norse playwright that rubbed him the wrong way, he was an excited follower and staunch champion of Ibsen in the nineties when "Hedda Gabler" and "The Master Builder" and the others were beginning to make their way on the English stage. In short, when it comes to recognising the dramatic character of James fiction in all his later years, I find I am unreservedly in agreement with Mr. Fergusson.

## X

But there is still another direction in which the work of James invites to classification and labelling by reference to historical genres or modes. The question arises as to where he stands in the traditional division of fiction into realism and romance. In planning to write this Introduction, I have had the very curious experience of being shocked to find James characterized as "romantic" by several most discriminating critics, and then discovering that I myself, in 1918, had devoted an entire chapter to the element of "romance" in him. And I have sometimes found myself quarreling with historians of American literature who have given James an important place in "the rise of American realism." It must be that Henry James is an odd number, not so easy to label as Balzac or Walter Scott, as George Sand or George Eliot.

The term realism implies, as I understand it, that the author is undertaking to represent human nature and life as they really are, objectively considered, whereas romance presents them to us as the heart would have them, with a high degree of sentimental idealization. Human nature as it really is, in the history of realism, generally means what we may call average humanity and not the character of exceptional men and women; or if they are exceptional, they are likely to be exceptional in the direction of vice rather than in the direction of virtue. The realist prided himself on taking subjects from lower social and cultural levels than had been the rule with the romancer. And, in addition to this, realism generally implied a more detailed, a more minutely documented, presentation of the human scene than had been the case with romantic writers.

It may be observed that realism has had a markedly different slant in French, in Russian and in English fiction. The emphasis in French fiction of the nineteenth century was on what may be called objective or scientific truth. Human nature was regarded as one province of natural history, or as one department of what we now call the social sciences. It was to be approached with the kind of cool detachment and impartiality which characterize scientific studies. In 19th-Century Russian fiction we are struck by the reference of all human behavior to mystical religious standards, especially in Tolstoy and Dostoevsky. In the last analysis, human behavior with them is judged by reference to values derived not from the realm of experience as open to scientific study but from a realm that transcends purely human considerations. English novelists, on the other hand, though for the most part they pay lip service to religion, are predominantly moral in their point of view. They are not concerned so much with whether men's behavior is conformable to the will of God as with whether it conforms to the rules of good conduct prevailing in English society—whether men are honest, faithful, chaste and charitable.

It is clear that, in this respect, James takes his place in the main stream of English realism as compared with that of France and Russia. But he is English with a difference—with a special tone and emphasis that mark him off from nearly all our writers, English or American. He is not, I think, a religious writer in any strict sense of the word. I do not find in him any disposition to refer human nature to any standard outside of itself. What interested him in life was the gratifications to be found in ideal human relationships. It is the obligations of honor between man and man, between man and woman, and the satisfaction to be taken in meeting these obligations, which form the constant theme of his stories.

The difference between James and earlier English writers is the special refinement he gives to his conception of human relations and the obligations inherent in them and necessary for their successful maintenance. You will almost never find him referring to bad conduct as sinful, or criminal, or immoral, or socially harmful, nor to good conduct as moral, or virtuous or spiritual. Undesirable behavior is likely to be referred to as vulgar or ugly; desirable behavior is that of a gentleman or lady; it is civilized or beautiful or magnificent. It might be said that, in its essence, James's morality is indistinguishable from his esthetics—that his ethical system of values is essentially an esthetic system. What he is concerned with, from the beginning to the end of his writing, is *the fine art of living.* For his leading characters, especially in his maturity, he invariably chooses men and women who are consciously devoted to this fine art of living, and who are mostly ready to sacrifice everything to it. For his secondary characters he often chooses people who are also, in their way and according to their lights, devoted to this same fine art, but whose notions of what it involves fall short of what is necessary to make it ideally right.

One must concede that on this point James is far from a realist in the strict sense of the word. It is not average human nature that he takes for his subject. For we can hardly admit that the mass of men are devoting themselves to any such fine art of living. They are trying to make ends meet, or to become rich and powerful. They are seeking sensual gratifications, and often without regard for the human relationships involved. They are concerned more with getting what they want than with how they get it. They are playing a game, it may be, but a game in which the winner is the man who knows all the tricks of the card sharper, and when he wins, it is at the expense of those who lose.

In the game that James has in mind, one cannot win at the expense of another, and cheating is fatal; it is a game in which the players are so to speak partners, bound to seek their common advantage, and the gains are all those of partners winning together. For it is the successful conduct of the fine relation between them that is the object of the game.

If then realism is taken to mean the representation of human nature as it is statistically found to be among men in the mass, James cannot be said to be a realist. If he is to be labelled realist, we must add to this generic term some other word to signify the particular species of realism that he exemplified. Perhaps we might call him an *idealistic realist*.

It is also to be noted that, in choosing people who practise the fine art of living, James finds it convenient to choose people, for the most part, who are well-to-do, intelligent, and of a high level of cultivation. The possession of wealth and leisure leaves them free to pursue their fine art without being distracted by the need to make their way in the world. And even to conceive this fine art interestingly it is necessary to be intelligent and cultivated. James's people, then, are largely taken from social levels higher than those characteristically treated by realists. There are here no Charles Bovarys, no Gervaises or Lantiers, no Peggotys or Little Nells. And it is the intellectual refinement of these people even more than their social elevation that makes them so "unrealistic" as representatives of our species. It is their conscious awareness of themselves and the game they are playing that sets them off so from a world in which men are much more the creatures of instinctual drives than of deliberate choice. It is this which enables them to make a work of art of their living; and it is this, as many critics have noted, that distinguishes the literary art of James from the ordinary realistic recordings.

Thus Herbert Read, in "The Sense of Glory", quotes from Professor Edgar's keenly penetrating account of James's theory of art. "It was his theory that the artist is privileged to give the law to life, and to submit her haphazard processes, her waywardness, her profuse extravagance, or even her occasional meagreness, to a control more severe than the discipline she herself imposes." And then Mr. Read goes on to say: "And this, of course, is the truth of the matter: the imagination seizes upon one of the disjointed events of which life for the most part is made up, and develops that event into a fable which has not the casual and occasional aspect of existence but the harmonious autonomy of art. Art, in fiction, is not a true report, but a convincing fable." It is in the same sense that Mr. Spender declares: "(James's) characters are not meant to be real in the sense that they are copies of the people whom, in life, they represent.... They are not portraits, but symbols of the types they represent; in the same way as the characters in Shakespeare.... Constructive and living art is always struggling against a stream of mere phenomena in order to create life." And it is in a similar vein that Mr. Blackmur says of James that "he had need of both that imagination which represents the actual and that which shapes the possible." And then—he is speaking of those tales in which James's theme is "that of the artist in conflict with society": "For James, imagination was the will of things, and as the will was inescapably moral, so the imagination could not help creating—could not fail rather to recreate—out of the evil of the artist's actual predicament the good of his possible invoked vision."

Upon such a theory of fictional art, we are not obliged to conclude that realism is incompatible with the highest artistry. There is nothing to prevent the author from being consciously aware of the full significance of the life he is presenting. He is at liberty to struggle against, or with, the stream of phenomena, and from the haphazard processes of nature to develop a convincing fable, and so "create life." In such cases we may call his realism *normative;* it subjects the "casual and occasional" aspects of existence to a logical or spiritual norm and so gives them significance. But when it is the *characters in the story* who are so constantly and largely provided with this conscious awareness, we begin to say they are not true to life, not true to the ordinary run of life, and seek for some other term to describe this sort of fiction. If we are not content with either romantic or realistic; if we must have some special term for James's art, we might venture a new coinage in critical jargon and call it simply *normative*.

And yet, among literary historians, it is customary to give James a prominent place in what is called the "rise of realism" in American fiction. And there are plausible reasons for thus featuring him in this chapter of our literary history. In any survey of American romanticism, one is impressed with the thinness of our nineteenth-century literature as compared with European writing in the same period. With rare exceptions, our poetry and fiction of the last century do not seem to have the *body* which one finds in Thackeray or Browning, in Balzac or Flaubert, in Tolstoy or Baudelaire. This want of body is shown in several ways. It is shown to begin with, in a very narrow limitation of subject-matter. Our nineteenth-century writers do not in general attack the world and life with the boldness of European writers. They are for one thing more prudish, more reluctant to introduce their readers to vicious and depraved conduct, or to go deeply into the hidden springs of character. They are primarily concerned to give a bright and edifying view of the world.

Now, Henry James, while he was so much interested in the fine art of living, was inclined to show this in terms of life in the actual world, where even persons of cultivation and consequence are not invariably guided by the rules of conventional morality. In this he was taking his

cue from continental fiction—from Balzac and Turgenev,
from Tolstoy and George Sand.    The actual donneé of
his story, the situation with which he starts, is likely to
be one that might have scandalized his American readers
if he had been a popular writer, and if he had not envel-
oped his narrative in such a maze of subtleties and dressed
it up in a style so allusive and intricately woven that only
the alert reader was fully aware of what he was dealing
with.

    This was particularly the case with the novels of his
final period.    I remember very well a discussion that took
place in my presence between two of my women friends
with regard to James's intention in "The Golden Bowl."
It had reference to the intimacy that prevailed between
Charlotte Stant and the Prince Amerigo after Maggie
Verver had been married to the Prince and had "squared"
things with her father by marrying him to her friend
Charlotte.    What Maggie did not know was that, some
years earlier, Charlotte had been the mistress of the Prince.
And what she did not at first realize, during their life in
London, was that Charlotte and the Prince were returning
to their earlier intimacy.

    To a reader of any sophistication there can be no
doubt as to the actual relations subsisting between Charlotte and the Prince.    But not all American readers in the
early 1900's were persons of sophistication.    James's manner of referring to this situation is so refined and allusive,
and the line taken by Maggie so "high" and "civilized",
that an inexperienced young woman might be excused
for supposing that the conduct of Charlotte and the Prince
was, at the very worst, inconsiderate and ill-advised.    And
so it was with one of my young women friends.    They

were both of them persons of exceptional intelligence, graduates of one of our best colleges for women, both of them of excellent and well-to-do families, both widely read in world literature. The one of them maintained that the relation between Charlotte and Amerigo was "guilty," and the other maintained that it was technically "innocent" and "platonic." Of course I had my own opinion, but I am sure that I tried to hold the balance even between these two admirable friends and bluestockings.

It is easy to see the pertinence of this incident to our discussion. James was here featuring a situation of the kind generally tabu in American fiction, but he was treating it in such a manner as to give offence to very few readers. In this gingerly treatment of a scandalous subject, I do not suppose that James was simply trying to propitiate his public. He was treating the subject as best suited his temper and his esthetic ideal. It was not the technical guilt or innocence of these two lovers that interested him, but the occasion given for Maggie Verver to exercise her talents in the fine art of living.

James is obviously not a Puritan, nor even a Victorian, in his moral outlook. In his fiction, the morality of an act is not found in its technical conformity to any statute or commandment; it is found in the actual human quality of the relation involved. But it would be a mistake to say, simply, that his ethics is an esthetic and let it go at that. The fact is that in his system of values there is a hierarchy, or vertical scale, comprising several levels of value, and that, in any one story, there is seen a gradual passage from one level to another. Throughout all his life, there were for James three categories of values prized in human beings. There was the category of es-

thetic discrimination, the category of social expertness and
good taste, and the category of values that are strictly
ethical.

We have seen how these categories of value are exemplified in "The Wings of the Dove." Aunt Maud, for
all her wealth, is simply a vulgar woman. While she has
social force, she has neither social nor esthetic grace, and
her house is a model of sumptuous bad taste. Lord Mark,
simply by inheritance, is a man of taste and intelligence,
and a man of unusual social tact and pliancy; it is only
in the end that he betrays himself, in his relations with
Milly, as devoid of all those finer instincts that derive
from the heart and the heart's conceiving. As for Kate,
she is the most extraordinary villainess that ever undertook to accomplish ugly ends, but always in terms of the
finest taste and sensibility. On two of the levels of value
she shows herself to be almost incomparably fine; but on
the highest level, and that most decisive for the art of
living, her shoddiness comes out in high relief.

We have seen how James's dramatic techniques were
employed to implement the characters' conscious awareness
of the issues involved and to bring about, as the essence
of the action, a clarification and resolution of these issues.
And this brings us back to the subject of James's "realism." It is perhaps these dramatic techniques, and especially that of the limited point of view, that give James his
best claim to be regarded as a realist. For it is these
procedures, and the intensity and intimacy of imaginative
realization entailed, which lend his narratives that air of
solid actuality which is so often missing in earlier American fiction—that *illusion of actuality* which Maupassant
signalizes as the distinguishing mark of realism. This is

not, of course, the method of Maupassant. It is subjective where he is objective. But for many readers James's characters are quite as real as Maupassant's. They are puzzling, to be sure, but they are *intriguing,* for one thing, by virtue of our very uncertainty just how to take them. If there is one thing that makes us believe in characters more than what the author has to say of them, it is what they have to say of one another, especially when they disagree in their estimate of the same person. When once you have made a character the subject of discussion and disagreement, you have no alternative but to regard him as real.

Besides, it is always a point with James that every observation made upon a character is made in the context and framework of a particular situation and a particular scene. And the closeness with which one is confined to the particular setting and the immediate issue lends itself to that "solidity of specification" which James considered one of the chief merits of a work of fiction. This, perhaps, more than anything else is the mark of realism as it is conceived by those who speak of James as important in the development of realism in America. He had a predilection, in all art, for the sort of effect to which he applied the French word *touffu*—as a thick-piled carpet— an effect or depth, richness, luxuriance of detail.

It will not be forgotten that one of his most admired models was Balzac. But here a difference must be noted. James does not so much go in for fullness of detail, the piling up of detail, the multiplication of objects, as for fineness of discrimination in regard to effects. He was of course influenced by the Flaubert-Maupassant doctrine of the *mot juste.* But in seeking for the precise word, he was not looking so much for the word which was most precise in objective description as for the word most suggestive of discriminated quality. And in this he is so successful that places and situations are as well realized for the imagination as in writers notable for the lavishness of detail by which their pictures are built up. So that altogether, it does appear that, in some sense of the word realism, it properly applies to James. At any rate he is not open to the reproach of thinness in his effects.

Still, if realism is taken to mean the exploitation in mass of the crude substance of life and of average human nature driven forward blindly by instinct and appetite; if it precludes the featuring of men and women whose action is deliberately controlled and formalized by the will to fineness; if its typical exemplars are taken to be Zola, or Flaubert or Maupassant, or even Thackeray or Dreiser, then clearly the term cannot properly be applied to James. Mr. Spender and Mr. Leavis have signalized the strain in him of the poet. Mr. Blackmur has characterized the work of the latest period as "the fiction of fate." Dealing with people engaged in a sort of death-struggle with society, and subject to the mutilating conditions of life, the stories of this period are "the prophecy of life beyond and under, or at any rate in spite of, the mutilating conditions." Mr. Fergusson and Miss Stevenson, among others, do not hesitate to label James "romantic" in contrasting him with the continental realism of his time; but they carefully define the term in such a way as to rule out the most damaging connotations of the word, and Miss Stevenson indicates how the romance of the later stories is "impregnated with realism," having "the benefit of the rich experience of life which went into the middle period of living and writing." And I find that in "The Method" I have distinguished an element of romance in the extremes to which James carried his "cultivation of psychological niceties," and in the "rarefied and transcendental atmosphere into which he lifts us, an atmosphere in which there is nothing to impede the free action of spirits."

## XI

And that is as far as I am inclined to go with the attempt to classify James by reference to the historical trends. What I should like to do in conclusion is to touch upon a subject more neglected, and more elusive, and that is the mere seduction James's fiction exercises on the reader's imagination. For it is that which brings one back again and again to the reading of James over a lifetime of this sort of self-indulgence. What most impresses me, in looking over after such an interval this work of my youth, is the way in which that young man keeps his head critically speaking, and that in spite of his evidently intense admiration for James. He appears to have had a strong determination not to let himself be taken in by his prophet and idol. He is determined to maintain his sense of humor, of measure, and not make unreasonable claims for the author of his predilection. Perhaps he was unduly conscious of how many readers found James unapproachable, and was inclined to exaggerate certain of his peculiarities by way of concession, in hopes of bringing them round to an appreciation of what he had of appeal for any serious reader. Since that time, James's stock has risen several hundred percent on the readers' market; and since then, what is more important, a much older man has had plenty of time to verify the constancy of James's appeal. So that, if he were to write the same book over again, he would be inclined, with a minimum of apology, to insist mainly on what good reading James makes. But it would come to the same thing in the end; for the burden of his discourse would be simply that James makes such good reading because he tells such good stories.

Literary appraisals must, in the last analysis, be very personal. For they must be made, if they are to carry any weight, on the basis of the reader's personal experience with the work read. It is my invariable experience with the stories of James, long and short, heavy or light, that my interest is captured from the first page. As soon as a character is presented, in a given situation, I find I have an active concern for him. What the author has to say about him is so special that it arrests the attention and carries one out of the world of the standardized and commonplace. And before we have turned many pages, the author has aroused our curiosity by the suggestion of some mystery in connection with this character or his situation, something ambiguous and in need of clarification. And this sense of mystery, which we have from the beginning, stays with us throughout. For wherever the answer is given to one question, another is raised in the act of answering the first; or several others, for the more we know about any situation, the more vistas it opens into the unknown and unclarified. In short, the stories of James are always mystery stories, and one may as well acknowledge to begin with that the fascination they have is akin to that some people find in those pictured parcels one takes home from the drug store on Saturday night along with one's bromides and, strangely enough, without the necessity of a doctor's prescription.  And if some readers do not feel the need for these pictured parcels of murder and detection, it is because there are the voluminous works of Dostoevski and Conrad, of Henry James and William Faulkner, to satisfy our most inexhaustible craving for mystery.

For mystery, fulfillment and evasion.  In his effort to make life more convenient and save space and time for his real business, man has so cluttered up the ways that all the lights are red lights, and he wears himself out trying to break through to some spacious unencumbered haven of the spirit.  After one has fought the battle of life with gadgets throughout the daylight hours, it is a luxury, with lamplight, to enter into a region in which there is never any question of mechanical arrangements or budgetary adjustments, of mere dust and racket, in which there is nothing to frustrate and baffle but the spirit itself in its limitations and its labyrinthine windings, and in which the lights are so disposed as to illuminate particular corners and passages and not to weary and plague us with indiscriminate glare.

The world of James is at once more strange and more familiar than that of the traffic jam or the dime store.  It is a strange world indeed in which one is concerned with nothing but essentials.  It is strange, too, for people who keep constantly to the superficial levels of consciousness, when, like visitors to mines, a smoky lamp is fixed to their caps and they are taken for excursions through dark subterranean galleries of the mind.  Without the terminology of the psychoanalyst and without the assumption of his special premises in regard to the libido, James has given us types that would fit neatly into the psychologist's categories, and his artist's imagination works with the surgical precision and sharpness of the Freudian scalpel to lay bare the state of being of his patient. But he is not a psychoanalyst in the full sense of the word, for he seldom undertakes to explain the origin of the malady by reference, for example, to forgotten experiences of childhood. For prevention of neuroses, if that concerns him, he must rely on the promotion of self-knowledge through the cultivation of conscious awareness of self.

Thus in "The Beast in the Jungle," the rather colorless man named Marcher suffers from a sense that he is destined to receive some monstrous visitation of doom; and he spends his life, along with a woman friend to whom he has confided his secret, waiting for the lightning to strike, or the beast to spring out upon him. As the story progresses we are gradually made aware that his monstrous doom is all Marcher has to give him distinction and that his confident anticipation of its coming is simply his "super-compensation," as the psychologists say, for his sense of inferiority; it is all he has to make him feel good about himself,—this, and the sharing of it by his friend. The proof of his mediocrity is found in his not realizing, with the death of his friend, that a genuine love for her would have been the one thing that would have drawn him out of the fatal circle of his egoism. When he does at length feebly realize this truth about himself, it proves inadequate to satisfy his craving for distinction, since his sole distinction was that "he had been the man of his time, *the* man, to whom nothing on earth was to have happened."

There must be plenty of people who might recognise Marcher's case as a true picture of their own—that is, if they had the wit to do so, the moral courage for that, the habit of self-study with which so many James characters are endowed. This is no doubt under some form or another one of the most familiar situations in human experience. What makes it strange is first that, throughout most of the story, Marcher does not have the clue to his own mystery, even after the reader has begun to have intimations of it; and then that few people are crazy enough, or imaginative enough, to conceive this particular way of giving themselves importance. Monstrous dooms are something, however, which we can tentatively allow, in a story, to other people, and through half of this tale a glamour attaches to Marcher by virtue of the very obsession that we later come to recognise as the sign of psychological weakness. And the image of the beast in the jungle is powerful enough to lend an air of glamorous strangeness even to the pitiful conclusion. In any case, James never pins upon his character any invidious psychological label; he leaves it to us to do that and thereby to derive a gratification such as we can never derive from the labelled specimens of the clinic.

From the point of view of mere story-telling, it is the woman friend, evidently in love with Marcher, dying perhaps of his incapacity to reciprocate her love, who provides the means by which his case-history is carried forward through fine degrees of growing light to its final clarification. For it is in their conversations, and the ambiguous things she says in her effort to spare him her own enlightenment, that the reader is gradually let into an understanding of Marcher's case. And it is their conversations that supply the drama—ironic and pathetic—that raises this story so much above the level of a clinical study.

Since James's mysteries are psychological, and subject to protracted pursuit and unravelling, it is at once clear why they take hold of and keep hold of our imaginations in a way not possible for the mysteries of the "who-done it," which are primarily mysteries of mere *fact,* where it is necessary to supply only the barest motive for action, and where, since at all costs the reader must be kept from guessing the true solution before the end, there is seldom any possibility of doing justice to the human factors involved.

James's are psychological mysteries and moral too. With Marcher it is chiefly a moral lack, a sort of obliquity or incapacity, that is in question. And it will not be necessary to labor the point that more often, with James's leading characters, it is a positive moral ideal, it is actual moral insight and capacity, that is shown in action. And the beauty of it is that the issues are not such as to be resolved by a simple turn of the hand, but sufficient to carry us forward, through many obscure windings, with no relaxation of continuity or lowering of intensity. And they are important enough, humanly, to bear the weight of all this continued pressure.

Perhaps what most bespells the reader of James is the peculiar intimacy which we share with his characters, following so closely the idiosyncrasy of their thought, shut up with them in the closed circle of their problems, even confined with them to the particular house and room where if anywhere they must find their way to a solution. This sense of being in the know, even where, at each successive stage in its unravelling, it is an unresolved problem of which we have knowledge, constitutes an appeal to our vanity or pride, making us feel the satisfaction of the religious initiate. And it carries with it a sense of the individual reality of the people with whom we have formed this initiate bond. It is at any rate my own experience that the people of James become and remain personal friends much as the people of Dickens do, though in such a different way.

I judge that Mr. Quentin Anderson has not had the same experience, but perhaps that is because he is so determined to regard the characters of James, in terms of his father's theodicy, as mere "aspects of Man and God." He believes that James's morality is tied to, and at every point parallels, this theological mythology which is a formal scheme for charting the process by which the race is passing through its ugly stage of ethical individualism to become in the end "a selfless concert of creativity". And so he seems to consider himself bound to note that this theological morality "dissolves every ethical situation" and inevitably breaks down "the barriers of personality."

Mr. Anderson finds himself thus in something of a dilemma. He believes it is not true, as generally assumed, that James's was "a consciousness or sensibility whose morality has no sanction but taste," but that, with him, on the contrary, "belief seems a necessary concomitant of the ordered world of his art." By belief, Mr. Anderson clearly means religious or supernatural belief; and he supposes James to have made every character and incident in the later great novels a symbol of something in his father's very special variety of Swedenborgian theology. It is this which gives him sanction as a moralist, and yet it is just this which brings it about that "his view of men and women has little normative value."

One feels that in Mr. Anderson's essay on "Henry James and the New Jerusalem" (Kenyon Review, Autumn 1943) he suffered from lack of space, and did not do justice to the large and interesting critical considerations he raised. And in the subtle and challenging essay which serves as his Introduction to his "Selected Short Stories" of James (Rinehart, New York, c. 1950), while he further emphasizes James's prophetic role, he certainly advances no new evidence to support his contention that if the reader is to understand certain tales and novels of James, he must know how straight they come from his father's doctrinal teaching. To a system of allegorical interpretation as comprehensive and elaborately developed as Mr. Anderson's, one does not feel like saying bluntly, "This will not hold water", certainly without a great deal of study and thought. But one cannot but feel that Mr. Anderson, on his side, is much too sweeping and confident in his assertion that the three great novels of his major phase were intended by James to illustrate a particular system of theological faith; and that in James's intention Milly Theale symbolizes the "descent of God" into the spirit of man, Adam Verver symbolizes Divine Wisdom, Maggie Verver Divine Love, and the Principino Divine-Natural Humanity. "The Ambassadors," "The Wings of the Dove," and "The Golden Bowl" "deal respectively with the Christian, and the New Church." *"The Wings of the Dove* logically follows an account of the failure of the Law or Jewish Church to cope with evil, since it is a poem in which Densher is redeemed and constrained to accept the divine love; and to it, in turn, *The Golden Bowl* is a logical sequel, since it deals with the coming of the divine-natural humanity (the New Church)—or the 'marriage' of the infinite and the finite."

In thus equating every most natural and innocent-looking circumstance in James's social comedy with some very special and esoteric item in his father's ingenious and bizarre theology, Mr. Anderson relies more on what, in textual studies, is called internal than on external evidence. The evidence is some fancied likeness between an item found in one system with an item found in the other so alien system. Thus Milly Theale, conscious that she symbolizes a divine power that is to set up the New Jerusalem in America, and that just because it is there men have instituted a "saturnalia of greed" .... "Milly therefore calls herself the 'survivor of a general wreck'—a spiritual deposit produced by the moral electrolysis of American society." In such a case the internal evidence requires one to ignore the plain meaning of Milly's phrase as it appears in its own context: viz., that she, with all her money, is the sole survivor of a family the other members of whom have died.

In parallels of this sort historical criticism generally demands more of *external* evidence, which in this case would mean evidence from the writings or sayings of Henry James Jr. that he had ever regarded any of his stories as embodiments of his father's theological doctrines, or even that he had accepted his father's theology as matter of faith. And since we have both the famous prefaces and note books, as well as many letters and recorded sayings of James, in which there is much reference to the origins of these novels and his intentions in them, the greatest weakness in Mr. Anderson's argument is not to cite any reference by Henry James to his father's theology, whether or not in connection with his own writing.

Several generations of scholars have now written about James the younger without informing us whether or not he *had* any theology.

It is true that in 1910 James contributed to Harper's Bazaar an article in which he stated his belief, or rather his fervent hope, that human consciousness may continue after death. But there is nothing in this article to suggest that his qualified belief in immortality was grounded in any variety of Christian theology, let alone the peculiar variety evolved by his father. Indeed, James seems a little embarrassed to realize that there may be in his shaping of his thought a superficial resemblance to theological concepts which he is far from sharing; showing, as he says with a touch of humor, "how neatly extremes may sometimes meet." So far as I know, apart from this article, the nearest he came to the statement of a religious position was in a letter to Grace Norton in 1883 on the occasion of a death in her family:

"I am determined not to speak to you," James writes, "except with the voice of stoicism. I don't know *why* we live—the gift of life comes to us from I don't know what source or for what purpose: but I believe we go on living for the reason that (always of course up to a certain point) life is the most valuable thing we know anything about, and it is therefore presumptively a great mistake to surrender it while there is any yet left in the cup. In other words consciousness is an illimitable power, and though at times it may seem to be all consciousness of misery, yet in the way it propagates itself from wave to wave, so that we never cease to feel, and though at moments we appear to, try to, pray to, there is probably something in the universe that it is probably good not to forsake."

This is not quite all he had to say for comfort to his friend but this is as near as he comes to anything that might be given a religious interpretation, and there is not the remotest hint here of any theological system out of which might be made such an allegory as Mr. Anderson makes out of his three great novels.

But not everybody will agree with Mr. Anderson that in order to have "a principled attitude toward men and affairs" one must take one's position on the grounds of supernatural faith, or that "belief seems to be a necessary concomitant of the ordered world of (James's) art." That James has a "principled attitude toward men and affairs" not many readers doubt. That he had a mature and deeply grounded hierarchy of values seems clear enough to me. And I don't see why it should be any the better for being grounded in some system of theology, let alone the peculiar system his father had worked out for himself. Wouldn't that remove it one stage further from the possibility of rational proof or empirical verification? Is it the assumption that *any* system of theology is better than none? It may very well be that men derive their order of values from reflection upon human experience and then manage somehow to fit them in, more or less uneasily, to some system of theology. And perhaps a man as independent-minded as Henry James was able to maintain his system of values without any support from theology. Whether or not it would then have a "sanction" for others would depend, for one thing, on the need *they* felt for a theology to support it.

But this is indeed taking the long way round to bring us back to the subject of James's characters, and whether they do have individual life of their own or function merely as figures in a moral allegory. It is my own personal experience that they do exist as persons in a very special and very substantial world that James has created for and by them. They are, to be sure, very special people by virtue of their intelligent awareness of what it is all about. But this is what makes it possible for them to invite us into such a state of intimacy with them, at the same time that it opens windows on a world of receding horizons and expanding dimensions. Dimensions expanding and shifting with every change of scene, almost with every enigmatic exchange of words. But while we speak of spiritual dimensions we have not been deprived of physical settings and the presence of people with their marked idiosyncrasy of tone and appearance.

It is here that James's power over words is of capital importance. And it is the combination of verbal precision with verbal suggestiveness that best characterizes his style as an instrument of imaginative evocation. This is perhaps what one would find to be the case in all highly gifted writers of fiction; but it is writers like Conrad, Dostoevski and Faulkner that come first to mind as most resembling James in this respect, however dissimilar is the particular subject-matter on which their styles are exercised and the particular range of association from which their words are drawn. In all these cases it is the adding of connotative suggestion to the words of precise and objective notation that gives the desired extension of imaginative effect. The modicum of objective notation is necessary to supply the primary substance of informative detail; it is the something not strictly "nominated in the bond"—less factual and literal, but often even more imaginatively qualificative—that gives wings to the phrase and glamour to the tone. (Oh, you will find this in Scott

Fitzgerald, and of course in Flaubert, in Tolstoy, in Thomas Hardy, in all the wizards, major and minor. But it is perhaps more indispensable and more certain to appear in those whose wizardry is peculiarly found in the imaginative extension of the spiritual life.)

Much has been written, and much more is bound to be written about James's use of figures of speech. Many of them are used to build up an atmosphere of fairy-tale or dream. But for one who deals so much with qualities and values, with the subtle tenuities of discriminated sentiment, the remarkable thing is that the very dream-effects are as often found to be the physical sensations of shock, of coldness, of cutting instruments and dangerous gulfs, as those of boating, of swimming under water, or resting secure in hiding-places. His friend's illness brings to Marcher "the shadow of a change and the chill of a shock." The two of them, awaiting his doom, are conscious of "depths, constantly bridged over by a structure firm enough in spite of its lightness and of its occasional oscillation in the somewhat vertiginous air," which occasionally invited "a dropping of the plummet and a measurement of the abyss." Later on, as the dying woman more and more withdraws, "she communicated with him as across some gulf." They rather lose their way as death comes nearer for her. "It was as if their dreams, numberless enough, were in solution in some thick cold mist through which thought lost itself." After her death, when he visits the graveyard, he encounters a man "with an expression like the cut of a blade" whose face was "the image of a scarred Passion." He finds a meaning for himself in the stranger's face, "which still flared for him as a smoky torch." What was now revealed to Marcher was "the sounded void of his life. He gazed, he drew breath, in pain, he had before him in sharper incision than ever the open page of his story."

These figures are all taken from the one short-story entitled "The Beast in the Jungle," and I have left out of account the central and key-figure of the beast, which receives such impressive development as the story goes forward.

But it is not necessary to have recourse to his poetic figures of speech to illustrate the power of suggestion that with James goes along with his objective precision. One might cite the brief characterizations of Mr. and Mrs. Moreen in "The Pupil." In both cases what the young scholar is concerned with is to bring these genteel but elusive employers of his to make some definite statement of the salary he is to receive for taking charge of their son's education. There was to begin with "the large affable lady who sat there drawing a pair of soiled *gants de suède* through a fat jewelled hand and, at once pressing and gliding, repeated over and over everything but the thing he would have liked to hear." It took our young friend two whole pages of hesitation and hinting before he could bring his lady to say graciously but still vaguely: "Oh I can assure you that all that will be quite regular." But four pages and some days later he is still baffled by the elegant evasiveness of the Moreens, this time in the person of Mr. Moreen, now returned from his occupations in town. "Mr. Moreen had a white moustache, a confiding manner and, in his buttonhole, the ribbon of a foreign order—bestowed, as Pemberton eventually learned, for services. For what services he never clearly ascertained: this was a point—one of a large number—that

Mr. Moreen's manner never confided. What it emphatically did confide was that he was even more a man of the world than you might at first make out." This system of characterization is even more effective in the case of the pupil himself, who proves to be a person worthy of longer study than his mannered parents, and we are launched on one of the most engaging and human of tales.

This combination of precise notation with connotative suggestion is most indispensable where the author is dealing with phenomena which cannot be adequately reduced to terms of objective science. Such are certainly, in our day, the phenomena of the occult; and it is because of his command of the double method that James's ghost-stories have come to be recognized as *nonpareil* in this genre. And then we are reminded that his ghosts are in several cases not real ghosts but doubles of something in the mind of him who sees them—in two notable cases projections of the man's own spirit or twins of his spirit but of an opposite moral complexion. Thus in "The Jolly Corner" and in the uncompleted novel, "The Sense of the Past," the ghostly person encountered by the man in the candle-lighted interior of his own house is a purely metaphysical entity—in one case, the man he might have been had he chosen to stay in New York and go in for money-making, in the other the self he would have been if he had lived in London a century earlier, if he had been a representative of the Past he so cherishes instead of the Future of which he is so inseparable a part. And yet there are few passages in James in which we have a stronger sense of the present, palpable reality of the physical situation than that in which Ralph Pendrel in "The Sense of the Past", or that in which Spencer Brydon in "The Jolly

Corner," confronts the ghost of the man he might have been.

Well, these are indeed allegorical parables, and all that gives reality to these metaphysical notions is the vivid actuality of the character in the story who is capable of imagining them and of the haunted houses in which the materialization takes place. To the old-fashioned reader, however, some of the same spectral quality may attach to the *states of mind* that play so large a part in stories where there is no question of the intrusion of the occult. But to the reader with a natural taste for James, it is just this exploitation of states of mind that makes the stories so fascinating. Not that there is anything unreal about states of mind, and still less anything vague, so long as they are bent on the strenuous meeting of moral issues. But in comparison with the average subject-matter of fiction in James's day, the exploration of levels of thought that are generally not brought into the light of consciousness does carry with it some pleasing sense of rarity, as of a "sea-change into something rich and strange." In his Introduction to his "Selected Short Stories" of James, Mr. Quentin Anderson remarks of James:

"He saw more than half a century ago that if he wished to be a great storyteller, to exercise a real dominion over the imaginations of his readers, he must avoid the very themes that were coming to the fore in fiction: money-making, social reform, the patient exploration of the average, the celebration of the familiar, and, in general, whatever circumscribed the possible effects of his work by reinforcing our sense of the diminishing importance of individuals. He was as anxious as the present-day existentialist to establish the belief that men create themselves by their acts, and he saw that it would be fatal to occupy himself with those contemporary figures who were, in the eyes of his readers, finished products, told stories, parts of the great romance of the commonplace of which the newspapers tell us at breakfast."

I do not see how one can indicate more impressively a main source of the fascination of James's stories. I have already confessed my inability to share Mr. Anderson's confidence that he has traced James's moral predilections back to the theological system of his father. And I do not wish to seem frivolous in my disinclination to bracket James with Dante, Bunyan or Blake as one of a line of religious prophets: though I have no quarrel with Mr. Anderson's identification of one of the novelist's main themes as "the distinction between the selfish and selfless ways of taking experience," or of a main source of his appeal as found in our modern hunger for "the substance of the moral life." I do not doubt that, taken altogether, the reading of James is bound to have a refining effect on our ethical nature; I certainly do not see how harm can come from following him in his exploration of the labyrinths of the moral sensibility, since it is so regularly guided by the light of a serious moral ideal. I am perhaps by temperament more concerned with the satisfactions than with the responsibilities of the moral life; or perhaps I am too obstinately bound, in my present undertaking, to consider James first and last as a storyteller. The labyrinths of the moral life are, I find, the most enthralling ways for the storyteller to follow. The spell might be more intermittent, to be sure, if once the clue were lost; but with James the clue is very firmly held through the most blind and devious windings of his labyrinth. We never quite miss the scent and the trail. And we have always the sense that we are penetrating territory that is inexhaustible in its possibilities for new discovery, that we may come out from the dense undergrowth at any moment on the sources of uncharted rivers or a view of mountain ranges not yet named on any map.

Joseph Warren Beach

P.S.  It is only since these pages were in proof that I have made myself properly acquainted with Osborn Andreas's "Henry James and the Expanding Horizon" (Seattle, 1948), and realized that it should be listed here among significant recent books on James.  While Mr. Andreas's text consists mostly of succinct summaries of James's "one hundred and twenty-five novels, novelettes, and short stories" so as to bring out the central idea of each one, and while his intention is not literary criticism in the narrow sense of the word, the upshot is such an impressive display of James's "total view of life" that it cannot fail to operate as a corrective for much wrong-headed criticism.  It has a distinct importance in itself as a record of James's life-long "response to the spectacle of personal intercourse"; and it brings in by the way many acute critical insights.  Two sentences may serve to give some hint of Mr. Andreas's line of thought: "James considered the cultivation of consciousness to be the most rewarding activity of man, the greatest privilege of life, and the supreme affirmation of man's essential nature."  "The uniqueness of James, the single new thought in the world to which his fiction gives expression, consists in his recognition that sensitivity to other persons expands the consciousness."  And I must add that, in his Conclusion, Mr.

Andreas has some very interesting things to say in answer to his question, whether James's outlook might have value in our time as a "criticism of life" not merely on the level of individual behavior but on that of men in the mass. On this point he is better worth listening to than Ezra Pound.

J.W.B.

# EXPLANATIONS

It is natural that books should multiply on the subject of Henry James. His art of story-telling is so conscious and deliberate that it offers itself unusually well to critical examination. There is indeed in his work a quite sufficient measure of that happy inspiration which is beyond all analysis and subject to no principle. But his most striking peculiarity, in contrast to English novelists in general, is the prominence in his work of studied art. Not that the art obtrudes itself unduly upon the attention of the reader. On the contrary: it is uncommonly well-bred and self-effacing. But for all that, the mere skill of the craftsman is more essential to the effectiveness of his work than is the case, for example, with Hardy or Meredith, in later times with Mr. Bennett or Mr. Wells, or in earlier times with Thackeray, Scott or Fielding. These novelists, some of them so great, are taken up to such an extent with their material and their attitude towards it, as to have comparatively little attention left for the niceties of art in the disposition of it. They may be likened to those early romantic composers whose devotion is so singly given to the creation and development of melody. James bears relation to the more sophisticated composers of his own day in whose work melody has become subordinate to harmony, in which the effect of the whole is so largely dependent on the relations of part to part, and in which there is so much wider range for the exercise of the artist's cunning. Whether this "sophistication," in musical or literary art, may not be the sign of degeneration from the noble simplicity of the old masters, is of course an open question. I prefer the less contentious position that admits of admiration for beauties of either kind.

A special invitation to the study of James is found in what he has written himself about the art of fiction, above all in the prefaces to the New York edition of his novels and tales.[1] No writer of fiction, no literary artist in any *genre,* has ever told us so distinctly, and at such length, what he was trying to do. And no artist has ever explained to the world so candidly how far and in what respects he succeeded in realizing his intentions. It need not be inferred from this, however, that James is the one artist least in need of explaining by others. These prefaces were written since the year 1906, and in that ultimate style of Mr. James's which has been the amazement and the amusement of the "vulgar" in all his latest work. Deeply interesting as they are, few but professional students would have the hardihood and pertinacity to make their way through these explanatory reviews distributed over twenty-four volumes. It remains for the student to collect and·set in order these scattered considerations, to view them in connection with the stories themselves, and, from the whole, to put together some connected account of the aims and method of our author.

It should be observed that Mr. James included in the New York edition hardly more than half his work.[a] In consequence, we have no comment of his own on novels so important in the history of his development as "Wash-

---

[1] Announcement is made, when this study is already far advanced in the process of printing, of two unfinished novels of James, "The Ivory Tower" and "The Sense of the Past," together with the author's preliminary plans and sketches for the completion of the books, documents which should throw yet fuller light on his methods of composition.[b]

[a]
[b] See *Supplementary Notes* 1954, page 285

ington Square," "The Bostonians" and "The Sacred
Fount." There comes up in this connection the interesting
question of why certain stories were included in this collection of his work and why certain others were left out.
And the general question starts a dozen special inquiries
to which the author has not himself made explicit answer,
and some of which he has not even broached. And while,
moreover, it is highly interesting and of real importance,
to see any artist as he sees himself, we are naturally
most concerned with the way he appears to us.

In this study we shall be concerned almost exclusively
with the novels, that is, with stories long enough to have
made more than four or five installments in serial publication. This mechanical definition is practically the only
means available for distinguishing between his novels
and his "tales." Mr. James seems not to have conceived
the "short story" in the rigorous fashion now prevailing,
and there is little essential difference in technique between
his short and his long stories. His *"contes"* all tend to
become *"nouvelles."* There is but a step, and that a
matter of length, from "The Real Thing" to "Daisy
Miller," one step from "Daisy Miller" to "The Spoils
of Poynton," and but one more from "The Spoils of
Poynton" to "The American." "Daisy Miller" we may
call a tale, "The Spoils of Poynton" a novel. And the
novels of James are more interesting than his tales.[c]
While he has done many brilliant things in the briefer
form, his most significant work is in the more extended
narrative. The reason for this should appear in the
course of our discussion.[2] It is enough to note in passing
that, while the tale may be the natural instrument of any

[2] See, for example, p. 70; but compare also the fourth chapter
of Part Two.

[c] See *Supplementary Notes* 1954, page 285

writer whose forte is sharpness of outline, liveliness in rendering the surface of life, the novel is more congenial to one whose bent is for the fine stroke, the rich effect, and who revels in the leisurely development of character from within.

In giving any description of the novels of James, one must take into account considerable variations according to the date of composition. In order not to complicate matters, I shall postpone to the second part of the study what is a subject of special interest in itself, the evolution of his method, the gradual process by which he assumed the technique that is most characteristic of him. It will then appear that his writing falls into two main periods, leaving out of account the stories written before 1875, the year in which the young author found himself in "Roderick Hudson."[3] The period of his early prime is one of fourteen years, ending with the publication in 1889 of "The Tragic Muse."[3] These years brought to light several great novels, notably "The Portrait of a Lady" and "The Princess Casamassima," as well as several inferior ones, such as "Confidence" and "The Europeans." After this period James seems to have intermitted the writing of novels for more than half a decade.[d] The period of maturity begins in 1896 with "The Spoils of Poynton" and continues down to 1904, the date of "The Golden Bowl." "The Outcry" (1911) must stand by itself as a kind of belated exercise in technique.

The second part of our study will give particular attention to the product of the early period, during which the story-teller was still making excursions and explorations. In the first part I shall endeavor to give an account of the method as it was finally worked out, with little regard

[3] In each case I give the date of appearance in magazine.

[d] See *Supplementary Notes* 1954, page 286.

to exceptions and experiments. My illustrations will therefore be drawn more often in this part from the work of the later period.

For it is the latest novels of James that are most distinctive. His earlier novels show more likeness to the work of his contemporaries and predecessors in English fiction. It is perhaps largely on this account that so many of his lovers prefer him in the earlier phase. And they may be justified in their preference. It is just possible that "Roderick Hudson" is a greater book than "The Spoils of Poynton," that "The Tragic Muse" is greater than "The Golden Bowl." But there can be little doubt that there is more of James in "The Spoils" and "The Golden Bowl." There is no doubt at all that he takes greater satisfaction himself in the later works, and that he more often achieves in them the thing at which he was always more or less consciously aiming. Aside from his explicit statements, we have the further evidence of his rejections. Of the seven novels which he refused admission to the collective edition, all but one display the earlier technique in marked degree.[4] The artist who was unwilling to revive "The Bostonians" was an artist who took more pleasure in "The Wings of the Dove" than in "The American."[e] If we are justified in describing "The Princess Casamassima" as of all the earlier novels the one most characteristic of its author, this is because it anticipates most nearly the technique of "The Ambassadors," which he regards as "quite the best, 'all round,' of his productions."[5]

It will not do to put the later novels out of court on the ground of mannerism as we do the latest poems of

[4] The exception was "The Sacred Fount." For this, see Part Two, Chap. V.

[5] Preface to "The Ambassadors," Vol. XXI, p. vii.

[e] See *Supplementary Notes* 1954, page 286

Browning.   The latest novels of James are carefully
planned works of art.   They are doubtless often somewhat overdone; there is a certain miscalculation of the
effect of minute detail.   But their peculiarities are not in
general properly to be described as mannerisms.   They
derive too directly from the original plan of the work,
and are too essential to its execution.   A mannerism is an
excrescence upon a work of art; and the upshot of our
whole study will be to show the growing impatience of
James, as he proceeds, with anything that obscures the
rigorous simplicity of design.[6]

[6] In any case one can hardly put the blame for one's dislike
upon the *style*.   We shall have little occasion in this study to
discuss the style of James, to consider in detail the vocabulary,
the turn of the phrase, the structure of the sentence.   But there
is one word that may be said in passing.   The style of the later
novels is not so markedly different from that of the earlier ones
as is sometimes supposed; and a close study of alterations made
by James in the early stories in revising them for the collective
edition shows that the direction taken by his style in its evolution was not, in these cases, towards the difficult and the precious.
In dialogue there is a tendency in the later work towards greater
informality, towards a truly colloquial manner; in characterization, towards greater exactness.[f]   What may be called the density
of the style in the narrative passages must be referred to the
uncommonly detailed reflection of the thought of his characters,
of characters intensely self-conscious.   Here of course lies the
offense.   But the words of James are the suitable dress of his
subject-matter.   And his style is pretty well kept in order, in all
his narratives, by the jealous discipline of the story itself.   If so
much cannot be said of his interviews and prefaces, his reminiscences and books of personal observation, that is partly because
he has in these no story—no strict design—to keep him in order:
there is nothing to prevent his "letting himself go."   In reference to the novels, if we are to complain of eccentricity, it is
eccentricity not so much in the manner of expression as in the
manner of thought.   But before complaining we must understand.

[f] See *Supplementary Notes* 1954, page 286

It would be more logical to condemn the whole undertaking of James as contrary to the spirit and inherent method of the novel, and as foredoomed to failure. The following study offers plentiful material for such an interpretation, especially in the chapters on "Revelation," "Dialogue" and "Eliminations." In that case the merit of the novels would be practically in inverse ratio to the author's success in carrying out his program, and the best stories would certainly be found in the earlier period. I can find no fault with such an interpretation except that it does not agree with my own impressions and preferences.

It may be inferred from this program that I am not undertaking an authoritative appraisal of the work of Henry James. I shall make little formal attempt to grade his stories in order of permanent greatness. Still less shall I attempt to determine his exact order of merit among novelists. These are exercises for posterity,[7] matters that somehow insist on getting themselves determined without much regard for the opinion of contemporary critics. There is of course an implied judgment in the singling out of a writer for such extended study. Any novelist so compelling to serious consideration, any art so fascinating as this, must have a very high order of merit. In any time it is high praise for a work of art to call it a work of notable distinction. Assuming so much for the work of James, our aim is to make out its peculiar character. We are to look for the special ideal

[7] The discerning reader may infer from certain signs that this study was largely made during the first year of the War, while Mr. James was still living; and the critical reader will appreciate my reluctance to assume even yet the authoritative manner of "posterity."

and method of this story-teller, and to estimate the degree
in which this method is applied in the several stories,
the success with which they realize this ideal. If this is
not so much criticism as interpretation, it should be at
least a long first step towards criticism.


### NOTE

References to the novels and tales of James, are, so far as
possible, to the "New York" edition, Scribners, 1907-1909, with
the number of the volume in that set. In the case of certain
tales not included in the New York edition, reference is made
to the magazine in which the story first appeared. References
to novels not included are to the following editions: "Watch
and Ward," Houghton Mifflin, 1887; "The Europeans," 9th ed.,
Houghton Mifflin; "Washington Square," Harpers, 1881; "The
Bostonians," Macmillan, 1886; "The Other House," Macmillan,
1896; "The Sacred Fount," Scribners, 1901; "The Outcry,"
Scribners, 1911.

PART ONE: THE METHOD

# I

## IDEA

The work of James is of course not an isolated phenomenon. He is naturally a creature of his time. And it is most convenient to begin with a consideration of those aspects in which he is in agreement with the greatest of his immediate predecessors. The main point is this, that James builds his novels primarily upon a motive, or an idea. In this respect he is particularly akin to Meredith and George Eliot.

The difference between the earlier and the later Victorian novels is in no respect more marked than in this matter. The earlier English novelists had generally of course a *subject,*—an historical subject, for example, like Charles Reade in "The Cloister and the Hearth," or a social subject like Thackeray in his studies of high life and its Bohemian fringes. In these novels we find a certain unity of composition resulting from the author's interest in the historical setting or in social groups illustrating the manners of a given time. We also call to mind how several of the earlier Victorian novelists made fiction a vehicle for comment upon politics, the industrial order and social abuses. Still more striking, in Dickens, is the demonstration of a proposition in human nature by the story of "Hard Times,"—a satire upon a false ideal of education, and in that respect suggestive of "Richard Feverel."

But several things are to be observed. In most cases in Dickens, the exposure of social abuses is an accidental and inorganic element in the novel. Where the social motive is more constant, it is generally made so at the expense of the story. "Hard Times" is indeed a logical, well-planned bit of fictional architecture. But it is probably the least entertaining performance of Dickens. The characters are hardly more than algebraic symbols necessary to the mathematical demonstration. It requires but the most cursory comparison with the great canvases of "Middlemarch" and "The Egoist" to see that it makes no real anticipation of the work of the later Victorians. As for the political novels of Beaconsfield, they are so loose-jointed and sketchy that we call them novels only on condition of calling them bad novels.

Generally speaking, in the earlier fiction, the indispensable of the novel is plot; in the later, it is character. Of "The Portrait of a Lady" Mr. James tells us: "Trying to recover here, for recognition, the germ of my idea, I see that it must have consisted not at all in any conceit of a 'plot,' nefarious name, in any flash, upon the fancy, of a set of relations, or in any one of those situations that, by a logic of their own, immediately fall, for the fabulist, into movement, into a march or a rush, a patter of quick steps; but altogether in the sense of a single character, the character and aspect of a particular engaging young woman, to which all the usual elements of a 'subject,' certainly of a setting, were to need to be superadded." In this connection James quotes the apology of Turgenieff, who had been charged with not having "story" enough. For him, too, the idea started "almost always with a vision of some person or persons . . . interesting him and appealing to him just as they were and by what they were," and it was only then that he "had to find for them the right relations, those that would most bring them out."[1] All the story needed was the amount required to exhibit the relations of his characters.

In so far as we can distinguish plot and character, it is of course character in which the idea is more likely to be lodged. But what we have before us is much more than a contrast between plot and character as the main subject of the novel. Everyone is aware of the prime importance, in most of Dickens, of the *characters*. This is very different from the importance, in Meredith and George Eliot, of *character*. The chief aim of Dickens is to make us *see* his *figures;* in Meredith and George Eliot, and in Henry James, the aim is quite as much to make us *acquainted* with the *character* of the *dramatis personæ*. This is what James has in mind when, in an early essay on Turgenieff, he discusses the pictorial vividness of his characters as a thing by itself, and then goes on to point out, what is a very different matter, the "representative character" of his persons. He speaks of Turgenieff's great admiration for Dickens, which he attributes to the vividness of Dickens in the drawing of his characters. But he wonders at his rating Dickens so very high, since, he says, "if Dickens fail to live long, it will be because his figures are all particular without being general; because they are individuals without being types; because we do not feel their continuity with the rest of humanity —see the matching of the pattern with the piece out of which all the creations of the novelist and the dramatist are cut."[2]

With the big men of James's time, in France as well as in England and Russia, it is not the pictorial vividness of the *dramatis personæ* that is remarkable so much as

[1] Vol. III, pp. vi-vii. Compare also "Partial Portraits," pp. 314-316.

[2] "Partial Portraits," p. 318.

their representative character. These men are not so much concerned with particular figures or groups of figures as with general types of character, with certain more or less abstract ideas involving character. It is sufficient, for the French, to refer to Zola, to Bourget, not to mention names of more recent notability. In English the most striking examples of this tendency are offered by Meredith in the whole series of his novels, from "Richard Feverel" to "The Amazing Marriage." Underlying all the creations of his imagination is Meredith's conception of the natural way of living; and his stories are largely devoted to the illustration of certain long-lived fashions of violating nature. A similar treatment of character is marked in some of the novelists of our later generations, notably in Mr. Galsworthy; though, judging from the remarks of Mr. James in his essay on "The New Novel,"[3] he is not impressed with the prevalence of a shaping idea, even of a subject, in most novels of the present day.

The prevailing idea, or motive, of James is the radical opposition of the American and the European ways of taking life. In "Daisy Miller" the European point of view is represented by the young American who, in the course of a long schooling at Geneva, has lost his understanding of American character, and who comes too late to appreciate the candid innocence and loveliness of the somewhat "fresh" American girl. In "The Wings of the Dove," the new world, in the shape of a ghostly presence, proves the shaming and undoing of the old. In "The Portrait of a Lady," the new seems to become the living victim of the old. In "The Golden Bowl," the two attitudes, at first so sharply opposed in husband and wife, tend to become identical. Old world and new world come

[3] In "Notes on Novelists."

to understand one another. New world takes on some of the cunning of the old; old world, some of the spiritual insight of the new.

While an "idea" must be general, the first suggestion for a story may be general or particular.[g] Often for James it was, as he tells us, some actual situation, a morsel of real life picked up perhaps in conversation. The first hint for "The Spoils of Poynton" was something dropped by the author's partner at dinner about a lawsuit between son and mother over the ownership of certain valuable furniture. It was this "mere floating particle in the stream of talk" which, as he said, "communicated the virus of suggestion" for the large developments that followed.[4] The germ of "The Ambassadors," still to be found embedded in the substance of that story, consisted in the remarks made by a person of distinction one Sunday afternoon at a social gathering in a Paris garden. They were essentially the remarks made by Lambert Strether to "Little Bilham" in the second chapter of the fifth book, in which Strether acknowledges that he has made the mistake of not living, and advises his young friend to "live all he can."[5] The tale of "The Real Thing," similarly, had its germ in the actual experience of "my much-loved friend George Du Maurier." A man and woman of real gentility had applied to Du Maurier for engagement as artist's models, for the "social" illustrations he was doing in "Punch." He was already well served, it seems, by another couple who were far from being persons of gentility but who played the part to the entire satisfaction of the artist.[6]

[4] Vol. X, pp. v-vii.
[5] Vol. XXI, p. v.
[6] Vol. XVIII, p. xx.
[g] See *Supplementary Notes* 1954, page 287

But however particular the circumstance that attracts the writer's notice, it begins at once to be worked upon by his prepared imagination, to be assimilated to the general substance of his mental world. The subject of "The Real Thing" ceases to be a particular case and comes to be a sort of problem in human reactions. Which are likely to prove the more satisfactory models for an artist wishing to make convincing illustrations of genteel life,—actual gentlefolk who have no talent for posing, no plasticity, or sitters without social pretension who have yet imagination and the faculty of putting on whatever semblance may be desired? If it be the latter that win out in such a competition, behold an irony fit for the hand of a writer of tales. Nothing is said by Mr. James as to the outcome of the suggested competition in the case of Du Maurier's applicants, or whether such a competition was actually set on foot by their engagement. The circumstances very early left the realm of the actual and the particular and entered that of the general and the representative.

The case of "The Ambassadors" again illustrates how the particular circumstance is liable to fall into some category all ready for it. The author is always waiting to pounce upon whatever is "to his purpose." He has been musing more or less consciously all his life on such a situation or relationship. The idea has been in solution, as it were, and this thing heard precipitates it. In the present instance, that of the remarks that suggested to him the theme of "The Ambassadors," "the observation there listened to and gathered up had contained part of the 'note' I was to recognize on the spot as to my purpose . . . the rest was in the place and the time and the scene they sketched: these constituents clustered and combined to give me further support, to give me what I may call the *note absolute*."⁷ This is a characteristic and remarkable statement. The ultimate seed of "The Ambassadors" would seem to be something less concrete even than a situation, a problem or a relationship. It is best described as a "note." And a note is something only to be recognized by its vibration in unison with a similar note already sounding within one's self.

In the case of "The Portrait of a Lady," and in that of "The Wings of the Dove," each of which is built up around a single central character, we are not told of any particular suggestion for the character in real life. Isabel Archer and Milly Theale seem to be really embodiments of certain long-considered types,—types each of a human being of a certain sort, or of a human being in a certain predicament. It goes without saying that the predicament is a "psychological," or spiritual, predicament. For even Isabel Archer, a creation of James in his earlier period, finds her difficulty rather in the relation of her ideals to those of her husband than in the objective facts of the situation. Of "The Wings of the Dove" and its heroine Mr. James says: "The idea, reduced to its essence, is that of a young person conscious of a great capacity for life, but early stricken and doomed, condemned to die under short respite, while also enamoured of the world; aware moreover of the condemnation and passionately desiring to 'put in' before extinction as many of the finer vibrations as possible, and so achieve, however briefly and brokenly, the sense of having lived."⁸ In each of these

---

⁷ Vol. XXI, p. vi. The italics are mine.

⁸ Vol. XIX, p. v. In the act of reading proof I call to mind that, while my statement of the case is in exact accord with the account of James in the preface to "The Dove," he does suggest, in "Notes of a Son and Brother," the existence of a particular model for Milly Theale; for so I understand the allusion on the

novels then, while the subject is a person, it is a person, in origin, typically and abstractly conceived. This will appear in more striking fashion when we come to consider the process by which the author *developed* the germ-idea in the circumstances of the plot.

Other stories of James are still more obviously abstract in theme, starting as they do not with a central character but with some mere *problem* in human nature.

This does not mean that the books of James are to be regarded as problem-novels. This will be made clearer in a later chapter. A problem-novel or a problem-play, as I understand it, is a novel or a play which undertakes to solve, or at least to state, some knotty problem of conduct. It frequently sets forth the predicament of someone at odds with social convention or the law, and is supposed to recommend prudence by an exhibition of its contrary, or to condemn the social order by a demonstration of its disastrous effects on human nature. Of course such a problem is a kind of idea. But it is only one kind; and it is quite unnecessary for an idea to take on the practical intensity of a problem in order to rank as an idea.

The word problem, as used in reference to the themes of James, means something to be figured out by the author, like a problem in physics,—something related to the "problem" of present-day fiction merely by virtue of its abstractness. A remarkable example of a story originating in such a problem is the little tale entitled "The

last page of that book to the death of a dear friend.[h] All of which goes to show how difficult it is to distinguish the individual and the general in any of his characters. His books of reminiscence reveal how very early and how constantly he was typifying and making representative all human phenomena that came within his range of vision.

[h] See *Supplementary Notes* 1954, page 287

Story in It." This was suggested to Mr. James by the observation of a distinguished novelist on being asked "why the adventures he imputed to his heroines were so perversely and persistently but of a type impossible to ladies respecting themselves." His reply had been to point out that "ladies who respected themselves took particular care never to *have* adventures," and to challenge in his turn : "A picture of life founded on the mere reserves and suppressions of life, what sort of a performance— for beauty, for interest, for tone—could *that* hope to be ?" This, if we may trust the indications in the story itself, was the point of view of a Frenchman ; and the American novelist has ready the hint of an answer doing credit equally to his Puritan cleanliness and his Yankee inge- nuity. "The thing is, all beautifully, a matter of interpre- tation and of the particular conditions ; without a view of which latter some of the most prodigious adventures . . . may vulgarly show for nothing. However that may be, I hasten to add," says Mr. James, "the mere stir of the air around the question reflected in the brief but earnest interchange I have just reported was to cause a 'subject,' to my sense, immediately to bloom there." [9]

Equally abstract, so far as we can learn from the author, was in origin the theme of "The Awkward Age." And the abstractness of theme is emphasized by the account given by Mr. James of the function assigned to the ten books into which the novel is divided. He in- tended the novel for publication serially in "Harper's Weekly," and he explained his scheme to the editor in advance by a sort of chart or ground-plan of the work. He drew on a sheet of paper "the neat figure of a circle consisting of a number of small rounds disposed at equal distances about a central object. The central object was my situation, my subject in itself, to which the thing would owe its title, and the small rounds represented so many distinct lamps, as I liked to call them, the function of each of which would be to light with all due intensity one of its aspects. `. . . Each of my 'lamps' would be the light of a single 'social occasion' in the history and intercourse of the characters concerned, and would bring out to the full the latent color of the scene in question and cause it to illustrate, to the last drop, its bearing on my theme." [10]

Once given the germ of the story, its motive or *mère-idée,* the circumstances of the plot are evolved with consistent undeviating logic that has little to do with the older novelists' love of an effect for its own sake. This is well exemplified in "The Wings of the Dove," as Mr. James informs us in detail of the process of its conception. He starts, as we have seen, with the idea of "a young person conscious of a great capacity for life; but early . . . condemned to die under short respite, while also enamoured of the world." This tells us little of the particular circumstances and identity of the young person, though Mr. James seems always to have had his young person particularized as to sex. But the idea proceeds to take on concreteness by natural process. The surrender of everything by this girl would be enhanced

[10] Vol. IX, pp. xvi and xvii. Has "Harper's Weekly" changed so completely in character since 1898; or was the naïveté of Mr. James in hoping for success with its readers for such a venture only to be compared with his naïveté in supposing this series of dialogue to be in the manner of "Gyp" or of Lavedan? The question has lost no pertinence since the submersion of "Harper's Weekly" in a periodical of other kidney.

in poignancy by "the sight of all she has"; hence the old New York family and the great wealth. The wealth and the lack of relatives living also place her in the required situation of entire freedom of action, which in turn makes still stronger the sense of her being a Tantalus. And to the same considerations must be attributed her nationality. "I had from far back mentally projected a certain sort of young American as more the 'heir of all the ages' than any other young person whatever . . . ; so that here was a chance to confer on some such figure a *supremely touching value*."[11]

So much for the central character herself. And now for the plot, now for the other persons involved with her in the web of circumstance. Such a person as this, says the author, falls necessarily "into some abysmal trap." "She would constitute for others (given her passionate yearning to live while she might) a complication as great as any they might constitute for herself. . . . Our young friend's existence would create . . . round her very much that whirlpool movement of the waters produced by the sinking of a big vessel or the failure of a great business."[12] So the author outlines for us the course of the logic by which the story is evolved from the idea. If it is a logic peculiar to his own imagination and experience of life, that is merely saying that it is the logic of all art, which is so much more subjective an affair than that of mathematics. The great point is that it *is* logic, of whatever order, and not the unlicensed play of fancy, still less a process admitting the deliberate search for entertainment without regard to fitness and consistency.

Referring to the invention of the plot of "The Ambassadors," Mr. James uses the very word logic. Having

[11] Vol. XIX, p. ix. The italics are mine.
[12] Id., pp. ix and x.

explained what was the original hint of an idea and
referred to Strether's outburst to little Bilham, he proceeds to set forth "that *supplement* of situation logically
involved in our gentleman's impulse to deliver himself
in the Paris garden on the Sunday afternoon—or if not
involved by strict logic then all ideally and enchantingly
implied in it. . . . It being thus the respectable hint that
I had with such avidity picked up, what would be the
story to which it would most inevitably form the center?"
How account for Strether and his "peculiar tone"? "It
would take a felt predicament or a false position to give
him so ironic an accent. . . . Possessed of our friend's
nationality, to start with, there was a general probability
in his narrower localism. . . . He would have issued,
our rueful worthy, from the very heart of New England
—at the heels of which matter of course a perfect train
of secrets tumbled for me into the light." Then further:
"What the 'position' would infallibly be, and why, on his
hands, it had turned 'false'—these inductive steps could
only be as rapid as they were distinct. I accounted for
everything . . . by the view that he had come to Paris
in some state of mind which was literally undergoing,
as a result of new and unexpected assaults and infusions,
a change almost from hour to hour. . . . *The* false
position, for our belated man of the world . . . was
obviously to have presented himself at the gate of that
boundless menagerie primed with a moral scheme of
the most approved pattern which was yet framed to break
down on any approach to vivid facts." [13]

Mr. James makes it clear that the logic of this evolution is not an arbitrary logic, subject to his capricious
manipulation. It may indeed follow the channels marked

[13] Vol. XXI, pp. viii–xiii.

out for it in the peculiar topography of his imagination. But it follows these channels without any vagabondage. He describes the process indeed as if he had little to do with it other than to record it. "The steps, for my fable, placed themselves with a prompt and, as it were, functional assurance—an air quite as of readiness to have dispensed with logic had I been in fact too stupid for my clue. . . . These things continued to fall together, as by the neat action of their own weight and form, even while their commentator scratched his head about them; he easily sees now that they were always well in advance of him."[14]

It is hardly necessary, I suppose, to dwell upon the contrast between this method and that of the early Victorian novelists. This confident, responsible inquiry after the characters and incidents most fitted to illuminate the carefully chosen subject of the picture is quite a different thing from the search for incidents and characters interesting and picturesque in themselves and for themselves. It is in this matter that one finds the closest likeness of the novels of James to those of Meredith and George Eliot. And indeed James has gone much farther than these late Victorians in the sacrifice of the ideal of variety to the ideal of consistency.

[14] Vol. XXI, p. xiii. Compare the similar language used in reference to the plot of "The Portrait of a Lady," Vol. III, p. xvii.

## II

## PICTURE

James is distinguished from his immediate English predecessors by his much greater preoccupation with matters of form. This is an affair not merely of surface, but strikes deeper and touches the idea, or theme, itself. Here shows the fundamental difference between the work of James and that of Meredith and George Eliot. All three novelists are given to the development of an idea or motive; the difference lies in the way in which the motive is conceived. The others conceive their motive more as thesis or moral; James conceives his as the subject of a picture.

The word picture thus used in reference to the themes of James[1] makes a figure of speech, an analogy, quite in the spirit of his own elucidations. It is intended to keep before our minds the inveterately esthetic bias of this author and to emphasize what is only a relative, but what is nevertheless a broad, appreciable difference between his attitude and that of the others mentioned. James's attitude is essentially artistic, theirs essentially philosophical. Of course in any novel, if there is an idea, it must get itself embodied in a plot involving characters, and the whole pattern of circumstance, with the characters grouped according to their relations and their qualities,

[1] Mr. Wells has some interesting animadversions on what seems to him (or his mouthpiece) the perversity of James in confounding the novel and the picture. They will be found in the fourth chapter of "Boon, the Mind of the Race," together with an amusing parody of the James method.

may be thought of as constituting the subject of a picture and a happy occasion for the exercise of the painter's skill. Only it is not generally so thought of by author or reader, especially in novels conscious of an "idea." And in the case of Meredith and George Eliot, if we may suppose these terms to be had in mind at all, they are put the other way round. The characters and incidents are intended to throw light upon the idea, to illustrate or prove it. The subject exists for the benefit of the idea, not the idea for the benefit of the subject.

The contrast is most striking in the case of Meredith, whose characters never get over that habit of representing abstractions which they contracted presumably from the example of Meredith's father-in-law, the author of "Nightmare Abbey," and in which they were confirmed by his own theory of the comic. His first work of fiction was a philosophical allegory expressed in fantastic narrative in the manner of the "Arabian Nights." In his last novel, the very names of the persons indicate their typical character in relation to the great debate between Nature and sentimental Romance. Woodseer is the clairvoyant prophet of Nature, Fleetwood the sentimentalist seeking an escape from the natural. And for practically every novel of Meredith it would be possible to draw up a table of persons suggestive of the table of "humours" prefixed by Ben Jonson to several of his plays. Nearly every character represents something in the philosophical scheme of the story. And many of them are little more than philosophical lay-figures. One has but to name such novels as "Sandra Belloni" and "One of our Conquerors" to call to mind whole groups of characters that are practically failures so far as pictorial effect is concerned. They were conceived and executed with originality and gusto; but they remain bizarre and puzzling in themselves and ill-composed in relation to one another. This is largely owing, I feel, to the author's almost total neglect of purely artistic considerations of the larger scope. The characters and incidents being logically evolved, Meredith's solicitude is practically confined to the logic of this evolution. If the evolution is perfectly accomplished, if each character says what he has to say to the thesis, if each incident is made to flash its facet of the idea, then all is well. The appeal being primarily to the mind, all conditions are fulfilled if once the mind is satisfied.

James, too, starts often with an abstraction. But it is not a thesis or a moral idea. It is a dramatic situation, a human relationship, perhaps a social irony,—in short, a composition. It is an arrangement of objects (that is, of the persons and incidents involved)—by likeness and opposition, by balance and cross-reference, with all regard to emphasis and proportion,—corresponding to the arrangement of figures, of background and foreground, of masses and lines, in a painting. Like the subject of a painting, it is chosen out of all other possible subjects as the one most amenable to the art of representation. Intellectual processes are plentifully there to guide the evolution of subject into story. But the appeal is made to the taste or imagination, and the intelligence, or logical sense, of author and reader is merely an instrument of the esthetic intention.

The difference is pronounced in the treatment of moral values. These earlier novelists are concerned primarily with the moral values as such. They wish their fable to make plain the nature of right and wrong, or at least of wise and foolish, and they wish to set the one in such a light as to recommend it for imitation. They are not, of course, crudely moralistic, being as they are enlightened artists. But their works of fiction are constantly devoted, like their other writing, to the exposition of a philosophy of life. Consider, for example, the care with which George Eliot made choice of her characters in "Middlemarch" so as to represent all the degrees of folly and wisdom. With what deliberation this positivist philosopher has noted the moral values and deficiencies of her Caleb Garth, her Fred Vincy, her Doctor Lydgate, not to mention the discriminated characters of "Adam Bede" and "Felix Holt"!

Our American novelist showed himself very early conscious of the issues involved. In an essay on George Eliot written in 1866, when he had not yet himself made public any story of novel length, speaking of her as a philosopher, and in that respect superior to Dickens and Thackeray, he felt it necessary to indicate his reservations on the side of the esthetic. "Considerable as are our author's qualities as an artist," writes the young critic, "and largely as they are displayed in 'Romola,' the book strikes me less as a work of art than as a work of morals."[2] Twenty years later, in his dialogue on "Daniel Deronda," he complains of the artificiality and unreality of all in that book that has to do with Daniel himself. Now the part that has to do with Daniel was precisely, as we know, a development of the sort of motive which appealed to George Eliot, which was a moral rather than an artistic motive. Readers generally agree with Mr. James that the character of Daniel Deronda is an artistic failure; and yet so deep is the appeal to our moral nature that few readers can have lost interest before the completion of the history.

James deals equally with moral values (as will be shown at length in our chapter on "Ethics"), but he is not concerned with them in their practical aspect. He

[2] "Views and Reviews," p. 33.

is not setting out to recommend the right and give warning against the wrong.  He is not even trying to make
clear their nature as right and wrong: his aim is neither
scientific nor ethical.  His concern is with the *appearance*
made by right and wrong, if we can even indicate his
scale of values in terms so downright as these.  They
are colors upon his palette, lines and masses available for
the comparatively transcendental uses of composition.
Hence the artist's delight in "ironies," which are patterns
of circumstance so revolting to the practical, the moral
sense, while often so pleasing in their appeal to the imagination.[3]

Only the artist could speak as James does of the subject of "What Maisie Knew."  His imagination had been
caught first, he tells us, by "the accidental mention . . .
made to him of the manner in which the situation of
some luckless child of a divorced couple was affected
. . . by the remarriage of one of its parents."  Here
were great possibilities for art.  "Sketchily clustered
even, these elements gave out that vague pictorial glow
which forms the first appeal of a living 'subject' to the
painter's consciousness."  But this subject could be
greatly enhanced in value by the addition of certain
elements to the plot.  The chief of these was the remarriage of *both* parents instead of merely one, and then

---

[3] It will now be clear how far the novels of James are from
being problem-novels.  One would hesitate to apply the term even
to the novels of Meredith; and James, we see, has Meredith,
not to speak of George Eliot, between him and the odious *genre*.
It would be easy to state the theme of "The Awkward Age," or
that of "The Ambassadors" in such a way as to bring into relief
a latent problem,—the problem, say, for "The Awkward Age,"
of the débutante and—to use the term in vogue—"sex-hygiene."
But this is precisely what Mr. James, in all his discussions of
these books, takes particular pains to avoid.

the formation of a new tie between the step-parents.
The beauty of the situation would be to have the innocent
young child made partly responsible for the formation
of the new guilty relation. Mr. James dwells with
reminiscent joy upon the gradual emergence of this idea,
so full of "charm," of "virtue" to the "intellectual nos-
tril." The upshot of all his pleasant exploration was the
discovery of what he calls "the full ironic truth" of the
situation. "At last . . . I was in presence of the red
dramatic spark that glowed at the core of my vision and
that, as I gently blew upon it, burned higher and clearer.
This precious particle was the *full* ironic truth—the most
interesting item to be read into the child's situation . . .
The child seen as creating by the fact of its forlornness
a relation between its step-parents, the more intimate
the better, dramatically speaking; the child, by the mere
appeal of neglectedness and the mere consciousness of
relief, weaving about, with the best faith in the world,
the close web of sophistication; the child becoming the
center and pretext for a fresh system of misbehaviour,
a system moreover of a nature to spread and ramify:
*there* would be the 'full' irony, there the promising theme
into which the hint I had originally picked up would
logically flower. No themes are so human as those that
reflect for us, out of the confusion of life, the close
connection of bliss and bale, of the things that help with
the things that hurt, so dangling forever before us that
bright hard medal, of so strange an alloy, one fact of
which is somebody's right and ease and the other somebody's pain and wrong."[4] It is interesting to reflect how
similar is the position of Milly Theale and that of Maggie
Verver to that of Maisie, and how completely all that
is said here of the theme of the earlier story applies to

[4] Vol. XI, pp. v-viii.

those of "The Wings of the Dove" and "The Golden Bowl."

In all his discussions Mr. James never speaks in any tone other than that of an artist appraising the points of a "subject"; and I recall no place in which he speaks at all of the moral tendency of his work save to glance with impatience at "the dull dispute over the 'immoral' subject and the moral."[5] The question about any subject that disposes of all others is simply, he tells us, "Is it valid, in a word, is it genuine, is it sincere, the result of some direct impression or perception of life?" The determining factor for a work of art is the artist himself and his way of envisaging the facts. And the chief difference between one sincere work of art and another would appear to be merely a greater poverty or richness of medium, the medium being, in Mr. James's figure, the "enveloping air of the artist's humanity." When Mr. James speaks of the subject of a novel as of "an ideal beauty of goodness," he means, as he at once explains— he is speaking of "The Ambassadors"—that it is a subject "the invoked action of which is to raise the artistic faith to its maximum."[6] It is an ideal theme not because of the value of its teaching, not because of the wisdom that one rubs off from it, but because of the intensity of its appeal to "the artistic faith."

It thus appears that Henry James was strongly imbued with the principle of "art for art's sake." And if he shows a divergence in this respect from the feeling of the great Victorian novelists, that is but the natural result of his position in time. It is not without significance that three of his tales—all dealing with literature and its makers—appeared in the early numbers of "The Yellow

[5] Vol. III, p. ix.

[6] Vol. XXI, p. vii.

Book,"[7] and that the first of his longer works in which he entirely found himself were likewise the product of the esthetic "nineties." Nor should we overlook, in this connection, the French influence. The reader of Mr. James's volumes of reminiscence will recall the important part played in the domestic economy of Henry James, Senior, by the "Revue des Deux Mondes." The novels of George Sand seem next only to those of Charles Dickens in the greediness with which they were anticipated and devoured by all members of the family. One recalls the later intimacy of Henry James, Junior, in the community of great French novelists of which the perhaps greater Russian Turgenieff was a naturalized citizen. Perhaps not less important as a shaping influence was the early haunting of Parisian picture-galleries by William and Henry James, with the short period of study at Newport under direction of William Hunt. Long before his first brief essay in fiction had found its benevolent editor, the young writer was thoroughly soaked in the terms and conceptions of pictorial art. And his later career was not such as to let him drop for a moment any of those dear solicitudes of painter and sculptor that are at once the bane and solace of the artist's life. In his interpretative prefaces, terms from the fine arts are next in frequency to those of dramatic reference, if indeed they do not actually exceed them in number.

The great word for Mr. James is composition. In the early essay from which I have already quoted, he writes of George Eliot as not remarkably strong in composition, and is much occupied in considering the relative

[7] These were "The Death of the Lion" (1894), "The Coxon Fund" (1894) and "The Next Time" (1895). Mr. James has some reminiscent remarks on his connection with this periodical in the preface to Vol. XV.

merits of her different works in the matter of "dramatic continuity" in distinction from a "descriptive, discursive method of narration."[8]    Many years later, at the end of his road, he is chiefly taken up, in his prefaces, with the subtleties, often the "super-subtleties" (as he calls them himself), of composition, because this alone is "positive beauty."[9]    The first obvious requirement of composition is unity, or pictorial fusion, of the diverse elements in a story.    This is considered at length by Mr. James in connection with his problem in designing "The Tragic Muse."    The idea of this book, as he first conceived it, involved two distinct subjects, what he calls his "political case" (the story of Nick Dormer) and what he calls his "theatrical case" (that of Miriam Rooth).    How put these subjects together so as not to "show the seam"? His own problem leads him to reflections on the want of "pictorial composition" in so many novels of great popularity and of classic distinction.    "There may in its absence be life, incontestably, as 'The Newcomes' has life, as 'Les Trois Mousquetaires,' as Tolstoi's 'Peace and War' have it; but what do such large loose baggy monsters, with their queer elements of the accidental and the arbitrary, artistically *mean?* . . . There is life and life, and as waste is only life sacrificed and thereby prevented from 'counting,' I delight in a deep-breathing economy and an organic form.    My business was accordingly to 'go in' for complete pictorial fusion, some such common interest between my first two notions as would, in spite of their birth under quite different stars, do them no violence at all."    And he tells us how he managed that difficult business.    "From the moment I made out . . . my lucky title, that is from the moment Miriam Rooth herself had given it me, so this young woman had given me with it her own position in the book, and so that in turn had given me my precious unity, to which no more than Miriam was either Nick Dormer nor Peter Sherringham to be sacrificed."[10]

Another pictorial consideration calls for the device described by the author as "foreshortening." This he must on occasion resort to for maintaining the desired balance between the first and second halves of a novel. He frequently fails, through excess of foresight, to get the "centre of his structure" actually placed in the middle of the book. "The first half of a fiction insists ever on figuring to me as the stage or theatre for the second half, and I have in general given so much space to making the theatre propitious that my halves have too often proved strangely unequal. Thereby has arisen with grim regularity the question of artfully, of consummately masking the fault and conferring on the false quantity the brave appearance of the true." His very mistakes are occasion for pleasurable exercise, for it is clear he takes great delight in meeting this grim question. "Therein lies the secret of the appeal, to [the artist's] mind, of the successfully *foreshortened* thing, where representation is arrived at . . . not by the addition of items . . . but by the art of figuring synthetically, a compactness into which the imagination may cut thick, as into the rich density of wedding-cake."[11] While the above remarks were made in special reference to "The Tragic Muse," the author often encountered the same fascinating problem, notably in writing "The Wings of the Dove." The latter half of that book he calls "the false and deformed half" because

[10] Vol. VII, p. xiii.
[11] Id., pp. xii-xiii.

of the recurrence of his "regular failure to keep the appointed halves of his whole equal." "This whole corner of my picture bristles with 'dodges' . . . for disguising the reduced scale of the exhibition, for foreshortening at any cost, for imparting to patches the value of presences . . . [showing] what a tangled web we weave when—well, when, through our mislaying or otherwise trifling with our blest pair of compasses, we have to produce the illusion of mass without the illusion of extent."[12]

Even the exigencies of serial publication give occasion for the exercise of the artistic faculty. Mr. James mentions, in connection with "The Ambassadors," the ingenuity called for in planning the "recurrent breaks and resumptions" of the story in such manner as to maintain consistency of effect in spite of them. Here again he mentions the difficulty not to complain of it but rather to rejoice in it as an opportunity for the exhibition of one's finest skill. By the time of the publication of "The Ambassadors," in 1903, he had long been accustomed actively to adopt this serial interruption "so as to make of it, in its way, a small compositional law."[13] It is evident that each of the twelve books of "The Ambassadors," or each larger section of the other novels, is to be regarded in the light of a separate panel of a screen or division of a wall-surface, and that the architectural conditions limiting the size and form of each are made to contribute their part to the effect of each division and of the whole. Did ever the passion for order and beauty more signally triumph over ugly disorder in the nature of things?

[12] Vol. XIX, pp. xviii-xix.
[13] Vol. XXI, pp. xiv-xv.

The pictorial conception of his themes is well exemplified in the series of stories presenting the American
abroad. The formula is most frequently something like
this: a simple, candid, but very fine and lustrous soul
seen against a dense murky background of sophisticated
manners and ways of thought. Most often it is an
American woman that is thus set in relief against the
European background. Such is the subject of "Daisy
Miller" and "The Portrait of a Lady" in the earlier
period, and, in the later period, of "The Wings of the
Dove" and "The Golden Bowl." Mr. James makes no
secret of his fondness for the "sinister" and the "portentous" as colors in his picture; these colors, combined
with the mystery which is a still more constant source of
interest, contribute to the rich complexity of which he is
so fond. And they serve moreover to heighten the contrast involved in the subject, to create an effect of
*chiaroscuro*. Most effective pictorially are the figures
of Isabel Archer in "The Portrait" and Milly Theale in
"The Dove." But the secret of this effectiveness lies
more in the background than in the main foreground
subject. As much art went to the creation of Madame
Merle and Gilbert Osmond as to that of Isabel. It
required a greater mastery of the brush to give us Kate
Croy than Milly Theale herself. If, by the way, the
relation of Isabel and Osmond suggests that of Gwendolen Harleth and Grandcourt in "Daniel Deronda,"[i] it
will be only to remind us how much more convincing
and more effective James made this background of the
cold and the dark. And the superiority of James in this
painter's job arises largely from his stronger consciousness of its being a question of painting.

I have pressed the comparison with George Eliot and
Meredith because they are the two novelists most like

[i] See *Supplementary Notes* 1954, page 287

James in procedure so far as the idea is concerned.[14] Many of the earlier English novelists, whom we have seen to be very little versed in the "idea," are often very great artists in the matter of picture. But it is not in the same sense as that in which James is such a master of picture. The droll and the grotesque figures of Dickens are of course drawn with an intensity to which no other maker of fiction can hope to approach. Hardly less remarkable is Dickens's faculty of making us see the London streets and buildings that form the setting of his dramas. In some of his later stories, moreover, he shows great ability in weaving plots of complex and studious pattern. But for composition proper he has no regard, if indeed he has any inkling of what it means; and it would be an over-great stretching of our figure to apply the term picture to the general theme or subject of any of his stories. Thackeray had more of the artist's sense for scale of values. But he was far from conceiving, let alone desiring, for his novels, that preserved consistency of tone, that constant reference to the center of all parts of the canvas, in which James took so much satisfaction in his own work.[15] We need not point out the complete want of coherent scheme in such an inferior work as "The Virginians." We may find our illus-

[14] I do not mean to consider the question of personal indebtedness of James to either of these writers. Most profound is his silence on the subject of Meredith, whom he mentions, so far as I have noticed, only as a contributor in early days to "Once a Week." He has much more to say, first and last, about George Eliot, and he was doubtless somewhat influenced by her work. But all that we need assume in reference to these three writers so near in time is that likeness of method natural to artists subject to similar influences.

[15] Note what he says on the subject in connection with "The Tragic Muse" in Vol. VII, pp. vii and xxii.

trations in Thackeray's greatest work, and note the comparative neglect of all but the central portrait in "Vanity Fair," or, if not neglect, the comparative failure then in the handling of the sub-plot, along with the correlative fact of attention squandered upon insignificant minor characters for whom a sense of proportion prescribes the scantiest treatment. We are here taking note merely, it may be, of an earlier fashion in the design of the novel. For it needs but the mention of George Moore, of John Galsworthy, of Joseph Conrad, to give assurance that the fashion represented by Henry James was to find a most respectable following if not actually to supersede that of Thackeray. And we have only to name Charles Reade, Bulwer-Lytton, Disraeli, to remind ourselves how much more striking is the contrast when we bring into comparison the second-class novelists of the earlier time. It is a chief distinction of James that he was the first to write novels in English with a full and fine sense of the principles of composition.

## III

## REVELATION

In naming points in which James has passed beyond this and that great novelist, we need not use the word surpassed. We must be careful not to write as if the world of readers, or even the world of critics, were agreed upon the merits of his work. Mr. James must have learned long since to content himself with the some-what frigid *respect* of the great world of reviewers, and to look, for a warmer and less guarded affection, to a small band of devotees. And this is largely because of the extremes to which he has carried his conception of the novel in terms of picture.

This pictorial preoccupation goes so far as almost to bring about a reversal of the essential method of fiction. The essential method of fiction is, or has always been, narrative. The earliest English novels consisted of a series of adventures, whose thread might generally be cut off anywhere with little damage to any plot there was. This is true for Smollett almost as much as for Defoe. Even in the case of Richardson, whose novels have a real story, with beginning, middle and end, and with narrative close-wrought and cumulative in effect, we have yet to make exceptions, and to acknowledge that the actual story of "Pamela" is contained in the first volume, while the second and third volumes are like instructive appendices. The early conception of the novel when conscious of form was in terms of the epic narra-tive, as appears in the theory of Fielding and in the practice notably of Fielding and Scott. And this continues to be the conception of the English novel down to the time of Henry James. With novelists like Meredith or George Eliot, to be sure, the logic remains incomplete till the end of the book, which as a whole constitutes the unfolding of all the implications of the subject. But still with them the narrative is felt to be essentially an affair of stages, of a series, of progression in time. Having learned to know the characters of the persons introduced, you are to see how these characters display themselves in action, you follow them from step to step of their fulfilment. Given the situation in which they find themselves, you are to follow the successive phases of the situation as it alters under stress of the dramatic action.

But in the most distinctive work of James the sense of progress, of story, is almost altogether lost.[j] You have rather a sense of being present at the gradual unveiling of a picture, or the gradual uncovering of a wall-painting which had been whitewashed over and is now being restored to view. The picture was all there from the start; there is nothing new being produced; there is no progress in that sense. The stages are merely those by which the exhibitor or the restorer of the picture uncovers now one, now another, portion of the wall or canvas, until finally the whole appears in its intelligible completeness. Or, once more to vary the figure, it is as if a landscape were gradually coming into view by the drawing off of veil after veil of mist. You become aware first of certain mountain forms looming vaguely defined. Little by little the mountains take on more definite shape, and something can be made out of the conformation of the valleys. And very slowly, at length, comes out clear one detail after another, until in the end you command the whole prospect, in all its related forms and hues.

[j]See *Supplementary Notes* 1954, page 287

It is almost as if Henry James had been affected by some of the metaphysics in which his brother William had so professional a concern. It is as if he had agreed, with certain idealist philosophers, that time—as well as space—is not a reality, but a condition of our consciousness, a convenient instrument of thought; that things do not really happen one after another, but that that is only the way in which they get themselves represented in the mind of the Absolute Being, in whom there is really no variableness neither shadow of turning. Among his many excursions in what are called "psychical" realms is a curious little tale entitled "Maud-Evelyn."[1] It has to do with an elderly couple who spend their days making up an imaginary history of their lost daughter. Never was story told at a greater remove from the persons most nearly concerned. The one who tells it to "us" gathered in the firelight is a certain Lady Emma. But she has picked it up in a series of conversations, extending over many years, with her protégés Marmaduke and the girl who loved him; and she gives it to us in successive installments as she received it. In the beginning the age of Maud-Evelyn when she died seems to have been left somewhat indeterminate, so as to suit the story her parents were to invent for her. When they made the acquaintance of Marmaduke, she was represented by her parents as old enough to have been engaged to marry the charming young man at the time of her death. And that is the first invention of their pious backward imaginings. We next learn that preparations had in fact all been made for her wedding, the bridal suite beautifully furnished and the presents laid out in shining order. (They were all really to be seen at the home of the parents; for the old couple and Marmaduke have spent their time getting

[1] It appeared in "The Atlantic Monthly" in April, 1900.

together the properties to suit their little domestic drama.) Eventually she is imagined to have been actually married to our young man, so that her parents may feel that she had fulfilled her beautiful destiny before death took her.

It is thus that we, in the present, "assist" at the gradual unfolding of events long past. "We," that is, in the present of the story; for the story consists in the process of the unfolding in the present, not in the events long past. We might take this as an exaggerated type of the method of James in his novels in which the successive moments of the present narrative impress one as the successive steps by which we are made acquainted with the set of facts already constituted. If you are to use the word story at all in connection with these novels. the story is not what the characters do, nor how the situation works out. The story is rather the process by which the characters and the situation are revealed to us. The last chapter is not an addendum, tacked on to let us know what happened after the wedding. It simply turns on the light by which the whole situation—which has perhaps long since taken shape in the dark—is at last made clear. And no one can hope to learn how such a novel "comes out" by turning to the last chapter, which is wholly unintelligible save as the last phase of the general situation, —last not necessarily in time, but the last to be displayed, and as meaningless by itself as a predicate without a subject.

This is obviously very different from the procedure of the earlier English novelists. Even in George Eliot you know by the time you have read a fraction of the book who it is you are dealing with. You know Adam Bede and Hetty Sorrel and Dinah Morris; you know Felix Holt, and Gwendolen Harleth, and Dorothea

Brooke.  And you know what they have to cope with.
You aren't quite sure how, given such characters and
such circumstances, the equation will work itself out.
That is the story.  But the elements are all given.  The
same is true for Meredith; and so *a fortiori* for Thackeray and Dickens, for Scott and Fielding.

There are indeed many instances in James of this
usual practice.  "The Bostonians" is a perfect example
of this method.  And this is probably one of the chief
reasons for its being denied admission to Mr. James's
collection of stories.[e]  The book is in three parts.  In
the first part, the situation is entirely set forth and the
problem stated.  The cards are all upon the table.  The
second and third parts show us a long-drawn-out playing
of the cards with which we have been made familiar.
There are some traces of this method in most of the
earlier novels of James, even those deemed worthy of
inclusion in the canon, such as "Roderick Hudson," "The
American" and "The Tragic Muse."  "Roderick Hudson"
reminds one of "Romola" in its record of the progressive
disintegration of a man's character.

But in the novels last mentioned, and still more in "The
Portrait of a Lady" and "The Princess Casamassima,"
there is a strong tendency towards the author's distinctive
method of gradual revelation.  This finds its application
in connection with certain characters and groups of
characters, like Madame Merle and Gilbert Osmond in
"The Portrait," and Christina Light in "Roderick Hudson."  In "The Princess Casamassima" we find the
nearest approach to the technique of the later period.
For here the story might be described as the gradual
unfolding or illumination of the character of this woman
so appealing to the curious imagination, and our hero and

the rest of the complement of characters, as essentially the spectators of this woman's performance.

It is, however, more constantly in the twentieth-century series that we have the full display of the method towards which all along the author was feeling his way. It is in these latest fictions that one feels most the want of movement, of that action which makes the indispensable, and the most striking element, of the ordinary novel. The sense at least of such objective performance is almost entirely lost; and incident, while it is implied in the situations presented, hardly appears in any state more naked than that of implication. The narrative is taken up with the gradual emergence of relationships and points of view, of attitudes and designs. Behind these subjective facts lurk indeed great cloudy masses of the objective. But they remain always in the mist, behind the subjective facts,—which seldom, for that matter, come out themselves into the clear, sharp light of plain statement.

The most amazing instance of this type of story is "The Sacred Fount," the first of the novels of James to make its appearance in the present century. It consists of a series of discussions at a week-end party concerning the sentimental relationships of certain men and women present. Not a single incident is brought into the narrative more important than the intimate look of two persons observed together in an arbor, a gentleman's appearance of age, or the waxing and waning of a lady's wit. The discussions are held largely between "me" and "Mrs. Briss"; and the climax of the story is found simply in the most extended of our debates, late at night in the hospitable drawing-room. Each one of us has developed an elaborate hypothesis to account for certain social phenomena,—phenomena whose actuality may itself be brought in question, being so much an affair of the interpretation (if not the imaginative invention) of appearances. "I" hold that the present wit and competence of Percy Long—heretofore a dull and unskilful member of society—have had to be paid for by the woman who loves him; and that this accounts for the nervous manner and peculiar tactics of Mae Server, who has lost her former cleverness and is trying to conceal the fact. On the same grounds I explain to myself the blooming of Mrs. Brissenden—my opponent in this debate—at the expense of "poor Briss," who daily presents an older face to the world. "Poor Briss," like Mae Server, has had to tap the "sacred fount," the limited source of vital energy, in order to give abundance of life to the one he loves. Following this clue, it appears to me that Percy Long and "Mrs. Briss," conscious of the similarity of their position, have formed a tacit league for concealment and the defence of their common interest. And again "poor Briss" and Mae Server seem to have been drawn together by a sense of their community and a common need for sympathy. It was Mrs. Briss in the first place who helped me to my theory. But it is obvious that, when she comes to realize how far I may carry its application, she must deny these facts and make her own independent interpretation of the facts she acknowledges. And Mrs. Briss is a most ingenious and plausible debater. So that "I" am obliged to hurry away from her neighborhood in order to maintain my own view of the facts. And so, in the end, the reader is left provided with two complete sets of interpretations of a group of more or less hypothetical relations. Nothing whatever, in the ordinary sense, has come to pass. But two distinct pictures of the same subject have been blocked out and painted in before our eyes.

And one thing further is to be observed. The nature

of the facts discussed by "me" and Mrs. Brissenden—
the personal bearing of them upon herself, not to speak
of her friends—makes it necessary that our discussion
should be conducted largely by indirection, in terms that
convey our meaning without ever putting it in plain
English.  Indeed the situation, as it immediately affects
her, must be altogether ignored so far as overt mention
goes.  The same thing is true for discussions between
"me" and Percy Long, "me" and Mae Server, "me" and
still other persons.  So that some of the terms of our
logic are like lines projected into space.  Some of our
weapons are perpetually hidden.  And we are perpetually
struggling for ends, and from motives, unmentioned but
vividly present in the minds of both parties.  It must be
clear how much all this contributes to the "nebulous"
character of the situations.  It is this that estranges so
many readers who insist on the author's keeping *them* at
least informed, and at once, of the precise meaning of
each play in the game.  The feelings of one such reader
have been amusingly expressed by Mr. W. C. France,
writing in "The Bookman."[2]  "Now," says Mr. France,
"though Mr. James talks a great deal in his novels about
'giving it' and 'having it straight' the thing you vulgarly want to know is *not* given you straight.  You must
guess it from that unemphasized fact of a later train,
that damning absence of an overcoat, . . . that otherwise
unaccountable burst of tears.  When Mr. James finesses
the essential incidents, when you are left to gather the
presence of a card of greater value from the very fact
that he plays low, he estranges the masculine attention,
and intrigues the soul of the feminine reader."

If Mr. France has correctly distinguished the reactions
of the sexes to the stories of James, and has given the

[2] March, 1905.

right explanation of the difference, then no story should more strongly repel the "masculine" nor more strongly attract the "feminine" reader than "The Sacred Fount." And no story can be more conspicuous for its difference from the ordinary fictitious narrative. It is perhaps unwise, however, to rest too great a burden of illustration upon this rather inferior work, which Mr. James did not think worthy of inclusion in the "canon." More authoritative evidence may be gathered from those later novels of which he so fully and frankly approves. And these quite sufficiently illustrate my description of his method. Of "The Ambassadors" we may say that there is no story except that a man goes to Paris on an errand and returns home without being able to carry it out. What you are really occupied with, in this story, is the discovery of Paris; or rather—and this is less objective still—the discovery of what Paris means. When you have made out what Paris means, you leave it there as it was. And the picture is complete. More strictly speaking, you— that is, Strether—have discovered the relation you bear yourself to that order of civilization; and this is the pictorial arrangement which is the upshot of the long process of laying on oils.

In "The Golden Bowl" there is a similar theme which we may describe as the discovery by the Italian Prince— creature of an ancient, sophisticated world—of the relation he bears to the fresh and fine ideals of the new American world. Charlotte and Maggie are the two touchstones by which his character and insight are tried out. Charlotte represents—in spite of her technical Americanism—the order of thought and of social accomplishment to which the Prince more naturally belongs and which he would more naturally appreciate. Maggie proves the finer, and in the end the more potent, influence;

and it is by his appreciation of her, his preference of her
to Charlotte, that he proves his fundamental worth, his
kinship below the surface with the finer and stronger
character. It is thus he shows himself—like the gilded
crystal bowl—of the finest material, and, though cracked,
not broken beyond repair and the hope of permanent
serviceableness. But we are very little sensible of the
*action,* of the movement by which this comes about. If
we are sensible of a process, it is the process by which
Maggie displays the strength of her nature. Or, taking
it the other way round, and so making clearer its subjective character, it is the process by which the Prince
becomes aware of the strength of his wife's nature. In
the earlier half of the book, which doubtless includes
reference to a larger number of objective facts, and those
of greater bulk and extension, what we are chiefly called
upon to view is the gradual emergence of the situation,
or the pattern of social units, made up of Maggie and
her father, the Prince and Charlotte. If it is true that
the situation comes into being before our eyes, what we
are conscious of is rather how we become aware of the
situation already in being.

These stories are not without incident. Only, as we
have seen, the author has a trick of referring to the past
each new incident he introduces. We are invited to look
back through the consciousness of one of the characters
upon a *fait accompli;* or we learn of the fact through
some dialogue in which the characters discuss the bearing
of what has happened upon their present situation.
James makes no use at all of the "dramatic" possibilities
of the death of Milly Theale in her Venetian palace or
of the last meeting of Milly and Merton. The facts are
of importance, but they are of importance merely as
forming the background and conditions of the final inter-

views between Merton and Kate Croy,—scenes in which
the theatrical is reduced to the minimum, and, while
actually making new decisions and taking steps which
determine the course of their lives, the characters give
the impression of merely working out the logic of what
has gone before.  So in the first part of "The Golden
Bowl" we are very little concerned with the action
involved in the love-making of Charlotte and the Prince.
They talk as if they were not actors in a drama but
figures in a pattern.  We do not see them doing this or
that; we become aware of the fact that they have arrived
at such a position in relation to one another and the other
characters.

In "The Golden Bowl" and "The Ambassadors," Mr.
James has justified his peculiar method, at least to the
lover of James.  In "The Golden Bowl" it proves not
incompatible—strangely enough, it might seem—with a
sense of dramatic struggle.  In neither book does it have
the effect of reducing the characters to puppets.  The
motives and issues are kept distinct, if indeed not at once
clear and fully understood; the interest ever deepens and
broadens; there is a steadiness and continuity of progress
that carries the reader forward in its strong sweep.  In
the case of "The Wings of the Dove" there is much
more doubt of the author's success.[k]  The difficulties of
the system here come out strong.  In certain parts of the
story, not only does nothing happen; we are considerably
puzzled to know what it is we are looking for.  That is,
we are not sufficiently admitted into the consciousness
of the character most concerned, or it is a consciousness
too troubled for us to follow with patience or comfort
its gradual enlightenment.  The indications are there, as
will appear upon rereading, but they are often too spar-
ingly supplied to let us in to the very mystery we are

[k] See *Supplementary Notes* 1954, page 288

supposed to gape at. Of course, if we like James at all, it must be for the mystery. But we must know what the mystery is about. We must know at least in what direction to look for light.

But if "The Wings of the Dove" betrays the difficulty of this system of story-writing, it none the less convincingly displays the system. And especially it reminds us again how impossible it is to take in any of these stories without the light supplied by the conclusion. "The Wings of the Dove" presents itself to me as primarily a study of the character of Kate Croy. That is the most interesting mystery of the book. And you certainly don't understand whom you are dealing with here, in the case of Kate and her lover, until the very last scene applies the test by which all that goes before may be interpreted. Similarly, in "The Golden Bowl," you do not understand until the last scene the appropriateness of this gilded and broken crystal cup which has been chosen to symbolize the princely husband of Maggie. And something similar is true of all the novels of the later period.

## IV

## SUSPENSE

Thus we are brought to one of the chief peculiarities of the method of James: his way of doling out his information in bits,—just enough each time to keep the reader from deserting, never enough to satisfy or finally enlighten him until the end. Something like this, in combination with other refinements of technique equally suggesting Henry James, is to be found in certain distinguished novelists of the present time who may be regarded as disciples of his. It is enough to mention Mrs. Wharton's "Ethan Frome" and Mr. Conrad's "Lord Jim." But Mrs. Wharton and Mr. Conrad have each of course a distinctive manner and a special line. Neither of them is in the remotest danger of being accused of slavish imitation of whomsoever; and they have left Henry James in undisputed possession of his own field. And the practice in question, in just this sort of novel, and in such completeness of execution, remains so far as I know unique. In this method the most subjective of psychological novels are in agreement with the most objective of detective stories. And they affect the reader in much the same way, keeping his curiosity forever aroused and never quite allayed until the end of the story. In my own reading, there is no fiction of any sort in which suspense is so constantly sustained. You are literally always in suspense, or at least always curious, always clamoring for more light.

It is perhaps some stretch of the meaning of the word suspense to apply it to these effects of James. In other novels we are in suspense as to the fortunes of our friends in the story, their success or failure in what they have undertaken, the nature of the dangers or difficulties they are destined to meet. The question is, What is going to happen? In James, the question is more often, *What is it that did happen?* where are we now? what did that mean? what is the significance of that act? what new light is thrown upon such and such a character, or upon our situation? Milly Theale, finding herself in the misty unfamiliar realm of English society, spends her days and weeks in making out now this, now that form, at first so indistinct in the fog, and so by degrees the general lay of the land. In particular she is engaged in the discovery, bit by bit, of the extensive personality of Kate Croy and the relation she bears to Milly and to Merton Densher. And then, through a large part of the book, we follow the gradual process by which Merton reconstructs, from her words and acts, the character and "system" of Kate, and, in a wider circle, from all that has befallen, the position in which he finds himself,—the state of his own mind and heart. This may not be suspense in the usual understanding of the term; but there is a continual appeal to our curiosity, to our concern for the characters. And there is more opportunity for the author to play upon this concern, or this curiosity, than in any other type of story,—more chance for him to "play" us as the angler plays his trout.

This method is very much in use in all the later novels and tales and in many of the earlier ones. But it finds perhaps its completest employment in "The Ambassadors." Nowhere has the author taken greater pains in turning on his light by slow degrees. In the first of the twelve books, prescribed by the twelve installments in a magazine, we do not even arrive at the Paris which is to be, we may say, the special subject of the study, nor do we make the acquaintance of any of the major characters other than the ever present observer and ambassador himself. The contrast between Maria Gostrey and Waymarsh, seen in the vestibule of England, the "rows" of Chester, is all the hint we are offered of that "Europe" which is the general category under which "Paris" is included as the particular instance. It is not till the end of the third book, and after careful preparation, that the young hero of the story is allowed to make his entry, with all the readjustments which his appearance requires in the views of Strether. In the next book, owing to the very favorable impression made by Chad, the attention of Strether is bent chiefly upon the woman who may be thought to have had a hand in turning out so fine a man. Strether now envisages the possibility that this is a "virtuous attachment," and begins to speculate on whether it is the mother or the daughter who is the object of an attachment as yet so little defined. Neither mother nor daughter enters until the fifth book, and it is not till the latter part of this book that Strether learns from Maria the outlines of the history of Madame de Vionnet. Chad's declaration that it is Madame de Vionnet and not her daughter whose friendship keeps him in Paris comes now to require the construction of some new hypothesis or interpretation. In the two following books we observe the process by which Strether so falls under the influence of the French lady as to make himself her champion, and becomes so absolute a convert to "Paris" as to grow sceptical of Woollett.

Meanwhile we have received from time to time some addition to our knowledge of the formidable Mrs. Newsome of Woollett, present only in the conscience of Strether. Light upon the American point of view begins to grow with the arrival of the Pococks. We want to know whether Sarah or Jim will see, as Strether has seen, the "values" of Chad in his later phase. We watch for the Woollett reaction. Before the formal announcement of this reaction by Mrs. Pocock, two new facts are "released" and call for assimilation. Mamie is to be an exception to the blindness of Woollett; she is to be on Strether's side. The other fact to be digested is the engagement of Jeanne to some gentleman we have not met. This announcement, made at this time like a move in a game, gives Strether the sense of depths in the situation not yet sounded by his imagination, and demands more extended discussions with Maria. Now follows Sarah Pocock's outburst of indignation against Strether for his friendly relations with Madame de Vionnet, which she declares to be "an outrage to women like us" and especially an insult to Mrs. Newsome. "She has confided to my judgment and my tenderness," says her daughter, reproducing the great lady's very words, "the expression of her personal sense of everything and the assertion of her personal dignity." In this interview we have the strongest light thus far vouchsafed on the personality of Mrs. Newsome; but it takes the comment of Maria Gostrey in the next book to bring out still more her quality as Strether himself has been brought to feel it. She has no imagination—that is the reason she can make herself felt so effectively. She has even, says Maria, imagined stupidly and meanly; or, what comes to the same thing, intensely and ignorantly.

The final chapters of this eleventh book furnish the last and—objectively—the most substantial fact necessary for Strether to determine his attitude in the whole affair, —the fact that this attachment of Chad and Madame de Vionnet is not a "virtuous" attachment after all. But

it requires the five chapters of the twelfth book to bring
out completely the final attitude of Strether,—how, as
Maria perceives, the shock of knowledge has come without bringing him any nearer to Mrs. Newsome or making
him any less ardent a champion of the French woman,
and how, for all that, he will not make his home in Paris,
not being—like Maria—"in harmony with what sur-
rounds him" there.

Thus from beginning to end of the story, we are
occupied with just *finding out* what it is the author is
hiding from us. And our eagerness is made no less keen by
the fact that in the story there are always several characters besieging every possible source of information and
that it is through their mouths our curiosity voices itself.
But the author is never to be shaken from his attitude
of serene imperturbability. He is never to be persuaded
to turn on more light than he thinks we absolutely need
at the moment. He is like some public personage constantly beset by a swarm of reporters hungry for a bit of
news, who does "release," bit by bit, such news as he
sees fit. The public personage sees fit to let the public
have whatever information, real or imaginary, will re-
dound to the credit of his party or will tend to build
up a particular reputation for himself. The author sees
fit to let his reader have whatever item will, at the
moment, best serve in bringing out the "subject" with
which he is engaged,—only making sure not to let him
have more than he can well manage at one time.

This extreme jealousy of his material is not to be
attributed wholly, or even principally, to a mischievous
love of teasing the reader,—however legitimate a motive
this may be in a writer of fiction. More important is his
concern that the reader may not have too big a helping.
He wishes him to master one position thoroughly before

be proceeds to the next. This both on account of the next position, which will be more securely seized if the first position is solidly occupied, and more especially on account of the earlier position itself. James wishes to express the last drop of human significance from whatever circumstance he puts into his press. This is required by that law of economy that he so cheerfully obeys. Any less deliberate rate of progress would make it impossible to "work" his story, as Mr. James would say himself, "for all it is worth."

# V

## POINT OF VIEW

The stories of Henry James are records of seeing rather than of doing. That we have seen to be, at any rate, the general impression of the reader. The process of the story is always more or less what Mr. James himself calls in one case a "process of vision." Of "The Ambassadors" he says, referring to the enlightenment of the main character, "The business of my tale and the march of my action, not to say the precious moral of everything, is just my demonstration of this process of vision."[1] Of "The Spoils of Poynton" he says, referring to the central character, Fleda Vetch, "The progress and march of my tale became and remained that of her understanding."[2] In a story so conceived, a matter of prime importance must naturally be the point of view from which the vision is had, the source of information or the medium through which what is to be seen is conveyed to the reader. There is no matter in which James has shown greater care for technique.

Mr. James is seldom or never, in his later work, the "omniscient author." He has a great scorn for this slovenly way of telling a story. It is only in his earlier work that he sometimes allows himself to step in and give special information to the reader,—information which he could not have had from the person or persons who are for the moment most concerned. Quite as little

[1] Vol. XXI, p. vi.
[2] Vol. X, p. xiii.

does he employ the device of having the story told in the first person by the leading character, with its great initial sacrifice of plausibility. His austere muse will not consent to that "terrible fluidity of self-revelation" that characterizes narratives like "Gil Blas" and "David Copperfield." [3]

This matter of the point of view is a most complex and difficult one, and the practice of story-tellers is manifold. It would be impossible to give a brief summary of the common usage, even if one had made a sufficiently careful survey of the field to feel certain of all the facts. But I can give some illustration of methods carefully avoided by James. And it will be interesting to take examples from the work of an earlier master to whom James owes a considerable debt. [4]

Hawthorne, in "The Marble Faun," is quite innocent of the scruples that so constantly exercise the conscience of the later American novelist. Not only does he indulge in the most extended descriptions and disquisitions, in which no pretense is made of following the discoveries and impressions of the characters; but he often rends abruptly the tissue of their impressions to throw in some observation of his own. In scene after scene, again, the author starts out telling his story from the point of view of one of the characters, recording simply what may be taken in by him, only to shift suddenly for a moment or for good to the point of view of another. In the scene of "The Marble Saloon," it is Kenyon who is first shown us observing the behavior and listening to the words of Miriam. It was he who watched for her arrival, he to whom "the feebleness of her step was apparent," who

---

[3] See Vol. XXI, pp. xvii-xix.

[4] Equally striking illustrations may be found in work so recent as that of Mr. Hardy.

"was startled to perceive" such an impulse of hers, who "could not but marvel" at such another. But we are not so sure of the point of view when we read, "She blushed, and turned away her eyes, knowing that there was more surprise and joy in their dewy glances, than any man save one ought to detect there." And in the following paragraph, there is an indubitable and disconcerting shift of the point of view. "Kenyon could not but marvel at the subjection into which this proud and self-dependent woman had wilfully flung herself, hanging her life upon the chance of an angry or favorable regard from a person who, a little while before, had seemed the plaything of a moment. But, in Miriam's eyes, Donatello was always, thenceforth, invested with the tragic dignity of their hour of crime; and, furthermore, the keen and deep insight with which her love endowed her [here we encounter the "omniscient author" in person] enabled her to know him far better than he could be known by ordinary observation." It is as if, in a dance, the spotlight, which has been resting long on the man, should be shifted for one intense moment to the figure of his companion. In the scene of "The Bronze Pontiff's Benediction," the spotlight is constantly shifting from one to another of the three performers, then to the "mob" of onlookers, to rest finally, for the curtain, on all three performers in a group.

In some cases the master of the puppets intrudes himself with the most amazing disregard for illusion, the highest impudence, as it would be judged by more modern showmen. In the chapter entitled "Reminiscences of Miriam," we have been following the track of Hilda's thoughts. It has been difficult to distinguish just what are Hilda's own reflections and what the interpretations and explanations of the author. But there is no doubt as to the line of distinction at this point: "Recurring to

**the** delinquencies of which she fancied (we say 'fancied' **because** we do not unhesitatingly adopt Hilda's present **view,** but rather suppose her misled by her feelings)— **of** which she fancied herself guilty towards her friend, **she** suddenly remembered a sealed packet that Miriam **had** confided to her." Here the author marks the distinction between his own and his character's view of the moral facts. In a later chapter, "A Frolic of the Carnival," we see him in the act of dangling before us his knowledge of certain material facts upon which he is not yet ready to enlighten us. It is at the moment of Hilda's appearance in the Englishman's balcony during the carnival, after her period of mysterious invisibility, "Whence she had come," says the author, "or where she had been hidden, during this mysterious interval, we can but imperfectly surmise, and do not mean, at present, to make it a matter of formal explanation with the reader. It is better, perhaps, to fancy that she had been snatched away to a land of picture ; that she had been straying with Claude in the golden light which he used to shed over his landscapes, but which he could never have beheld with his waking eyes," etc., etc. Thus does the author flout his patient reader, frankly acknowledging his substantial obligation and offering to pay it in the airy coin of poesy.

Such methods were suitable, it may be, to the easygoing "romance of Monte Beni," a tissue of poetic fancies, in which the characters are but vague symbols of moral truth, and in which, as he tells us himself, the last thing the author wishes to create is an illusion of "reality." They would not do at all for the close-woven psychological tissue of Henry James. Considering the sort of effect at which he aimed, he could not afford to risk the leakage of illusion (to use a favorite figure of his own) ; he could not afford to risk that blurring of effect caused by the arbitrary change of focus. He must take greater pains to conceal his art, and must never allow himself to be caught in the act of composing his stage effects. The realist, and above all the psychologist, in fiction has less margin of profit, as we may say in the language of the market, and is obliged to figure closer in regard to "overhead costs." He comes—at least Mr. James had come—to take great pride in his ingenuities of economy. In the choice and maintenance of a point of view, he is seeking a steady consistency of effect, the intensity and concentration that come of an exact centering of attention upon the chosen plot of consciousness. In the preface to "The Wings of the Dove," he says, "There is no economy of treatment without an adopted, a related point of view, and though I understand, under certain degrees of pressure, a represented community of vision between several parties to the action when it makes for concentration, I understand no breaking up of the register, no sacrifice of the recording consistency, that doesn't rather scatter and weaken."[5]

In some cases James chose to present his scene in a highly objective manner, as it would be followed by an imaginary spectator. In "The Outcry" and "The Awkward Age" he will hardly record the slightest subjective reaction of one of his characters without some reference to this postulated observer. "Hugh might at this moment have shown to an initiated eye as fairly elated."[6] "Unmistakably—for us at least—our young man was gaining time."[7] The great thing is not to go outside the present scene for enlightenment. In "The Awkward Age," he

[5] Vol. XIX, p. xvi.

[6] "The Outcry," p. 143; compare also pp. 177, 211, 227.

[7] Id., p. 85.

tells us, he wished always "to make the presented occasion tell all its story itself, remain shut up in its own presence and yet on that patch of staked-out ground become thoroughly interesting and remain thoroughly clear."[8] He follows the same plan in "The Outcry." We read of a certain lady that she had a certain gentleman's "announced name ringing in her ears—to some effect that we are as yet not qualified to discern."[9] Such is the tone the author assumes to put in his place any reader undertaking to see more than is allowed by the conditions of the exhibition.

But this is not his happiest way of securing consistency in the point of view. His happiest way is one which admits our following more closely the thoughts and feelings of his characters. "Again and again, on review," he writes in the preface to the last novel of the series, "the shorter things in especial that I have gathered into this Series have ranged themselves not as my own impersonal account of the affair in hand, but as my account of somebody's impression of it—the terms of this person's access to it and estimate of it contributing thus by some fine little law to intensification of interest."[10] The great charm of such a narrative as "The Spoils of Poynton" resides in that intimacy with the mind of Fleda, that sense of identification with her feeling and thought, in all their intensity, in all their delicate shift and play, that comes of this consistency in the point of view. James speaks often in his prefaces of his desire to get himself and his reader "down into the arena"—to "live, breathe, converse with the persons engaged in the struggle that provides for the

[8] Vol. IX, pp. xvii-xviii.
[9] P. 39.
[10] Vol. XXIII, p. v.

others in the circling tiers the entertainment of the game."[11]

The most remarkable feat of Henry James in this order is the record of "What Maisie Knew," in which he chose deliberately for his "register of impressions" the "small expanding consciousness" of a little girl. The story deals with vulgar facts involving passions and relations far beyond the understanding of any little girl, however clever, let alone so innocent and "nice" an understanding as this one. And yet the whole history is given without appeal to any other source of information than the natural observation of the little girl. This was the challenge of the subject to the artistic temper of Henry James. Given such an observer, he tells us in the preface, the design "would be to make and keep her so limited consciousness the very field of my picture while at the same time guarding with care the integrity of the objects represented." As she wouldn't *understand* much that occurred, the author was obliged to "stretch the matter to what his wondering witness materially and inevitably *saw.*" He determined on "giving it *all,* the whole situation surrounding her, but . . . giving it only through the occasions and connexions of her proximity and her attention. . . . This would be, to begin with, a plan of absolutely definite and measureable application—that in itself always a mark of beauty."[12]

Not merely the plan of "measurable application," but the economy of means involved in this particular plan was prized by Mr. James as "in itself always a mark of beauty." Over and over again he lets us know how much he loves to pack his material into the smallest possible compass, to make one stroke do duty for several, to

[11] Vol. XXIII, p. vi.
[12] Vol. XI, pp. ix-x.

secure that intensification of effect which comes of the double functioning of any given element in the pictorial composition. Such economies are to be secured by various means, but none are more gratifying than those which flow from an ingenious choice of a point of view. Mr. James notes with no little complacency the way in which, in "The Golden Bowl," the Princess, in addition to playing her part in the drama as required, serves as interpreter to us. Thus "the Princess . . . in addition to feeling everything she has to, and to playing her part just in that proportion, duplicates . . . her value and becomes a compositional resource . . . as well as a value intrinsic."[13] As usual Mr. James reserves his extremest expressions of satisfaction for the technique of "The Ambassadors," of which the "major propriety," the great "compositional law" was "that of employing but one centre and keeping it all within my hero's consciousness." There were to be plenty of other people with their motives and interests. "But Strether's sense of these things, and Strether's only, should avail me for showing them; I should know them but through his more or less groping knowledge of them, since his very gropings would figure among his most interesting motions, and a full observance of the rich rigour I speak of would give me more of the effect I should be most 'after' than all other possible observances together. It would give me a large unity, and that in turn would crown me with the grace to which the enlightened story-teller will at any time, for his interest, sacrifice if need be all other graces whatever. I refer of course to the grace of intensity."[14]

Now the most notable peculiarity of the stories of Henry James—regarding conception rather than execu-

[13] Vol. XXIII, p. vii.
[14] Vol. XXI, p. xv.

tion—is the refined, not to say fine-drawn interpretation of character, of motive and of personal relations. And if the situations and the reactions of character are to be conveyed to the reader exclusively through the consciousness of persons in the story, the persons thus serving as interpreters must necessarily be persons of fine discrimination, of keen penetration, of delicate sensibility. And this is, I think, almost invariably the case.[15]

As early as the time of "Roderick Hudson" James had created such an interpreter in the person of Rowland Mallet. As he says himself, "The centre of interest throughout 'Roderick' is in Rowland Mallet's consciousness, and the drama is the very drama of that consciousness—which I had of course to make sufficiently acute in order to enable it, like a set and lighted scene, to hold the play. . . . It had, naturally . . . not to be *too* acute —which would have disconnected it and made it superhuman: the beautiful little problem was to keep it connected, connected intimately, with the general human exposure . . . and yet to endow it with such intelligence that the appearances reflected in it, and constituting together there the situation and the 'story,' should become by that fact intelligible."[16]

But our best instances of this intelligent interpreter from within are to be found in the leading characters of the later stories. Every reader of James has been impressed—some have been bored—by the constancy with which the characters bestow upon one another the epithets "wonderful," "beautiful," "complete," "splen-

---

[15] Even Maisie is all of this, wanting only in maturity and experience to make her a satisfactory recorder of the objective as well as the subjective facts, that is of the incidents themselves as well as her youthful impressions of them.

[16] Vol. I, p. xvii.

did," and others to the same effect. Probably the person most lavishly praised for "wonderful" is Lambert Strether, and it is no less competent a judge than Maria Gostrey who thus passes judgment upon his insight and discrimination. It was for similar gifts that Mrs. Gereth made choice of Fleda Vetch for her friend and the depositary of the precious Spoils. Fleda appears from the beginning to be as well endowed as Mrs. Gereth with esthetic and practical intelligence; and we are made to feel before the end how much she surpasses her patron in moral and spiritual fineness. There is no character in fiction upon whose spiritual intelligence was put a harder and more unrelenting strain; and it is largely the success with which she supported this strain that gives her little story so high a place among all the novels of James. Her creator is fully conscious of all that is involved in this fact on the technical side, of the technical problem confronting the artist who undertakes such a subject, and the rewards higher than technical crowning his success. "Once more," in reviewing this work he perceives "that a subject so lighted, a subject residing in somebody's excited and concentrated feeling about something . . . has more beauty to give out than under any other style of pressure. [Such is his own somewhat confused combination of figures.] One is confronted obviously thus with the question of the importances; with that in particular, no doubt, of the weight of intelligent consciousness, consciousness of the whole, or of something ominously like it, that one may decently permit a represented figure to appear to throw. . . . This intelligence, an honorable amount of it, on the part of the person to whom one most invites attention, has but to play with sufficient freedom and ease, or call it with the right grace, to guarantee us that quantum of the impression of beauty which is the most fixed of the possible advantages of our producible effect. It may fail, as a positive presence, on other sides and in other connexions; but more or less of the treasure is stored safe from the moment such a quality of inward life is distilled, or in other words from the moment so fine an interpretation and criticism as that of Fleda Vetch's [*sic*]—to cite the present case—is applied without waste to the surrounding tangle."[17]

In some of his stories in which he has provided several such intelligences, or at any rate several minds sufficiently suited to act as "registers," James has experimented with the device of alternating points of view. This method was adopted in the more objective narrative of "The Tragic Muse," in which not too much is expected of Nick Dormer and Peter Sherringham in the matter of interpretation. More distinctive is the work in "The Wings of the Dove," in which if the story must get itself told from at least three different points of view—those of Kate, of Milly and of Merton—it is in point of fact the mental topography of these characters that we are most interested in exploring. In any case the situation seemed to the author one best exhibited now from one side and now from another; and this made a technical problem strongly appealing to the artist in him. "There was the 'fun' . . . of establishing one's successive centres—of fixing them so exactly that the portions of the subject commanded by them as by happy points of view, and accordingly treated from them, would constitute, so to speak, sufficiently solid *blocks* of wrought material, squared to the sharp edge, as to have weight and mass and carrying power; to make for construction, that is, to conduce to effect and to provide for beauty. Such a block, obviously, is the whole preliminary presentation

[17] Vol. X, pp. xiii-xiv.

of Kate Croy which, from the first, I recall, absolutely declined to enact itself save in terms of amplitude."[18] Mr. James speaks, changing the figure again, of his instinct in this case for the "indirect presentation of his main image" (that is, of Milly); this "proceeds obviously from her painter's tenderness of imagination about her, which reduces him to watching her, as it were, through the successive windows of other people's interest in her."[19]

It is clear that we have nothing here in common with that arbitrary and unconsidered shift of point of view within the chapter, within the paragraph, that visible manipulation of the puppets from without, which is so great a menace to illusion and intimacy. It is equally clear, however, how much the author pays, in this method, for the privilege of seeing the situation from more sides than one. He pays with the loss of that growing intensity, that larger consistency, which derive from uninterrupted continuity of the same conscious observation such as we have in "Poynton," in "Maisie," in "The Ambassadors," and—to name one instance from the earlier period—in "Roderick Hudson." At any rate, one gets from "The Dove" much less of a sense of unity and distinctness, in the whole, and in many of the parts, than from "Poynton" or "The Ambassadors," or, for that matter, from "The Golden Bowl." "The Golden Bowl" lies, in method, between "The Ambassadors" and "The Dove"; since here there is a change in point of view, but just the one change, between the first and second parts of the story. "The whole thing," Mr. James points out in the preface, "remains subject to the register, ever so closely kept, of the consciousness of but two of the characters. The

[18] Vol. XIX, pp. xii-xiii.
[19] Id., p. xxii.

Prince, in the first half of the book, virtually sees and knows and makes out, virtually represents to himself everything that concerns us. . . . The function of the Princess, in the remainder, matches exactly with his; the register of *her* consciousness is as closely kept."[20] It may well be partly this large division, in which one entire half of the story is given to the development of the situation in each of these minds, and in which the narrative does not keep making a fresh start, as in "The Dove," that accounts for the greater force and distinctness of effect in "The Golden Bowl."

Readers well acquainted with James's shorter stories will meantime have been wondering at my failure to mention another device employed in so many of his tales. I mean the introduction of some observer not concerned personally, or but slightly concerned, in the incidents recorded. This person is not, like Strether, an important actor; he is simply the narrator and interpreter of all that we are offered. He is often, says Mr. James, "but an unnamed, unintroduced and (save by right of intrinsic wit) unwarranted participant, the impersonal author's concrete deputy or delegate," etc.[21] Yet by means of him, the effect is at least made objectively pictorial without any recourse to the "mere muffled majesty of irresponsible 'authorship.'" Through him the facts are given with greater authority than can attach to the "omniscience" of any writer of fiction.

One at once recalls instances of this comparatively unconcerned observer in tales from every period except the very latest. Such are the persons who tell the stories of "A Passionate Pilgrim," "The Madonna of the Future," "The Pension Beaurepas" (all products of the

[20] Vol. XXIII, pp. vi-vii.
[21] Id., p. v.

70's); those of "The Patagonia," "The Author of Bel-traffio," "The Aspern Papers" (all from the 80's); those of "The Death of the Lion" and "Europe" (from the 90's). In all of these tales the account is given in the first person, since the objections to the autobiographic method do not hold when there is no question of the revelation of one's own character and affairs. Sometimes, however, as in "Pandora," "The Liar," and "The Two Faces," the third person is used even of this objective observer of the scene.

Of course this observer is not represented as an intrusive person with no more legitimate interest in the story than our universal human curiosity. That would be to make him too disagreeable for the purpose; or it would be too obviously a device for plausibility. His relation to the other characters must always be a natural one. The situation has come to his notice, in the first instance, in a perfectly natural manner; and if he goes on to pursue his inquiry, this is the result of a friendly or professional interest proper enough. In a considerable number of cases he is a man of letters for whom the interest in a literary phenomenon comes to reinforce his friendly sympathy for the persons concerned. Often, as in "The Figure in the Carpet," he has some little axe of his own to grind; sometimes, as in "The Beldonald Holbein," a little grudge of his own to gratify. And so, by insensible degrees, this character passes over into that of the interested observer, the actor himself. But we are at present considering the observer whose concern in the action remains slight and secondary.

It will be observed that this device of the non-interested observer is used by James only in his shorter stories, or tales, and not in his novels. The reason is not far to seek. The real inwardness of any situation, the intimate personal feeling, cannot be rendered thus from the outside. But then it is scarcely possible for the intimate personal feeling to be rendered, for the real inwardness of a situation to be developed, by whatever means, in any but the longest of *tales*. It takes *time* to get up momentum in the subjective world, to achieve the effect of weight and depth of feeling. And it is clear that the tales of Henry James are very seldom as subjective in method or intention as his novels. They are not so full and deep in conception as the novels. They are but episodes, fragments, glimpses of life caught on the wing. And they can often best be realized through the narrative of a comparative outsider. In the later stories, novel and tale alike, the subjective tendency is much greater. And it is remarkable how little use is made in the twentieth century tales of the device which was earlier such a favorite. "The Beast in the Jungle," "Crapy Cornelia," "The Bench of Desolation"—these stories follow from within the feeling and fortunes of the characters most concerned.[22]

Whether the situation is presented from without or from within, James has frequent recourse to another device for throwing additional light upon it. This is the introduction of a confidante—for this person is almost invariably a woman—with whom the (generally male) observer or actor may discuss the situation, comparing notes and checking up theories. This device is common in the novels and not infrequent in the tales. There are hints of this character in the early period, such as Mrs. Draper in "Madame de Mauves," Mrs. Tristram in "The American," Blanche Adney in "The Private Life." But

---

[22] The two last-named published in "The Finer Grain" (1910), and first appearing in magazines in 1909, too late to be included in the New York edition.

she becomes much more important, and maintains her importance more steadily throughout the course of the story, in the later period: witness Mrs. Munden in "The Beldonald Holbein," Mrs. Wix in "Maisie," Maria Gostrey in "The Ambassadors," Mrs. Assingham in "The Golden Bowl." It is Mrs. Munden who first gives his cue to the portrait-painter who tells the story as to the leading motive of Lady Beldonald, and who follows with him each stage in the situation resulting from the importation of her ugly-beautiful American cousin. It is with Mrs. Wix that little Maisie works out the moral problem involved in the relation of her step-father and her step-mother. It is Maria Gostrey who gives Strether his gradual initiation into the spirit of "Europe" and who receives his regular reports on the progress of his curious embassy. It is to Mrs. Assingham that the Prince Amerigo brings the perplexities occasioned by his marriage into so different a world from that in which he has been bred. These persons do not tend to confuse the point of view. They serve rather to strengthen the light thrown upon the situation from the mind of the chief observer. They are his confederates, acting and above all making observations in his interest. They give information and suggestion without which he could hardly arrive at a proper understanding of the case. They set him right when he goes astray. Above all, as sympathetic and intelligent listeners, they encourage him to express in words his view of the case he is observing and of his own position in relation to it. They are thus serving him and the author at the same time. They serve to transfer the record from the mind to the tongue of the observer, to dramatize the point of view, as it were, realizing it, or objectifying it in speech, and so rendering it fit for the purposes of fiction.

## VI

## DIALOGUE

The confidante bears her part in the drama almost exclusively in the way of talk. She bears a very large part, especially in the later period. And this brings to mind what is one of the most remarkable features of the stories of James, above all in this later period. That is the peculiar character and function of the dialogue. One need have no hesitation in saying that the dialogue is one of the strong points in the novels of James—providing one is prepared to explain the statement.

A great disappointment is in store for anyone coming to the dialogue of James in the expectation of finding those features which make the peculiar attraction of the dialogue of novelists in general. His forte does not lie in this direction, or in these directions. In Thackeray, one principal charm of the talk is the highly colored and amusing reproduction of "manners,"—the varying degrees of breeding, of social elevation; the ignorances and snobberies, the pride and sycophancy, of the characters. In Dickens we have the widest range of drollery in the manner of speech,—the jerky puppet-utterance of a Mr. Jingle or a Betsy Trotwood, the humor and impudence of a Sam Weller, the quaint solecism of his low-life characters. In Hardy we have a more poetical rendering of the quaintness of rustic conversation. In Meredith we are dazzled with the wit of the drawing-room and the erudition of the library; in Scott with the heroic audacity or the noble dignity of speech of historical personages. In Alexander Dumas (*père*), we run through page on page of "snappy" dialogue, in which a Gascon swagger and the constant "springing" of surprises keep us forever enlivened and on the *qui vive*. In almost all the standard novels, the "great" scenes are those in which some strenuous conflict of wills comes to a head in a "crack-crack" of words,—each speaker laying down, if I may change the figure, trump card after trump card until the hand is played out.

But James very seldom draws upon any of these funds of interest. The contrast of cultures—in the Thackerayan sense—is seldom a part of his subject. Rustics and eccentrics are almost wholly wanting. He is at no pains to make his characters witty or grandiloquent or magnanimous in any spectacular manner. And "great" scenes of the sort described above are outside his scope and aim. There are strenuous conflicts of will; but they are carried on between masked combatants, concerned above all to prevent a violent explosion, or any exposure to the gaze of the vulgar. When they play their trump card, it is not with a great smack down upon the table. They drop it rather out of their voluminous coat-sleeves and slip it on the green baize with discreet and apologetic gesture. Thus in general we may say of the dialogue of James that in comparison with the work of the great masters of fiction in English, it is colorless and featureless, wanting in variety and intensity of flavor, little given to rendering the "characters" and surface-effect of the drama. Its merits are of another order.

It is true that, in his earlier work, Mr. James made many experiments in the more usual modes. In "The Bostonians," we meet at Miss Birdseye's gathering in South Boston a group of eccentrics done, as nearly as the American author knew how, in the manner of Dickens. In "Roderick Hudson," in "The American," even in

"The Portrait of a Lady," we have characters of the milder Thackeray infusion, but still recognizable as Victorian "humorists." In the earlier chapters of "The American,"[1] the author has devoted considerable care to rendering in conversation the "character" of the two Americans in Paris, Mr. Tristram and Christopher Newman,—the vulgar sprightliness and man-of-the-world assurance of the one; the freshness, the directness, the quaint humor and abounding energy of the other; the American colloquialism and want of acquaintance with old-world standards of them both. Much is made too of the degrees of proficiency, or want of proficiency, of Newman in his use of the French language. Similarly the author has "laid himself out" on Mlle. Noémie Nioche and her father, types smelling strongly of Thackeray's Boulogne,—with which, by the way, in the book and out, James had been saturated from the earliest days.

Somewhat cruder is the humorous touch upon characters in "Roderick Hudson," the earliest of all the novels later acknowledged. There is Mr. Barnaby Striker, the Northampton attorney, of quaint gestures and attitudes, whose expressed view of his own career and character faintly reminds us of Mr. Gradgrind in "Hard Times." There is Mr. Leavenworth, patron of art after his retirement from the proprietorship of large mines of borax in the Middle West, whose pompous manner of speech smacks not a little of the earlier Victorian style. "You'll find me eager to patronize our indigenous talent," he says, for example. "You may be sure that I've employed a native architect for the large residential structure that I'm erecting on the banks of the Ohio. I've sustained a considerable loss [referring, if I remember rightly, to the death of his wife] ; but are we not told that the office

[1] On the other hand, Mrs. Bread speaks as we all might wish to.

of art is second only to that of religion?"[2] More specifically of the Thackeray tradition are the adventurers and adventuresses who figure in this book. There is the tropical envoy described in the thirteenth chapter, with the other "queer fish" whose company was for a time frequented by Roderick, although they were "outside of Rowland's well-ordered circle." But these characters make no talk. Among the more important characters of Thackerayan flavor who do make talk are Madame Grandoni, the Cavaliere and Mrs. Light, not to press the more remote resemblance of Christina Light to, say, Blanche Amory. The vulgarity and social ambition, the superstition and unscrupulousness, the plausible good-nature of Christina's mother make her remind us, as she reminded Madame Grandoni, "of some extravagant old woman in a novel—in something of Hofmann or Balzac, something even of your own Thackeray."[3] Her garrulity, extensively illustrated in the text, reminds us of Thackeray where it does not remind us more of Jane Austen.

Among the other more common uses of the dialogue to be found in "Roderick Hudson," we may mention the great "scene," in the twenty-first chapter, in which Roderick so frightens his mother and distresses his fiancée with the frantic confession of his failure. There is also the "high-brow" discussion of art in the sixth chapter, reminding one of "The Marble Faun," and not at all of James's later work. And there are instances likewise of what must have been intended for "witty" conversation, introduced to give the tone, or one of the

---

[2] Vol. I, p. 193.

[3] Id., p. 164. Again some woman met by Roderick at the Kursaal reminded Rowland of Thackeray's Madame de Cruchecassée; see p. 139.

tones, of smart society. The following interchange, for example, takes place in the course of a stroll in a Roman garden. Present are Roderick and Christina, Mrs. Light, the Cavaliere and the Prince.

"I should have liked to lie down on the grass and go to sleep," Christina added. "But it would have been unheard of."

"Oh, not quite," said the Prince in English, with a fine acquired distinctness. "There was already a Sleeping Beauty in the Wood."

"Charming!" cried Mrs. Light. "Do you hear that, my dear?"

"When the Prince says a brilliant thing, it would be a pity to lose it," said the girl. "Your servant, sir!" And she smiled at him with a grace that might have reassured him if he had thought her compliment ambiguous.[4]

It is obviously not in any of these directions that we are to look for peculiar excellence in the dialogue of Henry James. He did well to recognize the inferiority of his performances in the manner of Dickens or Thackeray or whatsoever humorous or dramatic English novelist. The characteristic dialogue of his maturer work is of a quite different order. The speakers, in the first place, are very little differentiated as to language and manner of speech, or, for that matter, as to any of the more obvious marks of character. They are all of approximately the same degree of culture and intelligence. They are generally persons of great social expertness. There is nothing formal or pedantic in their language, nor on the other hand any tincture of solecism, dialect or localism, unless it be those of London. They speak almost without exception what we may suppose

[4] P. 235.

to be the purest of London drawing-room slang. This must be qualified to the extent that they are often making points so fine they are obliged to take on some of James's own metaphysical vocabulary of analysis. Their sentences have often the double involution of metaphysics and extemporaneous colloquialism. They are sometimes long, frequently subject to qualifying parenthesis, abrupt transition, and breaking off without completion. These eager interlocutors are forever interrupting, politely contradicting, or earnestly confirming one another's statements.

These conversations may be divided into two more or less distinct groups, according as the speakers are to be classed as confederates or as antagonists; although we must take into account also a large number of scenes in which it is hard to say whether the character of confederacy or of antagonism predominates in the relation.

In extent and frequency of occurrence, the dialogue of confederates is much in the lead. And this we may consider the pure and simple type of all dialogue in the later period. This is the chief means by which the author develops his idea, or brings out his picture. It is generally in these conversations that we are informed as to the incidents or objective facts which make the backbone as well as the animated flesh of the ordinary novel, but which in James are relegated to the secondary position of subject-matter for talk. Indeed one of the chief functions of dialogue is here the gradual revelation of the facts of the story,—both the primary data, on which the story is based, and also the further incidents which take place within the proper limits of the story. It is thus, for example, that, during the play in London, Maria Gostrey gets out of Strether, bit by bit, with judicious questions, the antecedent facts of the story of "The Ambassadors,"—the character of Mrs. New-some and Strether's connection with her, the wonderful business possibilities at Woollett and the general situation there, Woollett's view of Paris, and the idea of the embassy. It is thus that, in their later meetings, Strether reports to her from time to time whatever discoveries he has made in Paris. It is thus that, near the end of "The Wings of the Dove," Densher gets out of Kate Croy the main facts of the story in Venice as regards Lord Mark.

Of course this use of the dialogue is not confined to James. But no English novelist, I think, has reduced it to such a system and made it so organic and indispensable a part of his method. They introduce it every little while in lumps as they feel the need of sweetening the drink. It is but an alternative means of relating the facts, displaying the characters or enlivening the action. In James it is much more deliberately used as a technical device. It is his trick for giving a dramatic cast to the narrative, for making the characters tell their own story.

But the facts are soon told—when once the author is ready to let us have them. And much more of the dialogue is given up to the *discussion* of the facts,—to the process of their assimilation. "What were the facts?" is a question that quickly gives place to the more important questions: "What do they mean?" "How do they affect the situation?" and (if "we" are more than mere observers personally unconcerned) "Where are *we* then?" In "The Golden Bowl," the Prince has two "confederates"—Charlotte Stant, his actual partner in guilt; and Mrs. Assingham, who in the first instance is merely the confidante of his perplexities and anxieties, but who becomes, in the course of the action, a critic to whom he and Charlotte must give an account of themselves.

The culmination of the first part of the story is in Book Three, where we are shown the four-cornered "situation" already constituted and needing only to be made clear. In the first chapters of this book, Charlotte and the Prince take turns in explaining it to Mrs. Assingham at the Ambassador's ball. In the third chapter Mrs. Assingham discusses what she has heard with the Colonel as they drive home. In the several ensuing chapters, it is the Prince and Charlotte who, in a succession of meetings *à deux,* work out to their own satisfaction what they choose to consider the beautiful completeness and symmetry of a situation in which all four parties are suited. In the final chapters of this third book, we learn from the discussions of Mrs. Assingham and the Colonel that a new factor has come in to upset the equation. Maggie's eyes have at last been opened to the presence of evil in the world, and she is now setting about really to secure the man whom she has married. In this quiet and indirect way we have been shown the climax of the story and its turning point,—the turning of this massive tide of human feeling and desire. There has been no attempt to exploit the "dramatic" aspects of the situation, the values for show and sensation. There has been consequently nothing showy or spectacular in the dialogue. It is the *significance* of the drama upon which author and characters have turned all their attention; and the talk in which the significance has been worked out naturally reflects the essentially intellectual character of the process.

Whether between confederates or antagonists, the pace of the talk is typically very slow, with occasional bursts of rapid fire in the exchange of views.

Between antagonists, it is a game they are playing, say a game of chess, in which each move must be studied with intensest concentration upon the manifold contingencies involved.

Between confederates the process may be represented by the figure of a puzzle-picture which they are putting together with one another's help, opposed only in the spirit of emulation in which one or the other fits in his piece. Between plays they are always giving one another significant looks, looks of inquiry or understanding, or even looks that amount to a move in the game, conveying as they often do more than the spoken word. It is a close and exacting occupation, taxing to the full the intellectual faculties of these partners. We are constantly being told how well they "follow" one another, or how one of them receives a momentary "check." In this co-operative game, a piece once placed is not necessarily put down for good, but may be taken back upon suggestion from one's companion, and another tried in its place. It is thus that is developed a special variety of talk peculiar to the characters of James, with a thousand recurring tricks or mannerisms if you please. It is often conducted by question and answer. One inquires first for the facts, and then the other offers, in the form of question, a tentative explanation of the facts, to be confirmed or to be refuted. The remark of one is taken up by the other, repeated with or without variation, and carried further. The ball is tossed from one to the other down the length of the field, and at last lodged in the basket with the finality of "there you are!" The reference of pronouns is often misunderstood, or in doubt, and we are then set right and carried further by our very mistake. Or else, the reference being unmistakable, the other party to the dialogue deliberately changes the pronoun and so throws some new and interesting light on the connection. By this means speech is tied to speech, all down the page, and over the page, by a sort of logical *liaison*.

To give an idea of this dialectic game of confederates, I cannot do better than transcribe portions of a typical conversation between Strether and Maria Gostrey from the eleventh book of "The Ambassadors." I shall take the liberty of italicizing words and phrases that blaze the trail of the argument, as well as writing in capitals those which emphasize the act and process of thought. Strether and Maria are discussing her tentative suggestion that Chad should pay his mother a short visit in Woollett.

"Why doesn't he *pay his mother a visit?* Even a week, at this good moment, would do."

"My dear lady," Strether replied—and HE HAD IT even to himself SURPRISINGLY READY— "my dear lady, *his mother has paid* HIM *a visit.*" [He refers to the coming of Mrs. Newsome's daughter, Sarah Pocock.] "Mrs. Newsome has been with him, this month, with an intensity that I'm sure he has thoroughly felt; he has lavishly entertained her, and she has let him have her thanks. Do you suggest he shall go back for more of them?"

Well, SHE SUCCEEDED after a little IN SHAKING IT OFF. "I SEE. It's *what you don't suggest— what you haven't suggested. And you know.*"

"So *would you,* my dear," he kindly said, "if you had so much as *seen her.*"

"*As seen Mrs. Newsome?*"

"*No, Sarah*—which, both for Chad and for myself, *has served all the purpose.*"

"And *served it* in a manner," she RESPONSIVELY MUSED, "so extraordinary!"

"Well, you see," he partly explained, "what it comes to is that she's all cold thought—which Sarah could serve to us cold without its really losing anything. So it is that we know *what she thinks of us.*"

MARIA HAD FOLLOWED, but SHE HAD AN
ARREST.   "What I've never made out, if you come
to that, is *what you think*—I mean you personally—*of
HER.*   Don't you so much, when all's said, as care a
little?"

This clue, followed in the same logical but labyrinthine
manner, leads them to the fact of his being thrown over
by Mrs. Newsome.   And they "work out" together the
character of Mrs. Newsome, and what must have been
her view of Strether and of her son Chad.

SHE TURNED IT OVER, but as hoping to clarify
much rather than to harmonise.   "The thing is that I
suppose *you've been disappointing—*"
    "Quite from the first of my arrival?   I dare say.   I
admit *I was surprising* even to myself."
    "And then of course," Maria went on, "I had *much
to do with it.*"
    "*With my being surprising—?*"
    "That will do," she laughed, "if you're too delicate to
*call it MY being!   Naturally,*" she added, "you came
over more or less *for surprises.*"
    "*Naturally!*"—he valued the reminder.
    "But *they were to have been all for you*"—she CON-
TINUED TO PIECE IT OUT—"and none of them for
her."
    Once more he stopped before her [he had been pacing
up and down in the manner usual with him in these
exciting moments of excogitation] *as if she had touched
the point.*   "That's just her difficulty—*that she doesn't
admit surprises,*" etc.   [She has her mind entirely made
up.]   "She's filled as full, packed as tight, as she'll hold,
and if you wish to get anything more or different either
out or in—"
    "*You've got to make over* altogether *the woman her-
self?*"
    "What it comes to," said Strether, "is that you've got
morally and intellectually *to get rid of her.*"

They continue to discuss Mrs. Newsome and her point of view, and two pages later we see Strether "coming up in another place." He explains that Mrs. Newsome had made up her mind that he was going to discover "horrors" in Paris, and that it didn't "suit her book" when he failed to discover them.

". . . That was her disappointment."

"You mean *you were to have found Chad himself horrible?*"

"*I was to have found the woman.*"

"*Horrible?*"

"*Found her as she imagined her.*" And Strether paused as if for his own expression of it he could add no touch to that picture.

His companion HAD meanwhile THOUGHT. "*She imagined stupidly*—so it comes to the same thing."

"*Stupidly?* Oh!" said Strether.

But she insisted. "*She imagined meanly.*"

He had it, however, better. "It couldn't but be *ignorantly.*"

"Well, *intensity with ignorance*—what do you want worse?"

"This question might have held him, but he let it pass."

"*Sarah isn't ignorant*—now; she keeps up the *theory of the horrible.*"

"Ah but *she's intense*—and that by itself will do sometimes as well. If it doesn't do, in this case, at any rate, to deny that Marie's charming, it will do at least *to deny that she's good.*"

"*What I claim is that she's good for Chad.*"

"*You don't claim*—SHE SEEMED TO LIKE IT CLEAR—that *she's good for YOU.*"

"But," he continued without heeding. "That's what I wanted them to come out for—to see for themselves *if she's bad for him.*"

"And now that they've done so *they won't admit that she's good even for anything?*"

"*They do think,*" Strether presently admitted, "*that

*she's* on the whole *about as bad for me*. But they're consistent of course, inasmuch as they've their clear view of *what's good for both of us."*

"For you, to begin with"—Maria, ALL RESPONSIVE, confined the question for the moment—"to eliminate from your existence and if possible even from your memory the dreadful creature that *I* must gruesomely shadow forth for them, even more than to eliminate the distincter evil—thereby a little less portentous—of the person whose confederate you've suffered yourself to become. However, that's comparatively simple. *You can easily, at the worst, after all, give me up."*

"*I can easily, at the worst, after all, give you up.*" The irony was so obvious that it needed no care. "*I can easily at the worst, after all, even forget you."*

"Call that then workable. But Mr. Newsome has much more to forget. *How can HE do it?"*

"Ah *THERE AGAIN WE ARE! That's just what I was to have made him do; just where I was to have worked with him and helped."*

These passages of linked remark and rejoinder, of co-operative and systematic exploration, are typical of the dialogue in the later stories whenever the persons engaged have an identity of interest, being purely what I have called confederates. When they are antagonists, or when at least they have some opposition of interest, some need for caution and reserve—as is the case, for example, with Fleda Vetch and Owen Gereth—certain modifications necessarily will appear. But even in such cases, the dialogue often conforms more nearly to this type than to the more usual types of dialogue in novels.

One point should be made before we go on to the observation of these modified forms of dialogue. It is by no means mere inquisitiveness, nor morbid self-consciousness, that inspires the characters so discussing themselves and others. For they almost invariably have a stake in the game quite sufficient to justify their demand for information. This fact seems to me to be ignored by Mr. Littell in his most interesting comment on this aspect of the later novels. "Each of his later novels," says Mr. Littell,[5] "is peopled by protagonists who watch themselves and one another, and by minor characters who watch the protagonists sleeplessly. They are not more interested than I, these minor characters, in the great relation we are studying together with such minuteness." And Mr. Littell finds it difficult to reconcile this "remorseless inquisitiveness" with "any remotest regard for the questioners' own notions of distinction." Now Mr. Littell has certainly characterized very neatly one of the most striking features of these stories—he is discussing specifically the "four supreme novels," "The Awkward Age," "The Wings of the Dove," "The Ambassadors" and "The Golden Bowl"—the intense light of observation from a dozen directions that beats upon every situation. But I am at a loss to know what particular characters he may have in mind who are not more "interested" than himself in what they are observing. Not Maria Gostrey, the minor character who does the observing in "The Ambassadors." She has certainly been given the utmost license and plenty of motive for her inquisitiveness by being made the confidante and assistant of Strether in his embassy,—not to speak of the presumption that she is in love with him. Not Milly Theale's companion nor Aunt Maud in "The Dove." Not surely the Duchess nor Mr. Longdon in "The Awkward Age." Nor finally can it be Mrs. Assingham in "The Golden Bowl," who spends so much of her time discussing with her husband the situation of Maggie and Charlotte, the Prince and Mr. Verver. We cannot surely

[5] "The New Republic," March 11, 1916.

lose sight of the fact that she was from the start the friend and confidante of the Prince, that he had invited her in so many words to be his "consort" on the strange voyage of his marriage, and that later on Maggie too had come to her for light and help. She had to understand the situation, the good woman, because she was obliged to "meddle," and she was obliged to meddle, among other things, the author is at great pains to let us know, in order to avoid the *"louche"* appearance of having conspired to render over-friendly services to the Prince in getting him married to the rich American. The only person I can think of in all the later stories who is a mere gossip is the man who tells the story of "The Sacred Fount"; and even he has grace enough to try to put his curiosity in the light of a general or philosophical interest in human reactions. And we must do Mr. James the justice of remembering that he did not include this story in the canon. It is more than likely that he had grave doubts himself as to the real "distinction" of this character. In general, however, his remorseless inquisitors have good reason for being remorseless. And it is this fact that gives to their talk a dignity greater than that of a puzzle or a game of chess. It gives to it some of the deeper human interest of drama.

# VII

# DRAMA

The exceptional importance and the systematic use of the dialogue suggest the playwright's method of telling his story. But we do not bestow the term "dramatic" upon scenes and situations which fail to show a marked opposition of wills. The dramatic character is naturally intenser whenever the persons approach the relation of antagonists.

There are many degrees to this approach in the stories of James, as may be seen best in those earlier novels of the final period, "The Spoils of Poynton," "The Awkward Age" and "The Sacred Fount." Fleda Vetch may be regarded as the antagonist of her own lover in so far as she feels in conscience bound to dissimulate her love for him and to prescribe for them both a line of conduct of a rigor beyond his strength. She is still more opposed to the mother of Owen, in spite of the confederacy at first established by her being chosen for a suitable daughter-in-law and custodian of the "spoils." Somewhat like Fleda's relation to Owen is that of Nanda to Vanderbank; and indeed there is hardly any pair in "The Awkward Age"—as, for example, Mrs. Brook and Van, Mrs. Brook and Longdon—who have not ample occasion for the display of caution and resourcefulness in the fencing matches in which they indulge perforce with one another. For while they always go outwardly on the assumption of being confederates, they are really working in each case for different, if not actually opposed, ends. And the universal style is one of strenuous eternal vigilance and elegant dissimulation under a bland pretense of disinterested candor. This variety of disguised antagonism finds its simplest case in the conversations of the narrator with Mrs. Briss in "The Sacred Fount." The narrator has no personal interest beyond his concern for the integrity of his hypothesis. But Mrs. Briss, under the guise of friendly rivalry in behalf of *her* hypothesis, is fighting with all her strength for the maintenance of her own private security.

It is but a step to those irreconcilable antagonisms, those relations of acute hostility, which mark the intenser moments of drama. Such are the relation of Maggie and Charlotte in the later parts of "The Golden Bowl" and that of Isabel Archer and Gilbert Osmond in the later parts of "The Portrait of a Lady." In these cases the elements of hatred, of horror, of intense fear, are added to that of mere opposition of aim. And thus we have drama in full panoply. Somewhat in a class with these is the situation of Fleda Vetch. For the agony of her struggle with temptation, as well as with her cunning human adversaries, raises the pitch to a level with that of the drama of Isabel Archer or of Maggie Verver.

Yet all three of these dramas have much in common with those less intense struggles that make the tissue of "The Awkward Age" and "The Sacred Fount." In both kinds the characters are fighting more or less in the dark. In every case they are doing their best to keep their own masks in place. Always in the heat of the struggle they must scrupulously maintain their *tenue.* One of the marks of the dialogue in all these relations is the anxiety of each party to get and keep a moral advantage over his adversary. They are all perpetually "sparring for position," as they might say. They can never therefore "give themselves away." They can never play, like Maria Gostrey and Lambert Strether, cards on the table. They must, on the contrary, keep their hands well hidden from one another; and they must never play a trump card when their purpose can be as well served by one of lower rank.

Naturally, therefore, the talk takes on a somewhat different cast from that between simple "confederates." It cannot show the same simplicity and completeness, the same beautiful continuity as of logical demonstration, which we observed in that of Strether and Maria, or in that of the Prince and Charlotte working out their position in reference to Maggie and her father. There is a greater mystery in this allusive talk playing above unsounded deeps. Often it requires, on the author's part, considerable explanation of what is going on in the minds of the parties to the conversation. And the dialogue proper appears greatly reduced in proportion to "psychological" narrative. In "The Golden Bowl," for example, in the great crucial scene between Maggie and Charlotte, the dialogue is to the narrative but as one to four or five,—so much need there was to set forth the nature of Maggie's "system" and the means other than words by which she managed to maintain her "advantage" of position over Charlotte—let alone the accompaniment of feeling which makes that scene so deep and moving. Where in such dialogue the method does not admit of so much editorial explanation, where the drama is all talk, the tendency is to put more of a strain on the attention of the reader. This, I think, is notably the case in "The Awkward Age," which seems to me the most "difficult" and the least satisfying of all James's more considerable works. In this book, the antagonisms are constantly present, but in so disguised a form as to keep the reader's brows knit more tightly than those of the characters themselves.

On the whole, however, whether the opposition is partial or complete, one is more impressed with the likeness than the unlikeness of the more dramatic scenes to those between mere confederates. The antagonists too are working out together, though in opposition, the situation in which they find themselves. One of them at least is trying to find out something, and that something is not so much an objective fact as a state of mind that constitutes a situation. Such, in "The Awkward Age," is the state of mind of Mr. Longdon,—not to mention that of Van, or that of Nanda. In "The Golden Bowl" it is the state of mind, or the "system," of Maggie. Poor Charlotte Stant, kept equally in the dark by her lover, her lover's wife, and her husband, the father-in-law of her lover, must relieve herself of the dreadful suspense as to where she stands by putting a question to her rival. When Maggie has assured her that she accuses her of nothing, and has submitted to that sisterly kiss upon the cheek, when the others concerned have arrived in time to witness that dramatic salutation, then Charlotte knows, and they all know, that a new pattern has arranged itself in their relations. In "The Portrait of a Lady " in all those scenes in which Pansy's marriage is in question, beneath all the struggle of Isabel and Osmond, there is for Isabel the great business of making out the character of her husband; and for us there is, through her consciousness, the gradual spectacle of the revelation of his baseness. The culmination of the struggle in "The Spoils of Poynton" comes with the full realization by Mrs. Gereth of the fundamental difference between her ethical scale and that of the two lovers. It is again a matter of question and answer, of following a trail.

Fleda has at last given in to Mrs. Gereth's importunity and agreed to "go to the Registrar" at once. But she has to acknowledge not knowing where Owen is.

"Find him, find him, [says Mrs. Gereth] come straight out with me to try at least and get *at* him."

"How can I get *at* him? He'll come when he's ready," our young woman quavered.

Mrs. Gereth turned on her sharply. "Ready for what? Ready to see me ruined without a reason or a reward?"

Fleda could at first say nothing; the worst of it all was *the something still unspoken between them.* [I have italicized these significant words.] Neither of them dared utter it, but the influence of it was in the girl's tone when she returned at last with great gentleness: "Don't be cruel to me—I'm very unhappy." The words produced a visible impression on Mrs. Gereth, who held her face averted and sent off through the window a gaze that kept pace with the long caravan of her treasures. Fleda knew she was watching it wind up the avenue of Poynton—Fleda participated indeed fully in the vision; so that after a little the most consoling thing seemed to her to add: "I don't see why in the world you take it so for granted that he's, as you say, 'lost.'"

Mrs. Gereth continued to stare out of the window, and her stillness denoted some success in controlling herself. "If he's not lost why are you unhappy?"

"I'm unhappy because I torment you and you don't understand me."

"No, Fleda, I don't understand you," said Mrs. Gereth, finally facing her again. "I don't understand you at all, and *it's as if you and Owen were of quite another race and another flesh. You make me feel very old-fashioned and simple and bad.*" [1]

This is the climax at once of the drama and of the "revelation." For in so far as James makes use of drama, it is in the interest of the idea. The idea having often

[1] Vol. X, pp. 221-222. Again the italics are mine.

to do with a strong contrast of character and point of view, drama is a natural by-product when the opposed views come into action. Or, putting it the other way round, the dramatic opposition is a means of bringing to light the contrast which is the main subject of the book. So it is in the scene from which quotation has been made. And being as they are a means to the development of an idea, it is to be expected that the dramatic scenes should partake somewhat of the nature of exposition.

This method is not, as we have seen, the ordinary method of telling a story. But it is not unlike the method of drama as practiced by some of the greatest modern playwrights, for whom the play is not incapable of developing an idea. It is not the drama of eloquence, the drama of "manners," the drama of "action." It is still less perhaps the drama of dialogue,—of the witty interchange of paradox and repartee. But eloquence, wit, manners, even "action," while all welcome as accessories, are none of them indispensables of drama. Indispensable alone is the personal struggle, brought within the compass of the "scene," and taken at a point acute enough to be capable of holding the stage.[2] Such a struggle, so limited and focussed, is the subject of "The Spoils of Poynton." And in its close weave, its quiet, steady, logical development of a human situation, it recalls the drama of "Ros-

[2] Of course, when I speak of drama in a novel, I do not mean to imply that the situation as there given is actually *presentable* on the stage. However similar to a play in logic and design, the novel has a technique of its own. Each form has its own exactions and its own exemptions. The great exemption of the novel is from making the speech of the characters self-explanatory and self-sufficient as a spectacle. And its main exaction is the correlative of this: the author of the novel must furnish his dialogue with full complement of setting and explanation.

mersholm" and "Hedda Gabler," the drama of *"Le Demi-Monde,"* the drama of *"Der Einsame Weg"* and *"Lebendige Stunden."* And we realize that it is not for nothing that Mr. James uses the language of the "scene" almost as much as that of the atelier in giving an account of the art of fiction. James is, of course, not by any means alone in being subject to the influence of the stage. Anyone familiar with the novels of, say, Mr. Galsworthy, not to go outside of our own language, will realize how profoundly the art of fiction has been affected by the art of drama since the time when the latter began to take itself with a seriousness worthy of its great traditions.

While his way of conceiving a scene has always, in the later years, something of the dramatic, the novels are comparatively few in either period in which James, rising to the pitch of drama reached in "The Spoils of Poynton," at the same time makes the drama serve so well the purposes of revelation. "The Tragic Muse" has only too abundantly the stuff of drama. The drama of Nick Dormer grows cold while that of Peter Sherringham is being warmed up. As for the nature of the material itself, it is obvious and abundant, but it lies too much on the surface for the kind of development that is the author's specialty. There is nothing here for interpretation. There is much for illustration—there are plenty of items. But they are all items for substantiating a simple proposition,—the incompatibility of the artistic and the practical temperaments. Nick Dormer must be given time to learn the strength of his inclination to the life of the artist. But there is nothing to be worked out, either in character or situation. There is no "System" to be tried, like the system of Maggie Verver or that of Gilbert Osmond's wife. There is no strategy called for.

And strategy is of the very essence of the drama in the best of Henry James.

The same objection holds in much greater degree for the excellent story of "Washington Square"; for "The Outcry," which of all novels of James approaches most nearly the technique of the play;[3] and for the exciting narrative of "The Other House." The last named, while it gives ample scope for the strategy of the unscrupulous "lead" (Rose Armiger), enlists this force in no better a cause than the defamation of a rival and the concealment of murder. And this is so far from being characteristic material for Henry James that we are for once inclined to dismiss the work with the vague speculation as to whether this master was capable, and at this point in his career, of resorting to the "potboiler."[1]

In other novels, while the material is amply susceptible of development and potentially dramatic, the inherent drama largely fails, for one reason or another, to get itself *realized*. This is the case with both "Roderick Hudson" and "The Wings of the Dove." We never really get inside the skin of Roderick, where the conflict may be supposed to rage, such is the limitation imposed by the choice of Rowland Mallet for interpreter. The struggle of Kate Croy and Milly Theale for the heart of Merton—for that is what it comes to in spite of the beautiful unselfishness of Milly—would be the best material for drama, were it not for the fact that the influence of Milly must work so much from a distance, as it were. The "scene" can never dispense with the personal presence of whatever forces are engaged. As for "The Ambassadors," the struggle there takes place too exclusively within the mind of Strether.

[3] See the fifth chapter of Part II.

[1] See *Supplementary Notes* 1954, page 288

We are thus brought back, for the really triumphant assertion of the dramatic sense, to "The Portrait of a Lady" in the early period, and, in the later one, "The Golden Bowl" and "The Spoils of Poynton." Each of these stories develops an idea involving contrasts in character and point of view. In each one the interest is centered upon the struggle of a single person—a woman—of a fineness and dignity and of an attractive humanity such as to enlist our full sympathy. Each woman is confronted with a problem bristling with difficulties. She is opposed by forces only less strong and subtle than herself. She is shown taking a line, devising a "system," which she carries out from point to point, while we follow without interruption and with ever growing intensity of concern.

And if one were to choose among all these for the drama *par excellence,* there would be little doubt of the pre-eminence of "Poynton." In stories so wide in scope as "The Portrait" and "The Golden Bowl," there must be much besides drama. There must be a dense marshalling of cohorts, a large unfolding of the human landscape. The drama is seen growing and putting forth leaves before the actual blossom unfolds. In plainer words, the dramatic scenes are but the culmination of the whole succession of scenes. This is implied in the very nature of the novel. But "Poynton" is largely exempt from the usual conditions of the novel by virtue of the more limited subject-matter, by the lucky conception of a conflict which can be shown always at its height. Perhaps we should simply say that "Poynton" is a *nouvelle* rather than a novel, and has the concentration proper to the briefer form. The drama takes but two of the twenty-two sections to get in motion. From the moment that Fleda Vetch determines to "cover" Owen, never to "give him away," from the moment that Mrs. Gereth so embarrasses Fleda by commending her to Owen for an ideal daughter-in-law, the forces have come to grips. The great scenes begin with the seventh section, on Owen's visit to Ricks, when Fleda must resort to such cunning diplomacy in drawing him out on the subject of Mona's ultimatum, and not betraying herself upon his contrast between her refinement and the vulgarity of Mona. There follows the still more difficult trial when she must pretend ignorance of Mona's attitude in the face of Mrs. Gereth's subtle inquisition. In the ensuing scenes, the ground is continually shifting. Fleda is driven back from one line of defense to another. She is obliged to invent a new ingenious strategy to suit each new position she takes. The tide of feeling rises higher and higher as she finds it harder and harder to satisfy her conscience within and to ward off the attacks of her foes without. We arrive at scenes of overt drama —such as would suit the visible stage itself—the shocking of Mrs. Brigstock, the breakdown in the arms of Owen, the final yielding to the importunities of Mrs. Gereth and the desire of her own heart. Here we have reached the climax; and the few remaining scenes are the quiet but highly emotional epilogue, with the last brief flaring up of grief at the burning of Poynton. There is much to be said for the large, slowly moving drama of "The Golden Bowl," with all its deliberate sumptuousness and amplitude. But for swift, unhalting onward movement, there is nothing in James—there is perhaps nothing anywhere—like "The Spoils of Poynton." And this may be taken as the type and classic instance of the "scenic" method in fiction.

Now it need not be inferred that dramatic effectiveness is the sole measure of success in the novels of James. Indeed we may go so far as to say that drama has never been one of the indispensables of fiction. Fielding is great without it, and it is by no means one of the most important elements in the greatness of Scott or Dickens. It must have been observed that among the novels of James largely wanting in drama are several of his best—notably, in the early period, "The Princess Casamassima" and "The Tragic Muse"; in the later period, "The Ambassadors" and "The Wings of the Dove." There can be little question of the superiority of "The Dove" to "The Other House," or of "The Ambassadors" to "The Outcry," in spite of the more dramatic character of the latter in each case. There are evidently other sources of interest still more important—at least when taken together—in determining the sum of interest of the work. All we can say is that, here or elsewhere, drama is one very great source of interest in the novel, and that, other things being equal, we shall prefer the novel that draws largely upon it. This is no doubt one of the chief reasons for the pre-eminence, in the early period, of "The Portrait of a Lady," and, in the later period, of "The Golden Bowl" and "The Spoils of Poynton."

# VIII

## ELIMINATIONS

The "scenic" method of narrative and the limitation of point of view carry with them certain corollaries in technique. They involve certain ideals important otherwise in determining the art of James. They involve—to put it in a word—intensive rather than extensive working of the subject. There are included in this "word" two propositions, one positive, the other negative. The subject is to be worked intensively; it is not to be worked extensively. To the first proposition too much time has perhaps been given already. It is in virtue of the second that James is most in contrast to the greater number of his English predecessors. For the novel, and especially the English novel, has seldom felt very strongly the obligation of art to selection and elimination. It seems from the beginning to have been exempt from the standards of severity in form. Being in origin a kind of literary mongrel, it might well pay no regard to prescriptions against the *mélange des genres*. Having for its function the mere entertainment of idle moments, having for jury the miscellaneous vulgar herd of readers, the only requirement was that it should entertain; all the resources of the author were drawn upon for diversity and abundance of entertainment, and little care was given to fitness, to the *bienséances,* to *vraisemblance,* to sobriety and consistency of effect. And this tradition has not failed to make itself felt in our day. Witness the popularity—to mention only serious work—of the novels of

Mr. H. G. Wells, of Mr. Gilbert Cannan, and of many other less gifted *improvisatori*.

But even in the novel there has been another tradition. There were signs of it in Fielding, and it was strong in Jane Austen and George Eliot. In our own time we have Mr. Galsworthy, Mrs. Wharton and several other devotees of the more sober faith. It would be neither politic nor critical to attempt to rule out either of these types of novel. We do not wish to cut ourselves off from any rich source of entertainment (and instruction) such as Mr. Wells has shown himself. And any such move could easily be countered with sarcasms upon the stricter form. It is easy to contrast the poverty and stuffiness of these selective writers with the large generosity and breeziness, the manifold suggestiveness and stimulation, of the rapid fire novelists. And indeed, so little authority have classic standards in our day, it is the more careful and limited novelist who is nowadays most likely to be put on the defensive. It is this type of novelist, in the person of its most notable exemplar in English, that is at this day most in need of explanation.

The appeal of James is not then the appeal of diversity. He makes no concession to the popular desire for a constant change of scene, for wonders and surprises, for sensations and facile amusement. You will find no airships or caravans to give you picturesque transit into the clouds or into gypsy-land. Neither politics nor literature, neither religion, morality nor social questions make the subject of his discourse. Indeed he is not inclined to discourse, nor his people either. His people seem to have no theories. Taken up with their own particular human problems, they show little interest in problems in general. Henry James may be the most psychological of novelists. He shows no inclination—at least in his

maturer work—to generalize his psychology. It is not
he who analyzes for us the motives of his characters. It
is they themselves who carry on any such investigation.
(That is indeed one reason why the stories seem so
"difficult" to the general reader, who is accustomed to
having his psychology straight from the author.) And
if our author does not psychologize, neither does he phi-
losophize, neither does he sentimentalize. You will find
no solid blocks of reflection upon "life" and human nature
scattered, Thackeray-wise, along the course of the narrative. You will find few producible nuggets of wisdom
such as catch the light from every ledge and cranny of
Meredith's work.

The appeal of James is not by diversity, but by fineness
of texture, closeness and subtility of weave, fastidiousness of workmanship. He is deeply concerned to produce
a surface at once rich and exquisite. For effects of this
order the most careful selection is required. The most
jealous watchfulness must be exercised against the intrusion of materials out of keeping with the design. There
is accordingly no place for the excursions and anecdotes,
the surprises and whimsies of the ordinary novelist.

The first concern of all is for the integrity and consistency of the scene, of what Mr. James calls the "discriminated occasion,"[1]—the "secret" of which, as he
points out, is "an adapted, a related point of view." The
reduction of the narrative to a series of "discriminated
occasions" and the strict adherence in each case to the
occasion so discriminated explain the strenuous elimination of the usual means of entertainment. Mr. James
has a horror of the "loose end," which, he says, has
found a perfect paradise in the English novel. In "The
Awkward Age," he tells us, it was his aim to compose

[1] Vol. XIX, p. xvi.

a series of scenes as objective as those of a play. In carrying out this aim he "participated in the technical amusement" of the playwright, finding the playwright's gratification in the neatly executed piece of work. "The play," he says, "consents to the logic of but one way, mathematically right, and with the loose end as gross an impertinence on its surface, and as grave a dishonour, as the dangle of a snippet of silk or wool on the right side of a tapestry. We are shut up wholly to cross-relations, relations all within the action itself; no part of which is related to anything but some other part—save of course by the relation of the total to life." [2]

Mr. James, in this same place, has a remarkable statement of the disabilities of the play in comparison with the novel, which latter may carry so much greater weight and richness of material. And he will never himself quite forego the advantage of the novelist. Even "The Awkward Age" is a novel and not a play. But he never, in his later period, loses sight of that ideal of the play. And he does forever seek to reduce all his material to the compass of the discriminated occasion.

James does not like to interrupt his story to go back to events beyond its proper limits in order to "catch up." That would be to let our present food grow cold. It is necessary, in "The Ambassadors," to let us know something of the history of Chad in Paris, as well as the fact that Strether was once himself in early years an eager pilgrim at Parisian shrines. But it is never Henry James who lets us know of these circumstances; nor are they presented to us in a general way. They come to us through the reflections of Strether upon a particular day, reflections naturally engendered and nourished by what he saw in a walk through familiar streets of Paris.

[2] Vol. IX, p. xx.

In this way "two birds are killed with one stone." We get our facts, and we get them colored and flavored with the feeling of the character. And besides all this, we never lose for a moment our intimate sense of the present experience. A still better means of rendering the facts, because more dramatic, more animated, is exemplified by the conversation with Maria Gostrey in which we are equipped, almost without suspecting it, with all the necessary data in regard to Woollett and the embassy. Incidentally Strether—and so the reader—has suggested to him reservations and interpretations that tend to modify the facts and make them still more a part of the present experience. They are not merely the subject of present discussion; they become the problem of the moment. And they serve to develop the characters at the same time that they advance the story. It is by such means that James avoids the boresome "seated mass of explanation after the fact," the "block of merely referential narrative," of which he speaks with so much dislike.[3] It is thus with his characteristic love of economy in the interest of luxury that he brings in so many other beauties of art in the very train of utility.

Similar considerations guide him in regard to the actual narrative,—the story of present events itself. The great thing is to make the account particular and not general,— to be forever dealing with some special occasion. Very seldom does the author take one of those bird's-eye views of a long period or a series of events so often resorted to by novelists for the sake of getting along with their story. Very seldom does he summarize or classify the experiences of his characters as Mr. Hugh Walpole, for example, in "Fortitude," summarizes the experiences of Peter Westcott at Dawson's school, or as Thackeray

[3] Vol. XXI, p. xix.

summarizes in "The Virginians" or even in "Vanity Fair." James does not like to let his character so far escape him,—to lose touch for so long with his immediate consciousness in particular circumstances. Summaries and classifications must come unmistakably through the consciousness of the character himself, or of someone else in the story who ought to know. Of course, in the later work, the problem is somewhat simplified for James by the comparatively brief time, the comparatively small number of events, covered in the story. In earlier novels, like "Roderick Hudson" and "The Portrait of a Lady," it must be acknowledged, many violations will be found of a rule not yet formulated for himself by the author.

The same rule requires the elimination of all description of persons, of scenery and of other "setting," except as they may be reflected naturally in the consciousness of the characters on a particular occasion. And this practically means the elimination of all blocks of description, of all but the briefest of suggestive phrases, or of details thoroughly assimilated and enlisted in the interest of some special bias of interpretation. Not often in his maturer work does James vouchsafe on his own authority a generalized account of the personal appearance of his characters. Nor does he often give the *items,* whether of the appearance in general or of the appearance on a particular occasion. What he strives to render is the main impression of the personality, with often the subtle change from day to day, the waxing and waning of beauty, the present condition of the soul as it shows through the earthy mask. The form and features, the dress and attitude are transparencies through which shines the light of thought and feeling.

Thus one might, in feeble imitation of his method, describe the author himself as he appeared to the French and to the American portrait painter, in each case so much more significant and beautiful than the man presented in the crude items of the photograph.[4] We are not told by Sargent and Blanche of the large extent of bald head, the heavy features and bulky figure of the anglicized American, the almost ferocious severity of his glance, the stiff formality of the coat and collar of a certain year. These were all doubtless facts of a certain kind, but negative, almost irrelevant facts,—facts interesting chiefly as illustrating the recalcitrant nature of the stuff of which human beings are wrought. The Henry James of Blanche is a thinker, seen in profile with the mild gravity of finely moulded features and far-seeing glance. It is a moment of thoughtful concentration. He is reflecting, it may be, upon that Future Life which he thought guaranteed to human desire by the boundless resourcefulness of the human spirit. And behind him in a rich and delicate pattern of leaves, we feel how, to his artist-imagination, experience flowers endlessly with the sense of our cosmic relations, the perception of which is the very process of conscious life.[5] The James seen by Sargent is the creator of human beings and the presenter of their dramas. He is shown here in the plenitude of creative power. Straight forward he looks from the place where he sits established in all the solid amplitude of entire possession. There is something almost portentous in his glance. It is so penetrating as

---

[4] There are indeed several most artistic photographs of James, notably those by Hoppe (reproduced in "The Craftsman," 25 : 31) and Coburn (see "The Bookman," 38 : 122 and "The Century," 87 : 150).

[5] Certain views of Henry James in regard to life after death were published in 1910 in "Harper's Bazaar," 44 : 26. They appear in condensed form in "Current Literature," 48 : 303-4.

to cause uneasiness were it not for the large indulgence, the gentleness of the philosopher, shed, as it were, from his shining brows. His eyes are darkened with thought, but his large features glow with the joy of successful labor, of understanding satisfied.

If I have read more into these portraits than is there in presented items, or if the painters have read more into the face of the author than they actually saw, we can hardly have gone further than the characters of James in their interpretation of one another's appearance. Thus Milly Theale learns from the mere look of Kate Croy, a person not given to easy betrayals, the substantial fact that Merton Densher has returned from America. "Kate had remained in the window, very handsome and upright, the outer dark framing in a highly favourable way her summery simplicities and lightnesses of dress. . . . She hovered there as with conscious eyes and some added advantage. Then indeed, with small delay, her friend sufficiently saw. The conscious eyes, the added advantage were but those she had now always at command,—those proper to the person Milly knew as known to Merton Densher. It was for several seconds again as if the *total* of her identity had been that of the person known to him—a determination having for result another sharpness of its own. Kate had positively but to be there just as she was to tell her he had come back. It seemed to pass between them in fine without a word that he was in London, that he was perhaps only round the corner. . . ."[6] Once more we come back to the "economy" of a writer whose description is so indistinguishable from the narrative itself. Of course this method requires an especially careful selection of the few items of appearance noted, since each bears so heavy

[6] Vol. XIX, pp. 272-273.

a burden of interpretation. James's later work in this respect compares with his earlier as the descriptions of Sterne compare with those of Smollett. We have much more data for the appearance of Commodore Trunnion than for that of Uncle Toby, but we feel much better acquainted with Uncle Toby, the details given in his case are so carefully chosen for what intimate things they tell us about him. In the later work of James we feel better acquainted with the characters than in his early work since everything that is told us about them is so immediately relevant. Facts are given us only so fast as we can digest them. But they are given us so unobtrusively that we are partly or wholly unaware of the means by which they are conveyed. This change in method might be likened to the change which Strether observed in Chad Newsome. "He had formerly with a great deal of action expressed very little; and he now expressed whatever was necessary with almost none at all." It is not that in his earlier characterizations James expresses very little; but that, in his later ones, with so few items, he manages to express so much more.

The same evolution is observable in his treatment of the setting. In the beginning he was precise and extensive in his notation of the details of setting. Dealing largely with European scenes, he shows the boundless hunger of the tourist for the picturesque and the pride of a youthful tourist in displaying his expert knowledge of the old world. Names of places are scattered through the story with lavish profusion. Public monuments and private dwellings come in alike for enthusiastic description. In the later stories there is no less rich a sense of "Europe," but it is conveyed in a manner much less ostentatious. Every detail admitted has now its direct bearing on the particular narrative and its intimate revelation of the characters involved. "Europe" is now a society; a world peopled with individuals living their natural and unpublished lives. Hotels and churches have yielded almost entirely to private homes as the scene of the story; and differences in atmosphere are now rendered much more delicately at a much smaller outlay of itemized description. The Parisian home of Madame de Vionnet is by no possibility to be confused in the reader's mind with that of Maria Gostrey or that of Chad Newsome. And yet there is very little offered in any of these cases for identification by the police. An instance of what James can do for a domestic interior without actually describing it is the account of Merton Densher's impressions of Aunt Maud's London residence:

Lancashire Gate looked rich—that was all the effect. . . . He hadn't known—and in spite of Kate's repeated reference to her own rebellions of taste—that he should "mind" so much how an independent lady might decorate her house. . . . Never, he felt sure, had he seen so many things so unanimously ugly—operatively, ominously so cruel. . . . He couldn't describe and dismiss them collectively, call them either Mid-Victorian or Early—not being certain they were rangeable under one rubric. It was only manifest they were splendid and were furthermore conclusively British. They constituted an order and abounded in rare material—precious woods, metals, stuffs, stones. He had never dreamed of anything so fringed and scalloped, so buttoned and corded, drawn everywhere so tight and curled everywhere so thick. He had never dreamed of so much gilt and glass, so much satin and plush, so much rosewood and marble and malachite. But it was above all the solid forms, the wasted finish, the misguided cost, the general attestation of morality and money, a good conscience and a big balance. These things finally represented for him a portentous negation of his own world of thought—of which, for that matter, in presence of them, he became as for the first time hopelessly aware. They revealed it to him by their merciless difference.[7]

Many sentences are omitted from this account in my citation, but none that add anything material to our knowledge of Aunt Maud's house. They all have reference to Densher's reactions in presence of this sumptuous ugliness. And that is the "note" of all the later work: the setting is given us through the reactions of the people in it, and carries all the color of their personality. In the case of Ricks in "The Spoils of Poynton" we are given several more precise details, as is fitting to a story having for its material subject the furnishings of a house. We learn of the "single plate of the window,"—the "one flat glass sliding up and down," with certain items of the wall paper and the doors. But this is merely the slender base from which Fleda conducts her higher operations of fancy, on the subject of the maiden-aunt who had informed this dwelling. There is nothing in which the difference between Fleda and Mrs. Gereth is brought out more delicately and yet more surely than in Mrs. Gereth's inability to feel the beauty of this maiden-aunt of Fleda's sympathetic reconstruction. It was here that, as much as anywhere, Fleda "took the highest line and the upper hand."[8] And thus we see again how description is made contributive to characterization,—nay, to the idea of the book.

As for natural scenery, there is practically none in the stories of James. That is significant enough. However much he may have loved mountains or the sea, the

[7] Vol. XIX, pp. 77-79.
[8] Vol. X, p. 248.

undomesticated aspects of nature—and as to this I cannot say—there was surely no place for these wild beauties among the clipped yews and formal terraces of his garden. No one, in reading Henry James, will have to skip the descriptions of nature. They were, of all luxuries in fiction, the first indicated for elimination.

Of course we must not give the impression that all the limitations of James were deliberately assumed for the sake of his art. Some of them are no doubt simply the limitations of his outlook. Such is notably the lack in all his work of what is sometimes called a larger social consciousness. By this is meant a realization of society as a whole made up of more or less disparate groups, with some understanding of the industrial and economic conditions that determine the life of each group and their relations to one another, and some active concern for the solution of our social problems. I suppose it is axiomatic that such a social consciousness is, if not the discovery of our time, at least one of the most striking marks of recent literature. And it does set a writer somewhat apart to be lacking in social consciousness in a period that has produced *"Die Weber," "Les Bienfaiteurs,"* "Widowers' Houses" and "Strife"; "The New Machiavelli," "Fraternity," "The Man of Property" and "The Harbor."

Many will be found to declare that no literature—perhaps no art of any kind—can be truly *great* in our day that is lacking in this essential element. It is a point upon which I cannot pronounce with authority. I certainly feel the lack in James. But there is one thing of which I am confident. Good art cannot be made out of materials of which one is not a master. Much harm comes to art from the attempt to handle material that is not one's own simply because it is supposed to be "the thing." This very social consciousness, when artificially taken on, or applied to life in a doctrinaire fashion, or unaccompanied by competent knowledge, has been the spoiling of much good art, in poetry, in the drama and the novel.

It happens that Henry James grew up in a world of thought to which these ideas seem to have been alien. His father was a man of independent means, not engaged in business, whose occupation was the pursuit of culture and the perfecting of a mystical philosophy. He was in no hurry to have his sons make choice of an occupation; he was loath to have them come to a decision, lest any given calling might limit the expansive life of the soul. In their household circle, the economic arts of production and distribution seemed as dull and sordid as the arts of the kitchen. So far from having formed an idea of "labor" and the laboring class, they do not appear to have taken into their horizon even the business man and the banker except as persons living on their incomes, and generally in Europe. Henry James gravitated inevitably towards the society of the leisured and well-to-do, and among them, the clever and highly cultivated. These he knew, with their complement of servants, bookbinders and telegraphers,[9] and with the outer fringe of artists, tourists, and the shabby genteel of European capitals.[10] It is idle to speculate on the greater social significance he might have had with a wider social horizon. He gave us a thorough and beautiful rendering of what he *knew;* and that, I must believe, is the one thing required by art.

[9] "In the Cage."
[10] "The Pupil."

## TONE

The same ideal which leads James to this simplification of the elements of the story expresses itself in a related character of his writings,—the consistency, or uniformity, of tone. I say consistency, or uniformity; but any one is free to say monotony who finds that these eliminations are in effect but limitations.

To a large extent the uniformity of tone reflects simply the uniformity of subject-matter. You do not find here the tone of low or violent passion since you are not dealing at all with people who employ such a tone. There are no low humors, and accordingly no suggestion of the manner of low comedy. The crude, the pathetic, the sentimental, in character and situation, are all ruled out, together with the atmospheres they carry with them.

But the uniformity of tone is not simply a result of homogeneity of the characters. With range of characters as limited as you please, the author would still be free to assume the tone of satire, of cynicism, of anxious morality, of sentimental concern. But James never takes advantage of this liberty. He is never sarcastic, never lachrymose, never moralistic. There is never any suffusion of his work with a cosmic poesy such as distinguishes the work of Hardy. It is always unmistakably the tone of prose in which he speaks. He has but a mild tincture of that gusto—that blend of irony and boyish high spirits—that makes the family likeness of male English novelists from Fielding and Scott to Dickens and Meredith. The tone of James is the tone of indoors and the tea-table. There is about him no smell of peat or sage-brush. You cannot imagine him peddling Bibles in Spain or "squatting" in California among the rattlesnakes. You cannot imagine him taking an interest in the soul of a planter up some river of Borneo. His words are never scattered and disarranged by any breath of the boisterous Atlantic.

Here again we are reminded of the importance of French influences in his training. All that we have just said of James may be said of Mr. George Moore. We recall that Mr. Moore wanted to be a painter; wanted it earnestly, it seems, and actually made a trial under Parisian masters. But we need not refer this quality in either case specifically to the influence of French painting. This uniformity of tone—this sacrifice of so many of the colors favored by English literary artists to an elegant consistency of effect—is a quality which has ever been highly prized by French writers, lovers of good form and refinement. And it is a quality which in every age has yielded in England to the love of variety, intensity and vigor. Witness Chaucer and Shakespeare, witness Thackeray and Browning. Witness even Congreve and Pope, who, in a period nominally devoted to the *bien-séances,* fell so far short of the simple good taste of Molière and Boileau. With the early periods, whether in France or elsewhere, James would seem to have been very little acquainted if we may judge from his allusions. But with nineteenth-century French writers (including the Gallicized Turgenieff) he was on terms of inti-macy; and it is among them that one finds the closest resemblance to his ideal in tone. Indeed his elimination of all the more markedly subjective colors in his writing may be regarded as but a corollary of the French rule of objective realism. In his case, however, as with the main French tradition, I feel this to be more an expression of temperament than subjection to any doctrine.

The simple fact is that James was extremely fastidious. If sometimes we find him violating good taste, as it must have seemed to him—as in "The American" by the oaths of his hero or by the mention of Swiss manure heaps, we may be sure *this* was the concession to doctrine. This was an attempt, by sacrifice of his own feelings, to propitiate the spirit of Balzac. Later on, I suppose, he developed an interpretation of the gospel which reconciled realism with good taste, at least for him. No one writer can treat the whole of life. Each one must devote himself to those aspects which he best understands. Such was the opinion of Maupassant quoted with seeming approval by Mr. James in his essay on the French writer.[1] And so the fastidious American was absolved from all commerce with the ugly and the cheap, his *forte* being the delineation of the fair and the fine. More and more, with the fixing of his taste, he chooses subjects to which the cheap and the ugly will not be relevant. More and more he chooses situations involving people of high goodbreeding and fineness of instinct. If there are vulgar people involved—like Jim Pocock in "The Ambassadors," like most of the characters in "What Maisie Knew"— they come to us strained through the consciousness of people not vulgar, and with all material offensiveness eliminated in the process. Our concern is for the other sort; and as for the author himself, we know how largely he sinks his own view in that of his Strethers and Fledas.

One thing particularly displeasing to such fastidiousness is any weight of emphasis incompatible with the nicest good taste. Neither joy nor sorrow, liking nor

[1] In "Partial Portraits."

dislike, neither fear, desire nor anxiety must be given strident utterance. For we are the most civil beings that ever took tea together; and we owe it to one another's feelings to keep our voices down to a sociable pitch. If readers get the impression that the people of James are without strong feeling, this is largely because of their preternatural good breeding. A careful reading of such a story as "The Spoils of Poynton" will reveal the presence throughout of a very strong undercurrent of emotion. But except at one or two critical moments it keeps well hidden beneath the surface.

There is another reason for the comparative want of expression of feeling in James. His characters are most of the time engaged in a strenuous exercise of their wits. However much their happiness may depend upon the solution of the problem that faces them, they must first solve the problem; and the energy concentrated on this intellectual process is so much energy diverted from the channels of emotional expression. It is also true that these people are generally actors, with good reasons for not betraying their feelings to one another.

But I had rather dwell here upon the other consideration. It is to a large degree the gentleman's ideal of *tenue* that requires him to maintain a quiet evenness of tone however strong his feelings may be. And the author himself, in those passages where he shows his people off their guard, feels the obligation of treating them—and the reader—in the same tone of smooth good breeding. In no respect have we a better gauge of the maturity of the work than in this matter of emotional emphasis, which shows a graduated decline from the first of the novels to the date[2] at which we may regard the method of James as fixed. In another connection I shall give

[2] Say 1896, the date of "Poynton."

instances of the heavier emphasis of "The American."
Here I will content myself with citing the words in which
are recorded Rowland Mallet's feelings when he learned
of the engagement of Mary Garland to Roderick Hudson.
It was on shipboard. "Rowland sat staring; though the
sea was calm it seemed to him that the ship gave a great
dizzying lurch. But in a moment he continued to answer
coherently."³ The early manner is here perhaps all the
more striking—at any rate it is all the more interesting—
because of the author's evident wish to indicate his
character's unusual self-control. His character was
indeed self-controlled; but the author indulges for him
in hyperbole to which he would never in later years have
committed himself. When in "The Spoils of Poynton"
we have had a particularly fine display of courageous
acting on the part of Fleda, and the author wishes to let
us know that she is at the emotional breaking-point, this
is the quiet way he does it: "At last . . . she made
a dash for the stairs and ran up."⁴ And it is not often
in this later period that James will record so animatedly
physical a manifestation of feeling as that, even of
characters "off the stage" like Fleda.

This subdued tone is in keeping with the general atmos-
pheric stillness which results from the narrative method
of "revelation." A more excited manner would accord
with a story full of the bustle of action or the clamor
of passion. But here we are bidden to follow with a
quiet intentness the growth of an idea. We have no
vagrant energy to spare for the mere pomp and circumstance of life. What we have most need of, after good
taste on guard, is a jealous intellectual self-possession.

There is no denying that, for most readers, James

³ Vol. I, p. 82.
⁴ Vol. X, p. 103.

carries too far this sterilizing or deodorizing process.
Even his fondest admirers have moments of irritation
with him for what must seem his excessive good breeding, his almost spinsterly fear of any note too loud, any
scent too strong.  However much we may love order and
regularity, the pruned and weeded garden, we cannot
but remember that some of our most pleasing impressions of beauty have been received from straggling weeds
that have escaped the gardener's hoe and come to flower
in saucy disregard of authority.  In English fiction, at
any rate, some of the finest effects are those which have
come by accident.  They are effects of inspiration rather
than of design.  Genius has blundered upon them almost
unawares.  Or at least they were possible only to the
artist painting with a broad stroke, with a large free
motion of the arm.

Not only was the ideal of James a different one.  He
seems to have had, in general, little patience with these
triumphs of straying genius.  Indeed he seems often to
have been incapable of recognizing them when he saw
them.  It would scarcely do to describe Thomas Hardy
as a straying genius, however triumphant a one we may
grant him.  But the attitude of James towards Hardy
will sufficiently illustrate his general insensibility to the
broader style.  It may be that Mr. James was later converted; but it must stand as symptomatic that a first
reading of "Far from the Madding Crowd" left him
cold.[5]  While that novel "at a cursory glance, has a rather
promising air of life and warmth," he is obliged to state
that "it has a fatal lack of magic."  It is indeed, he
acknowledges, a very clever book, and one having "a
certain aroma of the meadows and lanes—a natural

[5] So it appears from his unsigned review in "The Nation,"
Dec. 24, 1874.

relish for harvestings and sheep-washings." Otherwise
it is scarcely genuine. His account of the plot is most
illuminating. He enumerates the principal characters,
the several men and the heroine, Bathsheba Everdene.
"They are all in love with her," he says, "and the young
lady is a flirt, and encourages them all. . . . We cannot
say that we either understand or like Bathsheba. She
is a lady of the inconsequential, wilful, mettlesome type
which has lately become so much the fashion for heroines,
and of which Mr. Charles Reade is in a manner the
inventor. . . . But Mr. Hardy's embodiment of it seems
to us to lack reality; he puts her through the Charles
Reade paces, but she remains alternately vague and
coarse, and seems always artificial. This is Mr. Hardy's
trouble; he rarely gets beyond ambitious artifice—the
mechanical simulation of heat and depth and wisdom that
are absent. . . . Everything human in the book strikes
us as factitious and insubstantial; the only things we
believe in are the sheep and the dogs."

Ah well! We need not hold him too responsible for
an opinion expressed in 1874 in the Tartarly manner of
the periodical which had assumed, in America, the auto-
cratic mantle of the historical English reviews. Only,
we feel that he does betray here an insensibility that is
characteristic, the same insensibility that leads him to
question the greatness of Charles Dickens. There are
certain large ranges of life—and not so very remote
from common experience—in which he seems to be simply not at home. Otherwise he would not find it so easy
to dispose of Bathsheba Everdene with his label of flirt
and to dismiss everything human in this masterpiece as
factitious and insubstantial. I suppose the fastidious
taste of James could not put up with a certain awkward-
ness, a certain countrified homespun manner of Hardy's,

and that, finding heat and warmth and wisdom conveyed in a manner so uncouth, he was forced in self-defense to the assumption of their all being but a mechanical simulation. Instead of being too clever, Hardy was simply not clever enough, or not polite enough, to meet the exacting standard of his critic.

But it was funny indeed for Hardy, of all persons, to suffer the imputation of "a fatal lack of magic." Magic is, I suppose, the one thing in a book least susceptible of explanation, an effect not to be attained through any process of design and arrangement. It is the one quality which Hardy shows more often than any other English novelist. And it is a quality which only the most superstitious devotees of James would insist on ascribing to their idol. (His *charm* is unmistakable, and one must confess the at least etymological association of magic and charm.) It is seldom that his steady *recitative* breaks into the flowing curves of the aria, that sheer beauty disengages itself from the dense pattern of thought and experience. It is seldom that the reader is caught and swept along, as so often by Hardy, in the swift broad current of simple passion. That is not possible save at the sacrifice of his much-prized self-possession.

There are times in which the impatient reader is ready to damn his self-possession! We have epithets for describing the man whose manner is too perfect, who will never join us in any lapse from the drawing-room code. If we refrain from applying these epithets, it is because in the main we prefer good taste to bad, the quiet to the loud; and because we have so often found the most robust qualities lying beneath the exquisite surface of refinement. We may wish to remind our friend that one need not show himself robustious in order to show himself robust. We may be inclined to point out that the tea-table is all the better for an occasional excursion to the woods or even the tavern. But in the main we are content to visit the woods with Cooper and the tavern with Smollett, and to take our tea with James. We must not let an occasional irritation blind us to the rare beauty of tone which James was perhaps the first to demonstrate as a possibility for English fiction. The consistency upon which we have dwelt is a beauty implying many others. There is always positive enduring charm about work in which the materials are all so choice, in which the pieces are fitted together with such patient and jealous care. We cannot grow tired of these subdued harmonies of color, of this rare impeccable finish and glaze. However much we may admire the vivid canvases of the Salle Rubens, we are sure to return often enough to the cabinetwork, the tapestries and the porcelains of the Musée Cluny.

# X

## ROMANCE

The elaborate manipulation of suspense by James suggested comparison with the romantic *genre* of the detective story. And in more ways than one the novels of James make on me at least the impression of romances. I have to confess at once to a considerable insensibility to the charms of ordinary romance. But everyone has some craving for romance; and this craving is largely satisfied in my own case by the stories of James. And here I do not refer to the obviously and technically romantic manner of such a tale as "A Passionate Pilgrim" nor to the romantic circumstances in the plot of "The American." I have in mind that sober work of later years in which is carried furthest the cultivation of psychological niceties.[m]

This may seem a paradox, considering how generally psychological niceties are associated with the notion of realism. But the romantic impression here arises precisely from the extreme to which this tendency of James is pushed. The motives of his characters are refined to such a point as to make them seem not characters in "real life."

I should be the last to pronounce his characters not true to life. One reader at least has had the good fortune actually to know in person Maggie Verver and Kate Croy and Fleda Vetch. The circumstances may not have been the same—since life is often so much less generous of material than fiction—but the same qualities were present

[m] See *Supplementary Notes* 1954, page 288

to work upon whatever material offered. And that is surely enough to make one hesitate to question the reality of anything in James.

But still, how many of us are familiar with a society so "highly civilized" as this he paints? Figures like these are at most the rare exceptions, and are not often accompanied by satellites who can take and give cues and play out the scene with them. And again, as I have said, life does not always furnish material rich enough for such artists to work in; it is presumable that even they cannot make their lives one consistent pattern of this quality. What one finds in life are intimations, fragments, momentary and fleeting sensitivenesses and points of view, that remind one of the world of James. These very fine motives are not apparently such as govern constantly people's conduct, even that of those who most suggest his people. They seem indeed a luxury beyond the command of even the cultivated in ordinary circumstances. The people we know appear to be more governed by passions, by the primitive needs, by dull unromantic obligations, by the cruder social requirements and limitations. The professional character is more prominent in ordinary life: our friends have not put behind them their ambitions, have not so completely divested themselves as Christopher Newman or Chad Newsome of their industrial connections. And these things count for more in every move and calculation. There are things we simply *want:* there are things we must have; there are things we must do without; and all these things are present to limit and condition our thought and action. And then there is accident: there is that crude interposition of chance that Mr. Hardy can never bring himself to forget. This may not be so important in life as in the stories of Hardy; or it may not be significant enough poetically to justify its extreme prominence there. But it is a large item in life; it is a feature without which we can hardly recognize truth to life in fiction. And it is a most brutal and disturbing factor. It interferes with the weaving of patterns.

The people we know do not so consistently as the characters of James make a conscious art of life. They apply art to this or that detail or relation; but they cannot, or they will not take the trouble to make their whole life a work of considered beauty. The people of James are mostly rich or in some way raised above the necessity of earning their bread. Their relationships are greatly simplified to make them still more free. They are often free from the ordinary scruples of the man in the street, free from the New England conscience in its cruder aspects. Being very clever, they are free from the intellectual limitations under which plain people labor. They are preternaturally free, living in a moral vacuum, as it were. Moreover, the elements of life are simplified to an extreme degree, everything in any way irrelevant being shut out from all consideration. Under this head come the social and religious movements and struggles so prominent in George Eliot and Meredith and so many of their successors. It is perhaps just the irrelevant matters—as they would be for James—that create more than anything else in the ordinary novel the illusion of everyday life. So that it seems a rarefied and transcendental atmosphere into which James lifts us, an atmosphere in which there is nothing to impede the free action of spirits.

This atmosphere he has given a semi-physical counterpart in the air of the English country-house which he has so often described, and to which he returns so regularly for the scene of his action. It is an air of ample leisure-

liness, in which every provision is made for the convenience of people bent on liberal freedom of intercourse.
Such was the air in which Hyacinth Robinson made his
long visit with the Princess Casamassima; that in which
Nanda Brookenham and "Mitchy" disposed, under the
favoring auspices of Mr. Longdon, of the fates of themselves and Vanderbank and little Aggie; that in which
Maggie Verver and her father skirted and kept clear of
the subject of Maggie's great struggle with Charlotte
Stant. As James puts it in one of his tales,[1] "Life was,
indeed, well understood in these great conditions; the
conditions constituted, in their greatness, a kind of fundamental facility, provided a general exemption, bathed
the hour, whatever it was, in a universal blandness, that
were all a happy solvent for awkward relations." James
is fond of evoking a sense of lingering afternoon and
hours given over to the luxury of unhurried reflection.
"The day had been warm and splendid and this moment
of its wane . . . which seemed to say that whenever, in
such a house, there was space, there was also, benignantly,
time—formed, of the whole procession of the hours,
the one dearest to our friend, who, on such occasions,
interposed it, whenever he could, between the set of impressions that ended and the set that began with 'dressing.' . . . The air of the place, with the immense house
all seated aloft in strength, robed with summer and
crowned with success, was such as to contribute something of its own to the poetry of early evening. This
visitor, at any rate, saw and felt it all through one of
those fine hazes of August that remind you . . . of the
artful gauze stretched across the stage of a theatre when
an effect of mystery, or some particular pantomimic

[1] "Broken Wings," in "The Century," December, 1900.

ravishment, is desired." In such a world as this, all factitious impediments are smoothed away, and one may give oneself up, undiverted, to the cultivation of one's "impressions." No longer subject to the humiliating conditions of animal life, one may work out the pure spiritual pattern of one's experience!

There is nothing about all this that is not "true to life." Such happy combinations of character and condition are by no means inconceivable; and for the honor of our mortal estate, we hope they may be frequently found in fact. But they are not the combinations that stand out most prominently in a cursory survey of our surroundings. They must be, in a work of fiction, the result of the most deliberate selection. And they must strike most readers as being artificial to a high degree. If we do not yield ourselves willingly to the spell of this enchanter, if we find ourselves caught, in sterner moments, between our realism and his romance, then we are lost. Then we are likely to feel irritation at an author who asks us to take for granted so perfectly well-ordered a world. And our irritation is likely to extend to his people, who seem to have nothing to do but refine upon their motives, or—in more brutal English—split hairs. It is in such realist, sceptical mood that we ask of our friend "Mitchy" in "The Awkward Age," is he really a *man?* Would a real man have allowed himself to be persuaded to marry the girl he didn't care for in order to help the girl he did care for to make a better match? And would he have found his comfort for life in sharing, like a child, a *secret* with the girl he loved—[2] that being the means by which the two were drawn into confederacy? Is it not a comfort somewhat too metaphysical for human nature's daily

[2] See p. 352, Vol. IX.

need? Or again—in dissident mood—we grow impatient with the Prince Amerigo and Charlotte Stant as they spin the gossamer web of their relation to Maggie and her father. Is it a joke, this pretense of theirs that, because Maggie must be allowed to pair off with her father, they should lend themselves to the arrangement by pairing off themselves? Do they take seriously this way of justifying what in plain English we call adultery? We might more readily entertain the simple plea of their being in love. But being in love—in this simple fashion—is really too vulgar a fact, it seems, for a world no longer subject to the conditions of animal life. Too vulgar at least for mention in plain English. Meredith had a word, we remind ourselves, for people of this manner of thinking. He called them sentimentalists—and he never let them off as easily as they are let off here. He never let them go till he had made them ridiculous.

James has, in his essay on Maupassant, an interesting apology for the psychological method in fiction. He is speaking of Maupassant's opinion that "the analytic fashion of telling a story" is "much less profitable than the simple epic manner which 'avoids with care all complicated explanations, all dissertations upon motives, and confines itself to making persons and events pass before our eyes.'"

When it is a question of an artistic process, [Mr. James rejoins] we must always distrust very sharp distinctions, for there is surely in every method a little of every other method. It is as difficult to describe an action without glancing at its motive, its moral history, as it is to describe a motive without glancing at its practical consequence. Our history and our fiction are what we do; but it is surely not more easy to determine where what we do begins than to determine where it ends—

notoriously a hopeless task. It would take a very subtle
sense to draw a hard and fast line on the border-land
of explanation and illustration. If psychology be hidden
in life, as, according to M. de Maupassant, it should be
in a book, the question immediately comes up, "From
whom is it hidden?" From some people, no doubt, but
very much less from others; and all depends upon the
observer, the nature of one's observation, and one's
curiosity. For some people motives, relations, explanations, are a part of the very surface of the drama, with
the footlights beating full upon them. For me an act,
an incident, an attitude, may be a sharp, detached, isolated thing, of which I give a full account in saying that
such and such a way it came off. For you it may be
hung about with implications, with relations and conditions as necessary to help you to recognize it as the clothes
of your friends are to help you to recognize them in the
street.[3]

This critique appeared in 1888, at the close of the less
analytic period of his writing, and is like an anticipatory
apology for the work that was to follow. Only the most
irreconcilable enemy of the psychological will deny the
truth of his contention or begrudge him a reasonable
indulgence in what he calls himself "his irrepressible and
insatiable, his extravagant and immoral, interest in personal character and in the 'nature' of a mind."[4] But at
times one has the feeling that he has put the cart before
the horse,—that he is no longer interested in his friends
so much as in the clothes they wear. He seems willing
altogether to neglect his act, or incident, or attitude,
in favor of "the implications, the relations and conditions
necessary to help you to recognise it." And what is
particularly irritating to one in the critical spirit is that

[3] "Partial Portraits," pp. 256-257.
[4] Said in connection with "In a Cage," Vol. XI, p. xx.

not only the author but his creatures too have so largely abandoned themselves to the pursuit of motive for motive's sake. They seem at times to pride themselves on nothing but their cleverness, their penetration of one another's subtleties, the spirit of magnificent "general intelligence" in which they conduct their mutual relations. The height of this self-consciousness is reached in "The Awkward Age," where it is necessary for one of the ringleaders to suggest to another member of the coterie for them "not to be so awfully clever as to make it believed they can never be simple";[5] and where not merely the grown-up members of Mrs. Brookenham's circle prove themselves unfailingly "wonderful" or "beautiful" for the high line they take, but where even the *jeune fille* must needs have a "system" of her own,— and such a system!—and must needs work out with her suitors refinements one degree higher than her mother's.

Of course, we at once remind ourselves, "The Awkward Age" is intended for a picture of decadent society, and we must always reckon with the gently ironical light in which these characters are supposed to be shown. This consideration may apply still more to "The Sacred Fount" and the "marvel of our civilized state" presented there by the rival interpreters. But it does not so clearly apply to "The Wings of the Dove" and "The Golden Bowl." There is little to show that the author is not offering us Charlotte Stant and the Prince Amerigo, Kate Croy and Merton Densher, as genuine examples of the ideally civilized state. And certainly the self-consciousness and the passion for analytical refinements indulged in by these pairs of lovers are hardly less remarkable than those of Mrs. Brookenham's circle of dilettanti. I have referred to the process by which Charlotte and the

[5] Vol. IX, p. 303.

Prince persuaded themselves of the inevitability and beautiful propriety of their *liaison*. "The whole demonstration," it seemed to them, was "taking place at a very high level of debate—in the cool upper air of the finer discrimination, the deeper sincerity, the larger philosophy."[6] There has never been a more pointed illustration of the "fine shades" and "nice feelings" made ridiculous by Meredith in "Sandra Belloni." Perhaps we are to understand here that such sophistication is the only medium in which a guilty love may be made to assume an air of decency. But the innocence of Kate Croy and Merton Densher talks the same language on the occasion when they first pledge themselves to one another. . . .

They were talking, for the time, with the strangest mixture of deliberation and directness, and nothing could have been more in the tone of it than the way she at last said—[Well, it doesn't matter to us now what she said.] He gave a rather glazed smile. "For young persons of a great distinction and a very high spirit we're a caution!" "Yes," she took it straight up: "we're hideously intelligent. But there's fun in it too. We must get our fun where we can. I think," she added, and for that matter not without courage, "our relation's quite beautiful. It's not a bit vulgar. I cling to some saving romance in things."[7]

Any one who reads through the conversation that follows will agree that their relation is not a bit vulgar. As for Milly Theale, while she is not given the same opportunity in conversation to make fine points, she does it abundantly in the privacy of her own reflections. She makes the most beautiful of points in regard to Kate, who lends herself so well to such treatment. For Milly "had amuse-

[6] Vol. XXIII, pp. 300-301.
[7] Vol. XIX, p. 72.

ments of thought that were like the secrecies of a little
girl playing with dolls when conventionally 'too big.' "[8]
Perhaps the reader would like a bit of a reminder here
of the nature of the amusements referred to. In the following passage, Milly is interrogating herself as to her
sensations on realizing that the great doctor knows
"everything" about her condition.

Now she knew not only that she didn't dislike this—
the state of being found out about; but that on the contrary it was truly what she had come for, and that for
the time at least it would give her something firm to stand
on. She struck herself as aware, aware as she had never
been, of really not having had from the beginning anything firm. It would be strange for the firmness to come,
after all, from her learning in these agreeable conditions
that she was in some way doomed; but above all it
would prove how little she had hitherto had to hold her
up. If she was now to be held up by the mere process—
since that was perhaps on the cards—of being let down,
this would only testify in turn to her queer little history.
*That* sense of loosely rattling had been no process at all;
and it was ridiculously true that her thus sitting there
to see her life put into the scales represented her first
approach to the taste of orderly living. Such was Milly's
romantic version—that her life, especially by the fact of
this second interview, *was* put into the scales; and just
the best part of the relation established might have been,
for that matter, that the great grave charming man knew,
had known at once, that it was romantic, and in that
measure allowed for it. Her only doubt, her only fear,
was whether he perhaps wouldn't even take advantage
of her being a little romantic to treat her as romantic
altogether.[9]

It is hard to realize that all these fleecy paradoxes are
woven about the hard question of a bodily ailment; that

[8] Vol. XIX, p. 212.
[9] Id., p. 236.

nothing less important hangs upon this doctor's knowledge than the issue of *life and death*.

One thing must be granted for these people. They are not, like the ladies and gentlemen in Lyly's "Euphues," playing a mere dialectic game, a game that has no beginning or end. However fine their points may be, they *have* a relation to the general point at issue. And however roundabout a road they may be taking, it is a road that leads them towards their goal. This may be sufficient to acquit them of the charge of sentimentalism. For the sensations of the sentimentalist are beautiful on the sole condition of being sterile.

In any case our irritation is a passing cloud in the clear sky of our felicity. We have but to grant the premises of this philosopher, we have but to take his world as he offers it, to feel his own luxury in the contemplation of mental evolutions. We love to lose ourselves in the warm, thick-sprouting jungle of human nature as he conjures it up. He does beguile us royally. He flatters us to the top of our bent. He stimulates our imagination like a drug. Our own experience is colored by this medium in which we are plunged so deep. For a long time after reading James, we find ourselves living in this romantic world. We discover motives of a refinement hitherto unsuspected. Our own talk at the dancing club or over the bridge table is full of significances ordinarily not discerned. In short we are like the young ladies who used to read the romances of Mrs. Radcliffe or Mlle. de Scudéry, or the young men who still read "The Talisman," "The Last of the Mohicans" and "The Count of Monte Cristo."

## XI

## ETHICS

An earlier chapter is devoted to the uniformity of tone in James. It might have been called the neutrality of tone, since almost every possible attitude of the author liable to color the subject is ruled out in his ideal. Among other attitudes thus eliminated is a moral attitude. And so we have as a peculiarity of James among the masters of fiction in English his moral detachment or neutrality.[n]

The earlier English novelists all took pride in putting themselves into the story. They thought it right to show how much they were concerned in the behavior of their characters, to let the reader know how he should take them by means of the tone of satire, of sentiment, of moralizing philosophy. Fielding takes frequent occasion to pause and assure us he is not recommending the impiety of Mr. Square or the naughtiness of Tom Jones. Sterne is always making love to his characters. George Eliot and Meredith are still very far from the impersonal or "objective" manner so natural to French writers of fiction. But in James we have the same neutrality that has been since affected by Mr. George Moore, by Mrs. Wharton, by Mr. Galsworthy and so many other distinguished English novelists. Perhaps the likeness is greatest to Mr. Conrad. For at his best Conrad, like James, gets his effect of neutrality by means of—or is it in spite of?—his method of presenting the whole action from the point of view of the characters. The author in this method shows himself no *parti pris*. He passes

[n] See *Supplementary Notes* 1954, page 288

no judgments upon his creatures. He does not even ask you to pass judgment; he simply invites you to the enjoyment of his picture. If Fleda Vetch's philosophy is to be preferred to that of Mrs. Gereth, if Maggie Verver's to Charlotte Stant's, it is not the author who tells you so. You have to find it out for yourself.

It is interesting to speculate how other novelists would have treated the themes of James. In "The Spoils of Poynton," George Eliot would, I suppose, have agreed in preferring Fleda to Mrs. Gereth; and she would have let you know rather promptly how well Fleda typified the eternal beauty of a scrupulous conscience. Meredith would probably have taken sides with Mrs. Gereth as being a representative of common sense; and he would not have hesitated to call Fleda a sentimentalist, and to explain how she is preferring imaginary values to real ones and sacrificing the happiness of four people to her own spiritual vanity. It is clear that James admires Fleda most; but the only way in which he favors her is by making *hers* the interpreting consciousness.

This is not a method grateful to the "man in the street." It makes him too responsible. And that is not what he likes. For while he is generally moral, tremendously moral, he wants the responsibility laid elsewhere. And we are mostly ourselves the man in the street,—enough so to suspect this moral neutrality—when carried to such lengths—of being indistinguishable from moral indifference. Thus James falls under the general suspicion attaching to "foreign" writers of fiction.

This is one of the curiosities of literary history, that Henry James should be suspected of moral indifference and confused with the foreign sinners of his day. He has taken pains enough in his critical writing to make clear his attitude in the matter. He is indeed indulgent of any conscientious literary art, and he does not wish to coerce anyone against his bent or his natural philosophy. But it is plain that he prefers a view of life that takes largely into account moral considerations; and that while he deprecates the characteristic timidity of English novelists in regard to certain aspects of morality,[1] he yet on the whole thinks highly of them for their moral complexion. In an essay on Trollope, comparing English writers of fiction with French, James remarks that the English "have been more at home in the moral world; as people say today they know their way about the conscience."[2] Most penetrating criticism of non-moral tendencies in certain foreign fiction is to be found in James's essays on Maupassant and D'Annunzio. In the case of Maupassant, the American novelist was obviously confronted with a problem which he was anxious to solve. He was deeply concerned to find some way of reconciling the vile cynicism of this author with his high and serious art. This he does simply by denying to the French storyteller the possession of a moral sense.

The truth is that the admirable system of simplification which makes his tales so rapid and concise . . . strikes us as not in the least a conscious intellectual effort, a selective, comparative process. He tells us all he knows, all he suspects, and if these things take no account of the moral nature of man, it is because he has no window looking in that direction, and not because artistic scruples have compelled him to close it up. The very compact mansion in which he dwells presents on that side a perfectly dead wall. . . .[3] If he is a master of his art and it is discouraging to find what low views are compatible with mastery, there is satisfaction, on the other hand,

[1] In the essay on "The Art of Fiction" in "Partial Portraits."
[2] "Partial Portraits," p. 124.
[3] Id., p. 258.

in learning on what particular condition he holds his strange success. This condition, it seems to me, is that of having totally omitted one of the items of the problem.[4]

We may be sure that James did not intend himself to omit any of the items of the problem. These passages are from the essay quoted in my last chapter in which he defends the use of "psychology." The psychology of James is nothing but an extended delineation of the moral aspects of life. The sense of his moral indifference which some people get from a hasty reading must derive partly, as I have intimated, from the neutrality of treatment. And it derives partly too from the fact that the moral values of James are not at once recognized for those of the man in the street. It may be that James does manifest an indifference to questions of conduct on the ordinary plane, such questions as are gravely featured in "The Second Mrs. Tanqueray" and "The Notorious Mrs. Ebbsmith." He flies in a loftier air, where one has no encounter with the vulgar temptations, or where at least they are not seen in the simple vulgar light. There is— particularly in the later novels—scarcely a hint of the principle of duty as such, the principle that has figured so largely in the moral system of New England. We are not here concerned with the morality of the decalogue and the police court, with what is known as "conventional morality." Some of his most favored characters are at times shown indulgent to violations of this conventional code, if not actually indifferent to it. Thus Christopher Newman, while "going in" himself for the highest luxury in the article of love, does not feel called upon to break with, or preach at, his Parisian friend whose ideal

---

[4] "Partial Portraits," p. 284.

is so much lower. Merton Densher, who can with difficulty stomach the way his fiancée proposes to work their American friend, actually requires Kate to sacrifice her innocence, as we say, in order to prove her sincerity. Maggie Verver and her father cannot find it in their hearts to hate or condemn the unfaithful partners who have taken up so unnatural an alliance; and Maggie wins back her husband precisely through the magnanimous way in which she takes the situation. Lambert Strether, who is the very incarnation of the New England conscience, feels bound to declare in the end for the continuance of an adulterous relation—to put it in legal terms—as the clear mandate of gratitude and good faith.

It is true that, on the whole, the conventional morality does not come out so badly after all. It comes out much better in James than in most of his successors in the English novel. The case of Chad in "The Ambassadors" is really quite exceptional with James. One must remember how Madame de Mauves requires her chivalrous lover to sacrifice his passion to an ideal of fineness; how Isabel Archer goes back to her detestable husband; how Maisie's bewildered little conscience at last revolts against Sir Claude's living with Mrs. Beale; how triumphant is Maggie Verver in the end over the charms of her unscrupulous rival. James is by no means a revolutionary or a radical. He has nothing in common with those novelists and playwrights of our day who want to make over the structure of society. He is a gentleman of cultivated and conservative, not to say reactionary, instinct, who seems to take great pleasure in the present state of things. His instinct will generally in the end be found to favor the same line of conduct as that favored by the ecclesiastical and civil law, as far as the law goes.

The point is that it *is* instinct, or intuition, that determines these matters for him. And his ethical reactions seem to be very little affected by the practical bearing of the conduct under consideration. The avoidance of pain and the attainment of happiness are not the matters of first importance. In brief, his ethics are not utilitarian. Still less does he conceive of morality, in the fashion of those who make an "economic interpretation of history," as the product ultimately of industrial conditions, as accordingly relative and having no higher sanction than the social order that produces it. The morality of James is serenely unconscious of any such low origins.

Now the ethics of most of us, in so far as they are not conventional or traditional, are frankly utilitarian. We argue that such a line of conduct is wrong because it is socially harmful; that such a line of conduct is right because in the long run it leads to the greatest good of the greatest number. When we condemn horse-stealing or wife-stealing, we can cite the most practical of reasons. That is where James differs from us. The best reason he can find for condemning or approving a given course of action is that it is ugly or beautiful as the case may be. That is in the last analysis why he suffers suspicion in a world of practical people.

When we bring it down to particulars, we find it comes to much the same thing in the end. Our morality, like our food and our material arrangements, has been pretty well standardized; and the ethics of James are found, on inspection, to be the usual idealistic, or "bourgeois," or Christian ethics.

Let us enumerate the several virtues most highly recommended by the example of his heroes and heroines. We cannot do better than begin, however, with his criticism of the ethics—or sentimental esthetics—of his

Italian contemporary, D'Annunzio. The erotic adventures of D'Annunzio's people James finds most unsatisfactory because they remain so purely matters of sensation, so brief and isolated, bearing so little relation to the general course of life and conduct. I must cite but one or two from the many keen observations of our critic. "That sexual passion," says Mr. James, "from which he extracts such admirable detached pictures insists on remaining for him *only* the act of a moment, beginning and ending in itself and disowning any representative character. . . . Shut out from the rest of life, shut out from all fruition and assimilation, it has no more dignity than—to use a homely image—the boots and shoes that we see, in the corridors of promiscuous hotels, standing, often in double pairs, at the doors of rooms. . . . What the participants do with their agitation, in short, or even what it does with them, *that* is the stuff of poetry, and it is never really interesting save when something finely contributive in themselves makes it so. It is this absence of anything finely contributive in themselves, on the part of the various couples here concerned, that is the open door to the trivial."[5] One will note the terms of approval and condemnation. The great sin is to be trivial, and the great virtue is to have dignity. In order for love to have dignity, it must be more than "the act of a moment, beginning and ending in itself and disowning any representative character." To have representative character it must stand for something in sentiment, in personal relations. And in order to correspond to anything in sentiment it must have *duration,* so that there may be some wholeness or continuity in the pattern of one's conduct. "How otherwise than

[5] "Notes on Novelists," p. 292.

by the element of comparative duration do we obtain
the element of comparative good faith, on which we
depend for the element, in turn, of comparative dignity ?"[6]

Here then we have the first of the virtues that characterize the finest people of James, the virtue of constancy,
or faithfulness to a relation. When Isabel Archer returns
to her husband, in spite of the certainty of unhappiness
with him, it is not altogether, it is not mainly, I think,
on account of Pansy and what she owes to her unpro-
tected state. Or Pansy is thought of as but one factor
in the general matrimonial situation. Isabel returns because her pride requires that she shall carry through
what she has undertaken, that the stuff of her life may
not be left torn and ragged. Osmond himself had
expressed it for her in their last talk before her departure
for England. He had reminded her of their inescapable
nearness to one another, as husband and wife. It might
be a disagreeable proximity, but it was one of their own
deliberate making. "I think," says Osmond "we should
accept the consequences of our actions, and what I value
most in life is the honour of the thing." These words
"were not a command, they constituted a kind of appeal ;
and, though she felt that any expression of respect on his
part could only be a refinement of egotism, they
represented something transcendent and absolute, like the
sign of the cross or the flag of one's country."[7] It is
even more obviously this virtue of constancy that prevails
in "The Ambassadors" because of its being constancy
to a relation not conventionally right. To all intents and
purposes, it seems to Strether, Chad Newsome is the
husband of Madame de Vionnet. It is he that is bound
to her by gratitude for all that this relation has meant

[6] "Notes on Novelists," p. 286.
[7] Vol. IV, p. 356.

in the development of his personality. It is he whose moral dignity depends upon the continuance of a relation long established and grounded in sentiment and taste. He stands, in this story, in the same relation to his mistress as Cressida, before her breach of faith, stands to her lover Troilus.

So important is this virtue of constancy to an established relation, so important is duration in love, that when the heart of Merton Densher, in "The Wings of the Dove," begins to turn from his unscrupulous fiancée to the finer woman whom she wishes to "use," he begins to realize how far back *their* acquaintance really dates. It was not Kate and her aunt who first introduced him to Milly Theale in England. He had known her first, in the hazy period of his stay in New York. "Behind everything for him was his renewed remembrance, which had fairly become a habit, that he had been the first to know her. . . . Its influence had been all there, been in the high-hung rumbling carriage with them, from the moment she took him to drive, covering them in together as if it had been a rug of softest silk. It had worked as a clear connexion with something lodged in the past, something already their own. . . . He was not *there,* not just as he was in so doing it, through Kate and Kate's idea, but through Milly and Milly's own, and through himself and *his* own, unmistakably—as well as through the little facts, whatever they had amounted to, of his time in New York."[8] It is thus that he reconciles his conscience obscurely to the obscure transfer of allegiance that he is making by giving the greatest possible sense of intimacy and extent to the chronologically more recent of his relations. It is thus that he violates constancy in the very *name* of constancy.

[8] Vol. XX, pp. 185-186.

On this same branch grows the twin virtue of good faith. It is, we learn, comparative good faith which is indispensable to comparative moral dignity. There is very little of the *comparative* in the good faith which James exacts of his principal characters. Nothing short of absolute is that of Rowland Mallet and Mary Garland. Isabel Archer comes back to assured misery in order to meet what her mean husband calls "the honour of the thing." Fleda Vetch makes a still greater sacrifice to what many would deem a Quixotic sense of honor. If we have the feeling that Chad Newsome will in the end prove unfaithful to Madame de Vionnet, this arises from our very suspicion that his character is not up to the standard of his personality. Merton Densher finds he cannot lie to Milly Theale as required by Kate's program. If he had lied about their engagement, he explains to Kate, he would have been obliged to make the lie true.[9]

But there is a virtue more distinctively Christian than honor that figures largely in the stories of James. That is unselfishness, or self-devotion to the happiness of others. Rowland Mallet is the shining example in the earlier novels. But the largest number and the most interesting of these martyrs are to be found in the later group. For here it is that we have Fleda Vetch and "Mitchy" and Milly Theale. Here also we have the interesting case of Maggie Verver, who, in order to get back her husband and yet spare the feelings of her rival, consents in one scene even to play the part of a mean and jealous woman, and so make a sacrifice of what is perhaps our most precious asset, vanity.[10] Of course she does not make her sacrifice for nothing, and yet it is a beautiful exhibition of generosity of spirit. She wins her own personal

[9] Vol. XX, p. 325.
[10] Chap. V. of the Fifth Book.

end by sinking herself so completely. Lambert Strether, on the other hand, like Fleda and Milly and Mitchy, gives up all and has nothing to show for it. He might have had Maria Gostrey, and a very good bargain it would have been. But as he explains to her, in order to be right he must "not, out of the whole affair, have got anything for himself."[11]

Not anything, that is, of course, but the consciousness of being "right," or some such insubstantial gain as that. The capacity for self-devotion implies an unusually high appreciation of immaterial values. The ethical values of James are always of the most immaterial. They are never represented in religious any more than in utilitarian terms.[12] The rewards of a future life count for nothing with the characters of James. Self-sacrifice is not a word in their vocabulary. They never think of their sacrifices as being made for some "far gain." Their morality is an affair of sentiment, or of taste. Their creator is capable of speaking of his characters' moral good taste.[13] The art of life which they are all practising so assiduously is an art the materials of which are what we call moral—only, as we have seen, they are so presented that the man in the street might utterly fail to indentify them as such. We can best express it perhaps by calling it a transcendental morality. It is all conceived in that spiritual realm where the bounds of taste and morality run together and become indistinguishable.

So far as I know, James has found appreciation, where

[11] Vol. XXII, p. 326.

[12] I am not forgetting either that the finer type of Utilitarian has place for many immaterial things among his more substantial "utilities."

[13] Apropos of "Aunt Pinnie" in "The Princess Casamassima," Vol. V, p. 68.

he has found it at all, almost exclusively among English and American readers. And while I cannot at all clearly explain what I mean, I feel that his appeal is necessarily limited to the Anglo-Saxon moral sentiment. The peculiar quality of spiritual life here delineated is English, or still more perhaps American, and a quality not readily intelligible to the French mind, for example. The same quality is to be felt in Emerson and in Wordsworth. The reader may remember the passage in "Madame de Mauves" in which M. de Mauves appeals to the young American who is paying attentions to his wife, on the subject of her reading. It is a passage of the highest irony for the Anglo-Saxon reader. " 'I doubt if your English authors,' the Count [remarked] with a serenity which Longmore afterwards characterized as sublime, 'are very sound reading for young married women. I don't pretend to know very much about them; but I remember that not long after our marriage Madame de Mauves undertook to read me one day some passages from a certain Wordsworth—a poet highly esteemed, it appears, *chez vous*. It was as if she had taken me by the nape of the neck and held my head for half an hour over a basin of *soupe aux choux:* I felt as if we ought to ventilate the drawingroom before any one called. But I suppose you know him—*ce génie-là*. Every nation has its own ideals of every kind, but when I remember some of *our* charming writers!' " He recommends Alfred de Musset; and he wishes his wife might do a little traveling, presumably in company with Mr. Longmore. "It would enlarge her horizon . . . it would wake up her imagination."[14] We have a way, *nous autres,* of considering Wordsworth very much of a stimulus to the imagination. I am aware that one of the finest studies of Wordsworth has been

[14] Vol. XIII, p. 265-266.

made by a French scholar. But I suppose it is not rash to assert that M. de Mauves represents better the general taste of his nation in this matter than M. Legouis.

At any rate foreigners have shown very little inclination to take to their bosoms Henry James.

This is not, I think, because of his extreme niceness in psychological analysis. Some of the continental writers have carried very far this same practice. It is rather because of the peculiar psychology to which he applies his analysis. With them the psychological details must make up together a picture of the broad passions and moral forces. They must foot up to something Byronic or Balzacian. And this the niceties of James would not seem to them to do. Mr. James tells us that Turgenieff didn't take the trouble to read the novels which he regularly sent as tribute to the master. Had he read them, Mr. James opines, they would not have appealed to him. "He cared, more than anything else, for the air of reality, and my reality was not to the purpose. I do not think my stories struck him as quite meat for men. The manner was more apparent than the matter; they were too *tarabiscoté,* as I once heard him say of the style of a book—had on the surface too many little flowers and knots of ribbon." [15] I wonder if Mr. James did not make too much, in this guess, of the style of his work, the beribboned *surface.* Was there not a deeper reason why they would not have seemed to the Russian novelist "quite meat for men"? Was there not another reason for their failing to have for certain readers "the air of reality"? I fancy the great bar to appreciation by foreigners would be that peculiar transcendentalism or other-worldliness of motives in James. Was not James in all this traceably a product of that mystical New

[15] "Partial Portraits," pp. 298-299.

England spirit represented so strongly in his Sweden-borgian father and his religio-philosophical brother? James may have been as expatriated an American as you will; his stories laid at home may be particularly thin and wanting in quality. But his most typical characters are, with few exceptions, Americans; and while the background is European, the psychology is Anglo-Saxon, and what is more, Anglo-Saxon of Concord and Cambridge, Mass. What "foreigner" could be expected really to appreciate the character of Milly Theale or Maggie Verver, of Lambert Strether or even of little Maisie?

This is all, to be sure, a highly speculative matter. No one knows what are the traits of the American character at the present moment, or what our national ideals are going to show themselves when formed. But we do know something of a certain American spirit that flowered about Boston in the days of Theodore Parker; and I find a strong tincture of this spirit in the ethics of Henry James. If my finding be correct, it should make us hesitate the less to rank James not merely as the greatest novelist born in America, but as our greatest American novelist. He may not be American as Mark Twain or Benjamin Franklin or Edgar Lee Masters are American, but he is American as Emerson and Thoreau and Hawthorne are.

# THE FIGURE IN THE CARPET

There is one group among the shorter stories of James that has a peculiar interest for anyone seeking hints and revelations of the personal experience, the temper and ideals of their author. It comprises nearly a dozen tales dealing with writers of fiction. It is of course a hazardous business making inferences in regard to James from any of these stories. The information we may suppose ourselves to derive from them is neither so substantial, so technical, nor so authoritative as what he offers us in the Prefaces. But it is not the less precious on that account. If, with tact and discretion, we do learn something from these stories about his attitude towards his art, it will be something of an intimacy nowhere else to be felt. It will be something, say, which modesty and pride forbade him to let us have straight from himself; but something he might be willing for us to learn by sympathetic inference, laying upon us the whole responsibility of assertion.

Most fascinating of all these tales, and the one which constitutes the greatest temptation for the interpreter of James, is "The Figure in the Carpet."[1] For here he shows us a novelist of rare distinction flinging down to the eager critic the challenge of his secret. The critic is a clever fellow, a "demon of subtlety"; but he has failed, like everyone else, to discover the "little point" the novelist most wishes to make. In fact he has to be informed that there is any such little point to be discovered, that there is a "particular thing" the novelist has

[1] Vol. XV. Quotations are from pp. 229-235 and p. 240.

"written his books most *for.*" "Isn't there for every writer," asks Hugh Vereker, in their momentous midnight talk, "isn't there a particular thing of that sort, the thing that most makes him apply himself, the thing without the effort to achieve which he wouldn't write at all, the very passion of his passion, the part of the business in which, for him, the flame of art burns most intensely? Well, it's *that!*" And on a demand for more particularity he adds, "There's an idea in my work without which I wouldn't have given a straw for the whole job. It's the finest fullest intention of the lot, and the application of it has been, I think, a triumph of patience, of ingenuity. . . . It stretches, this little trick of mine, from book to book, and everything else, comparatively, plays over the surface of it. The order, the form, the texture of my books will perhaps some day constitute for the initiated a complete representation of it. So it's naturally the thing for the critic to look for. It strikes me . . . even as the thing for the critic to find." To the other's query, "You call it a little trick?" the novelist replies, "That's only my little modesty. It's really an exquisite scheme." It is later that the critic hits on the figure of speech by which this "little trick" is best to be described. "It was something, I guessed, in the primal plan; something like a complex figure in a Persian carpet. He [Vereker] highly approved of this image when I used it, and he used another himself. 'It's the very string,' he said, 'that my pearls are strung on.'"

"It's naturally the thing for the critic to look for," said Hugh Vereker of his "little trick." "It strikes me even as the thing for the critic to find." What head is cool enough to resist the suggestion that James had here in mind his own well-nigh desperate case? Was there not some "intention" of his own which had been regularly overlooked by reviewers in their hasty mention of his work? It was not that he *wished* to be difficult and esoteric. It was not so at least with Hugh Vereker. "If my great affair's a secret, that's only because it's a secret in spite of itself—the amazing event has made it one. I not only never took the smallest precaution to keep it so, but never dreamed of any such accident. If I had I shouldn't in advance have had the heart to go on. As it was, I only became aware little by little, and meanwhile I had done my work." But now his secret had become for him the great amusement of life. " 'I live almost to see if it will ever be detected.' He looked at me for a jesting challenge; something far within his eyes seemed to peep out. 'But I needn't worry—it won't!' " One cannot but wonder if Henry James, like Hugh Vereker, did pass away without ever having his secret put adequately into words.

We need not take this tale too gravely as a revelation of the artistic soul of Henry James. We need not set ourselves, with confident assumption, to solve the hinted riddle of his work. But we should be missing a rare occasion if we did not take up this metaphor and let it guide us in our summary of his art. Perhaps we should say there is not one, there are many figures in the carpet, —as many figures as there are fond, discerning readers. For me the figure in the carpet is that which gives life to the whole work. It must be implied in all that we have found to be true of it; it must be the inner meaning and the motive of all that is included in his method. This too is suggested by what Hugh Vereker says of his "secret." It is not a "kind of esoteric message": at least it cannot be adequately described "in cheap journalese." He will not limit it by saying it is "something in the style or something in the thought, an element of form or an element of feeling." "Well," says Hugh Vereker, "you've got a heart in your body. Is that an element of form or an element of feeling? What I contend that nobody has ever mentioned in my work is the organ of life."

"Esoteric message" is "cheap journalese." The same red lantern warns off from any statement of James's "philosophy of life." It may be James has no philosophy of life. But he has something which will serve the purpose as well. He has a scale of values, a preference in human experience, an absorbing preoccupation. From first to last he is preoccupied not with men's lives but with the quality of their experience; not with the pattern but with the texture of life. Most novelists seem by comparison all taken up with the pattern. In Fielding and Scott, in Balzac and Zola, in Thackeray and Tolstoi, it is the adventures of the characters that we are bidden to follow. The contrast is the more remarkable when it is the English contemporaries of James that are brought into comparison. In Meredith and George Eliot, a matter of prime importance is what the characters bring to pass in a practical way. These authors may indeed reconcile themselves to the littleness of accomplishment on the part of their heroes; but it is accomplishment of some sort on which heroes and authors alike are determined. Meredith and George Eliot had both a philosophy of life. They were both strongly imbued with perfectionist and utilitarian ideals. They staked their all on the progress and improvement of humanity. A better world was the cry they had taken up from the lips of Rousseau and Voltaire, Bentham and Mill. The fact is deeply hidden under romance and sentiment of the later day; but George Eliot and Meredith are still in the practical and materialist tradition, of, say, Benjamin Franklin. It is another tradition, as we have seen, to which James owes allegiance; an idealist tradition deriving ultimately from romantic Germany and reaching its finest expression in Wordsworth, Emerson and Hawthorne. Writing in the time of Gladstone and Bernard Shaw, James seems hardly to have given a thought to the political destinies of men or to the practical consequences and bearings of personal conduct. It is not in the relative terms of cause and effect that he considers human action. He is content, like some visionary Platonist, to refer each item of conduct to an absolute standard of the good and the beautiful. This is one reason why he is so strange a figure in our world all bent on getting results. We have, mostly, no such absolute standards. We know nothing of any Ideas in the mind of God.

In the stories of other writers, men and women are shown us obsessed with desires and ambitions and opposed by material difficulties. And our interest is absorbed in the process by which they overcome their difficulties and realize their desires. The characters of James too have ambitions and desires. But that is not the thing that strikes us most about them. What strikes us most about them is their capacity for renunciation— for giving up any particular gratification in favor of some fine ideal of conduct with which it proves incompatible. Common men and women have a more desperate grip on material values. There are things they insist on having. It may be money, or professional success, or social position, or some person indispensable to their happiness. And there is for them no immaterial substitute for these substantial goods. There is nothing in thought or feeling that can reconcile the lover to the loss of his mistress, nothing he will prefer to the woman he has set his heart upon. But the characters of James are not common men

and women; and for the finest of them there is always
something of more account than the substance of their
experience,—namely, its quality. They may, like other
mortals, long for the realization of some particular desire;
but they long still more fervently for the supreme comfort of being right with themselves. We know what a
capacity for happiness was Isabel Archer's; but we know
that happiness was far from being the thing she most
sought, and we know with what deliberation she chose to
embrace her fate, when she was once made aware of
"what most people know and suffer." We are gratified
and appalled by the meekness with which these people
accept their dole of misery and deprivation,—this Mitchy
and Nanda, this Christopher Newman and Fleda Vetch.
It seems that we must not use words of unhappy connotation to describe such exalted fervency of renunciation.
It is only because we ourselves require the objective
realization of our desires that we so misrepresent them.
They seem in point of fact to take some higher ground
inaccessible to our feet. They seem to say: Lo, we have
in not having. We were denied the shadow, but we have
always possessed the real substance. One fantastic creature even ventures to contend that, in the realm of art,
realization—concrete achievement—is inimical to the
true life of the soul. Gabriel Nash is actually afraid
Nick Dormer will prove a successful painter and so spoil
the beauty of his testimony to the artistic faith. He
prefers to "work in life" himself. Nick is so practical:
he wishes Gabriel "had more to show" for his "little
system." "Oh," says Gabriel, "having something to
show's such a poor business. It's a kind of confession
of failure." [2] One does not need to measure one's acts
by their consequences. "One is one's self a fine

[2] "The Tragic Muse," Vol. VII, p. 178.

consequence." [3] This is the very inner citadel of intransigent idealism. On this system we may interpret the story of Fleda Vetch as the triumph of Fleda. Let her cover her face in sorrow as she will. Her vulgar rival may have her lover, and the flames may have devoured the Spoils. But somehow we are given to understand that, of all the people in her world, she remains the wealthiest. She remains in substantial possession of beauty and of love.

What counts in the world of James is not the facts themselves,—what one does or what happens to one, but the interpretation put upon the facts. James has a great fondness, especially in his tales, for subjects very slight and off the common track of observation. There is little in the circumstances themselves to attract attention, and the people are, on the surface, entirely wanting in romantic interest. The challenge is all the greater to an author who prides himself on seeing below the surface of human nature, who is like a naturalist delighted to bring home flowers of rare and neglected beauty from spots unnoted by vulgar eyes. Such a flower was the homely American kinswoman of Lady Beldonald, who was intended by that handsome woman to be her foil, her dull and unremarked companion, and who was declared by the portrait-painter to be as distinguished and "beautiful" as a Holbein. It is himself that James describes in the words of the painter. "It's not my fault," he says, "if I am so put together as often to find more life in situations obscure and subject to interpretation than in the gross rattle of the foreground." This note is forever recurring both in the stories themselves and in the author's comment on them. We hear it in Miriam Rooth's naïve explanation to the great French

[3] "The Tragic Muse," Vol. VII, p. 33.

actress that "there were two kinds of scenes and speeches: those which acted themselves, of which the treatment was plain, the only way, so that you had just to take it; and those open to interpretation, with which you had to fight every step, rendering, arranging, doing the thing according to your idea."[4]   The note is sounded more delicately and modestly in the case of Mrs. Blessing-bourne and her romantic and at the same time Platonic feeling for Colonel Voyt.   That gentleman, who is in full enjoyment of the love of another woman, is inclined to regard such merely Platonic love as but thin material for romance.   But in his discussion of the matter with his own mistress, he agrees that the pathetic lady's very *consciousness* "*was*, in the last analysis, a kind of shy romance.   Not a romance like their own, a thing to make the fortune of any author up to the mark . . . but a small scared starved subjective satisfaction that would do her no harm and nobody else any good."[5]   We may be sure it was not the creator of Fleda Vetch and Milly Theale who is applying to Mrs. Blessingbourne's experi-ence this supercilious description.   As he says himself in the preface, "The thing is, all beautifully, a matter of interpretation and of the particular conditions; without a view of which latter some of the most prodigious adven-tures, as one has often had occasion to say, may vulgarly show for nothing."[6]

The same point is made still more significantly in refer-ence to the "adventures" of Isabel Archer, which he seems to think are but mild ones by the ordinary romantic

---

[4] "The Tragic Muse," Vol. VII, p. 194.

[5] From "The Story in It," Vol. XVIII, pp. 434-435.

[6] Id., p. xxiii.   The reader will pardon my quoting a second time a sentence so illuminating; the first time was in the chapter on "Idea."

measure. "Without her sense of them, her sense *for* them, as one may say, they are next to nothing at all; but isn't the beauty and the difficulty just in showing their mystic conversion by that sense, conversion into the stuff of drama or, even more delightful word still, of 'story'?" He vouchsafes two "very good instances of this effect of conversion." One of them is

. . . in the long statement, just beyond the middle of the book, of my young woman's extraordinary meditative vigil on the occasion that was to become for her such a landmark. Reduced to its essence, it is but the vigil of searching criticism; but it throws the action further forward than twenty "incidents" might have done. It was designed to have all the vivacity of incident and all the economy of picture. She sits up, by her dying fire, far into the night, under the spell of recognitions on which she finds the last sharpness suddenly wait. It is a representation simply of her motionlessly *seeing,* and an attempt withal to make the mere still lucidity of her act as "interesting" as the surprise of a caravan or the identification of a pirate. It represents, for that matter, one of the identifications dear to the novelist, and even indispensable to him; but it all goes on without her being approached by another person and without her leaving her chair. It is obviously the best thing in the book, but it is only a supreme illustration of the general plan.[7]

If Mr. James ever did trace out for us the Figure in the Carpet, it was in this passage, in which, concluding his review of the first book which really shows up the figure with any distinctness, he lets us know what is "obviously" the best thing in the book, and offers it to us as "only a supreme illustration of the general plan." We are reminded of the terms in which Hugh Vereker adumbrates for his young friend the "exquisite scheme,"

[7] Vol. III, pp. xx-xxi.

the "primal plan," not merely of his latest work, but of the whole series of his novels. We are further reminded of Hugh Vereker's attitude towards his public by Mr. James's apologetic and somewhat exasperated remark— it is in connection with his other instance of "the rare chemistry" of the character's sense for her adventures— "It is dreadful to have too much, for any artistic demonstration, to dot one's i's and insist on one's intentions, and I am not eager to do it now."

But however reluctant, he felt obliged on this one occasion to insist on his intentions. "The question here was that of producing the maximum of intensity with the minimum of strain. The interest was to be raised to its pitch and yet the elements to be kept in their key; so that, should the whole thing duly impress, I might show what an 'exciting' inward life may do for the person leading it even while it remains perfectly normal."[8]

"The Portrait of a Lady" was the first book in which James plainly showed his "little trick," which he went on showing more and more plainly from that time out. His little trick was simply not to tell the "story" at all as the story is told by the Scotts and the Maupassants, but to give us instead the subjective accompaniment of the story. His "exquisite scheme" was to confine himself as nearly as possible to the "inward life" of his characters, and yet to make it as "exciting" for his readers as it was for the author, as exciting—were that possible—as it was for the characters themselves.

Such an interpretation of his "scheme" would conform very well, at any rate, to Hugh Vereker's comprehensive description of his own: "It's the finest fullest intention of the lot, and the application of it has been, I think, a tri-

[8] Vol. III, p. xx.

umph of patience, of ingenuity. . . . It stretches, this little trick of mine, from book to book, and everything else, comparatively, plays over the surface of it. The order, the form, the texture of my books will perhaps some day constitute for the initiated a complete representation of it." I don't know how the scheme I have indicated would be represented in the *order* of the books of James. But it might serve as an explanation of their form and texture, and of all the peculiarities of his method as we have made them out. Naturally a book devoted to the inward life of a group of people would be nothing without its "idea." But the strict limitation of the action to the consciousness of these people would insure against undue abstractness in the idea, would transform idea into "picture." The succession of incidents in an ordinary story would in such a narrative be represented by the process of "revelation" of the picture. Suspense would have reference not to what might happen but to the subjective reverberation of what happens. In a record of inward life it is obvious how important must be the choice and maintenance of a point of view. It is almost absolutely essential that the center of interest should be a person of penetrating intelligence. It is plain how this subjective bias would affect the nature of the dialogue, making it less picturesque, more fine-drawn and close-knit, being the record of mental exploration carried on by several persons in concert. This is true of the dialogue even in those more dramatic situations involving tense oppositions of will, and gives its peculiar character to the "drama" of James. The exclusive interest in mental exploration explains to a large extent the wholesale "eliminations," which in turn relate themselves to the "neutral tone" of James's writing. And the almost complete abstraction from the world of common accident and circumstance, the confinement of attention to the realm of spiritual reactions, gives to the work of James its insubstantial, its romantic, even fantastic, character, which makes it the scorn of the "general," the despair of the conscientious, and the supreme entertainment of those who like it.

Above all does the exclusive concern with the inward life of his people explain the dominance of ethical considerations and at the same time perhaps the peculiar character of those involved. For the characters of James the faculty of supreme importance is the intelligence, or insight, the faculty of perceiving "values" beyond those utilities upon which everyone agrees. Of such immaterial values there are two general groups, both of great importance and of unfailing concern to the people of James. The first group includes social and esthetic values, which I class together because of their close association in the characters' minds, and because of their being on a common level as contrasted with the other group of values,—the spiritual.

Minor classifications we must here ignore. We must ignore those contrasts in social ideals which play so large a part in the earlier stories of James, but which in the long run prove to be of secondary importance. Social ideals may appear on the surface to be relative; but at bottom they show themselves, for this conservative philosopher, as absolute as any Platonic Ideas. Tact and discernment, fairness and modesty, the preference of the fine to the vulgar, the instinct for the nice and the proper, are after all traits in which practically all his favored characters agree, whether they be of Albany or London, Paris or "Woollett," "Flickerbridge" or Rome. There is one notable instance in which the contrast is drawn between a sense for social and a sense for esthetic values. The drama of "The Tragic Muse" arises from the inability of Julia Dallow, socially so complete, to comprehend the esthetic life of Nick Dormer; Nick Dormer is himself never quite able to make up his mind whether so thoroughly artistic a spirit as that of Gabriel Nash is capable of the refinements of gentility; and Peter Sherringham is in a similar perplexity as regards the character of Miriam Rooth. Generally however the social and the esthetic senses are inseparable for the people of James. Mona Brigstock and her mother are as incapable of the social as of the esthetic shibboleths of Fleda Vetch and Mrs. Gereth. Isabel Archer receives in one undivided flood her impressions of the esthetic and the social qualities of Madame Merle and of Gilbert Osmond. The world of refinements typified to Hyacinth Robinson by the Princess Casamassima is a world in which he cannot distinguish the esthetic from the social felicities. So that, on the whole, we should be justified in employing the hyphenated term of social-esthetic to distinguish that type of intelligence which is shared by practically all the important characters of James. Or we might serve our purpose with the simpler, and equally comprehensive, term, good taste.

There is at least one important character who is lacking in good taste so understood. I mean Daisy Miller, whose peculiarity lies in her possession of a rare spiritual beauty quite unaccompanied by social tact and artistic discernment. But Mr. James has expressed doubts himself as to the reality of this charming poetic creation; and the one romantic exception will but make more notable the almost universal prevalence of good taste as a qualification for admittance into the gallery of Henry James. This is the first qualification,—that is, the one first to be considered: one must successfully stand this test before being advanced to the higher one reserved for heroes and heroines. It is good taste which unites in one great shining company the otherwise so various Gilbert Osmond and Isabel Archer, Mrs. Brookenham and Nanda, Kate Croy and Milly Theale, Chad Newsome and Lambert Strether.

The *ideal* of James is clearly a combination, or rather a *fusion,* of good taste with spiritual discernment, and perhaps the most complete, if not the most dramatic, instance of this fusion is the last named, Lambert Strether. For him there seems to be no such distinction between esthetic and ethical as perplexes most of us mortals. Madame de Vionnet has a claim upon Chad, he thinks, because she has worked upon him so fine a transformation; and this character of Chad's, of her creation, is all described in terms of esthetic and social connotation. No doubt the idea of an *obligation* is a moral idea at bottom; but this obligation is in direct opposition to the legal and religious code, and never were greater pains taken to translate moral concept into the language of simple good taste. In the mind of Lambert Strether there seems to be no clear dividing line between the categories of beauty and goodness.

Somewhat the same condition prevails in the psychology of "The Awkward Age"; and the tendency is always in this direction in the stories of James. But in many cases the distinction is much sharper between good taste and the moral sense. And whenever the distinction appears, the moral sense is clearly preferred as the higher and rarer, and as something added to the other or built upon it. Fleda Vetch is preferred to Mrs. Gereth as being capable of spiritual discernment in addition to possessing the mere good taste of which the latter is such a miracle. We must do Mrs. Gereth the justice to acknowledge that her devotion to the Spoils was an ideal and unselfish devotion, altogether different from the "crude love of possession," and that it gives a hint of spiritual quality. But in any other and more human connection, she was an unscrupulous because an unseeing woman. "She had no imagination about anybody's life save on the side she bumped against. Fleda was quite aware that she would have otherwise been a rare creature, but a rare creature was originally just what she had struck her as being. Mrs. Gereth had really no perception of anybody's nature—had only one question about persons: were they clever or stupid? To be clever meant to know the 'marks.' Fleda knew them by direct inspiration, and a warm recognition of this had been her friend's tribute to her character. The girl now had hours of sombre hope she might never see anything 'good' again: that kind of experience was clearly so broken a reed, so fallible a source of peace." [9] Owen had no more sense for the "marks" than Mona or Mrs. Brigstock.; but he was capable of rising to Fleda's spiritual bait. And so we are given the impression of him as really more clever than his mother, being in a class with Fleda. And Mrs. Gereth comes to recognize Fleda and Owen as "of quite another race and another flesh." [10]

So it is that Milly Theale is preferred to the superb and socially incomparable Kate Croy; that Mitchy and Nanda are preferred to the infinitely clever and subtle mother of Nanda; that Isabel Archer is preferred to the charming and accomplished Madame Merle and to Osmond, who had both so long a start of her in social and esthetic

[9] Vol. X, p. 138.
[10] Id., p. 222.

cultivation. In each case the one preferred has, in addition to the common good taste, the wit to distinguish moral beauty.

It is all, as we have seen, a matter of insight. The less favored characters, the false and the shady people, are morally color-blind. It is always the same story throughout the whole series of novels. It is so in "Roderick Hudson" at the beginning and in "The Golden Bowl" at the end. In "The Golden Bowl," it is a question of whether the Prince Amerigo has enough discernment to perceive the superiority of his wife to his accomplished mistress. The "style" of Charlotte has indeed been "great" in the closing scenes of the drama, but great in a way far below the spiritual fineness of Maggie. Maggie is "great" enough to perceive the greatness of Charlotte. "Isn't she too splendid?" she asks her husband. "That's our help, you see." . . . "See?" says Amerigo, triumphantly meeting his final test, "I see nothing but *you*." Roderick Hudson is an artist of genius, with endowments infinitely superior to those of his friend and benefactor in every respect except this of spiritual discernment. It is only at the end of his life that he has a glimpse of what he has missed. It is in his last conversation with Rowland, in which the latter has finally told him of his own love for Mary. Roderick comes to see how "hideous" is the appearance he has made. "Do you really care," Rowland is prompted to ask, "for what you may have appeared?" "Certainly. I've been damnably stupid. Isn't an artist supposed to be a man of fine perceptions? I haven't, as it turns out, had *one*."[11]

The stories of James are a continuous record of such

[11] Vol. I, p. 512.

"fine perceptions" had or missed. The stuff is as airy as gossamer: not at all

"Things done, that took the eye and had the price."

Hence the notorious difficulty and inaccessibility of James. And hence the romantic exhilaration of his work for so many denizens of a world in which the realization of ideals is so rare and hard of accomplishment. May this be the secret of his great following among women? His greatest appeal is perhaps to those whose lives have yielded the minimum of realization, to those who have the least control over the gross materials of life.

# PART TWO:

## THE METHOD OF HENRY JAMES

# I

## OBSCURE BEGINNINGS

Young writers who have had little success with their first ventures may take comfort in the contemplation of the early work of Henry James. He is one of those writers of great distinction who have had a long road to success. It is not that he had difficulty in placing his early experiments in fiction. Some acquaintance with editors gave him access very early to American magazines of the best sort. Not merely did the "Nation" and the "North American Review" make a regular practice of printing his compact and competent critical reviews. No less an organ than the "Atlantic Monthly" printed over his signature story after story of much more doubtful merit. Is it possible that the conductors of the great "Atlantic" applied in the seventies less exacting tests to candidates for publicity, or that we have been overestimating the general quality of the literature produced in those palmy days? Or did they perhaps, with miraculous insight, discover in these green shoots the promise of our story-teller's rich maturity, and deliberately offer him their pages for that public exhibition which is so needful a step in literary apprenticeship? There was doubtless promise in these early tales; there was certainly very mediocre performance. And most remarkable is the contrast between these commonplace stories and the mature work of an author who—whatever else may be said of him—can hardly be denied the title of distinction. For the length of nearly two decades, at least, his path is strewn with the remains of feeble and abortive experiment.

If in this chapter I dwell more than elsewhere in my study upon the tales, it is because they were his very earliest work. Mr. James was later well aware of the quality of this early work; and he took some pains to cover his tracks. In the years 1907 to 1909 appeared the "New York" edition of his novels and tales, in which he established the canon of his works of fiction. Most of his earlier tales, as well as one full-fledged novel, were designedly shut out from this company of his cherished offspring. Half of the earlier tales had never even appeared in book form; and most of the rest languish still in the oblivion of rare and little-sought volumes. It is only the curious historian, bent on tracing the path of genius, who does him the doubtful service of bringing to light these repudiated children of his brain. And the present historian will make as brief as possible the earliest chapter of this chronicle, that dealing with the twenty-five tales and the one novel published before the year 1875. Not all the tales, nor by any means all the novels, produced since 1875 were included in the New York edition. But after that date we may say the author had struck some kind of a gait, and what he produced in this middle period can never be dismissed without more careful scrutiny. The very crudeness of the early stories, however, gives them some title to consideration in any analytic study. What was the matter with these stories? In what respects do they fall short of the author's notion of a good story?

A curious circumstance meets us at the start. If we divide his tales into two groups of "realistic" and "romantic," we instantly observe that it was in the romantic tales that James first struck his vein. I suppose one would naturally apply the term realistic to the best-known work of Henry James. At any rate he will hardly be thought of as a romantic story-teller in the ordinary sense. And yet the first of all his tales to merit admission to the canon were the distinctly romantic stories, "A Passionate Pilgrim" and "The Madonna of the Future." The first tale of a soberer cast thus to be honored is "Madame de Mauves," which appeared just before "Roderick Hudson." One significant fact here stares us in the face. The first stories good enough for the collective edition were all laid in Europe. A glance at the New York edition will furnish the correlative fact that, of all the novels and tales included in its twenty-four volumes, not half a dozen are laid in the native land of Henry James.[1] And one further observation will complete our enlightenment. In every one of the realistic tales preceding "Madame de Mauves," the story is laid in the United States; and this is true of four out of five of all the novels up to 1886 excluded from the canon. If it was in romance that the young author first found himself, it was because in romance he first found himself in the old world.

At first blush one might be inclined to indict Mr. James for want of patriotism, thus to repudiate his distinctively American stories. Can it be that—in contrast to one of his characters—he had never felt "certain natural, filial longings for this dear American mother of us all"?[2] Such an impression will be at once dispelled by the reading of Mr. James's reminiscences of his youth, in which he recalls with such fondness his life in New York and Newport, Cambridge and Boston, during the intervals of the family's foreign sojourn. His passion for "Eu-

---

[1] This does not include stories, like "Roderick Hudson," in which the scene is American for a very small part of the whole narrative.

[2] From "A Light Man," in "The Galaxy," July, 1869.

rope" seems always to have left room in his heart for a strong, if not uncritical love of his native land. And second thought will lead us to exclaim: What great sacrifices he did make on the altar of patriotism! Unless, after all, we had better say, on the altar of realism! For I fancy the poor man ridden in the early years with a notion that telling the truth in fiction means telling the truth about your own people "located" (as Americans say) on your own familiar heath. How could he disregard the examples of Balzac and George Eliot and Turgenieff? And so he kept up for years the bootless effort to make stories of Americans in New York and Boston, in Newport and Sharon Springs. As late as 1885 he was still cultivating the forlorn hope with "The Bostonians." That was his last attack in force.[3] And a touching tribute it was to his New England conscience.

The main reason for James's failure to make anything of "the American scene" is obvious enough to anyone familiar with his most characteristic work. If his central figures are likely to be women of a certain beautiful clear simplicity of soul, his backgrounds, as we have seen, are even more likely to consist in a social order full of sophistications and complexities, giving the effect of a darker and more troubled coloring. If his ethics are transcendental New England, his manners are social Europe. But if he can sometimes find the right ethics in the old world, he can never find the manners anywhere else. If his central figure is most often American, his background must be invariably European. And the background is in the stories of Henry James as dominant in the final effect as the harmonic background in a song

---

[3] Unless we take into account "The Ivory Tower," left unfinished at his death, and published posthumously, the scene of which is laid in Newport.

of Debussy. The melody itself is transformed by the magic of harmonization. The developed art of James is greatly an affair of relationships and adjustments, of carefully disposed lights and qualified shadows, of nice gradations and subtle intimations. Mr. James often tells us how fond he is of "thickened motive and accumulated character." He likes to deal with situations in which action and motive are much affected by the pressure of convention, by traditions and points of view implying a long-established, deep-rooted, widely ramifying society. He finds more for explication and representation in the refinements and indirections of a somewhat decadent order than in the brusque downrightness of social pioneers. All this implies a longer cultivation of the arts of leisure, a longer familiarity with the fruits of social privilege, than could be found in his Boston, where culture was so largely literary and foreign in its reference, in his Albany and New York, where—as he tells us in "A Small Boy"—a young man had no alternative to the counting-house but a short life of cheap dissipation.

This European background was prized both as physical setting and as social *milieu*. For many readers the interest of these stories is to a very large extent the interest of Paris and London, of Venice and Rome. Of course, in the simplest material way, the parks and monuments, the drawing-rooms and country houses of Europe contribute an element of the splendid and sumptuous, as the titles of Lord and Princess lend their glitter to the social effect. When Nick Dormer and Julia Dallow take their *bocks* in the open air of Paris, we note that "beyond the Boulevard des Capucines [the city] flared through the warm evening like a vast bazaar, and opposite the Café Durand the Madeleine rose theatrical, a high artful décor before the footlights of the Rue Royale." When

Milly Theale comes abroad to make what she can of the few brief moments of her life, she must needs commandeer a Venetian palace for the scene of her international drama.  The dark domestic struggle of Maggie Verver is spaciously enacted in the gardens and along the terraces at Fawns; and her terrible quiet encounter with Charlotte takes place in the midst of the grand drawing-room "under the old lustres of Venice and the eyes of several great portraits more or less contemporary with these."  When the other members of the party arrive "at the open door at the end of the room" to witness the "prodigious kiss" with which the interview is sealed, we cannot fail to realize the scene as one mounted handsomely upon a stage of regal distances. One is struck on review with the large number of instances in which we have to do with precious works of art like Mr. Verver's collections and the "old things" of Poynton, as well as the more modest furniture of Gilbert Osmond and Chad Newsome, of Edward Rosier and even Maria Gostrey.  Even the socialist Hyacinth Robinson was gradually reconciled to an order of things which had made possible so great an accumulation of beauty.  And the prime element in the beauty of things European is that "tone of time" which was so rarely felt by James in connection with anything American.[4]

But however seductive the European settings in a physical way, it is the social *milieu* that is most indispensable to the logic of the story.  It was quite as much in the social order itself that Hyacinth Robinson felt the beautifying effect of the tone of time.  It was there above all that he and his creator found that high orderliness and *convenience* enjoyed at least by the privileged

[4] It is, to be sure, of old New York society that the phrase is used in the tale of "Crapy Cornelia," in "The Finer Grain."

few. The social order in Europe was actually an *order*. It had long since taken on its recognizable forms. It was therefore so much *found* for the painter of life in the way of arrangement, pattern, composition. And for the painter of social life, it was pre-eminently a social order. The characters of Henry James are never naked souls meeting in some uncharted realm of romance. They are social beings locally conditioned and very much clothed. And it is not in khaki and broad-brimmed hats and the riding-boots of the "greaser" that they are clothed. It is in the discreet and conventional, if often shining, garb of the tea table and the dining room. The kind of relationships in which they are involved are only such as can be maintained in connection with the normal contacts of organized and, to use a very up-to-date term, of standardized society. Everybody has been delighted with certain refreshing scenes in George Meredith,— the scene in which one heroine is discovered as a "haggard Venus" perched on some inaccessible crag of the Alps, the scene in which an athletic hero and heroine plight their unconventional troth beneath the waters of the Atlantic. Such things are impossible to the less vivid creatures of our American novelist. These persons never dream of any excursion beyond the strict bounds of social etiquette. The very air they breathe—from the moment they get to Europe—is the purged and walled-in air of the *bienséances*. They are creatures of a system in which everything is done decently and in order. They would be quite lost without the smooth-running social machine which carries them so securely through their day of morning calls and afternoon teas.

It was long before James could bring himself to make an acknowledgment so wanting in filial piety. He hated no doubt to confess himself beaten on his own ground.

And then he had not yet really made out his formula. But all the while the truth was there before his troubled eyes: the settings that he needed were not to be found at home. Our sun is too fierce and bright, our shadows too wanting in richness and mystery, for the purposes of his fine brush. Our society was too crude and unformed, our tongue untutored. There was here no drift of centuries. There was no elegant and cultivated leisure. It might all be symbolized by the institution of five o'clock tea. In one of his latest tales, James represents a poor English tradesman as having his first personal introduction to this custom "known to him only by the contemporary novel of manners and the catchy advertisements of table linen."[5] What should our author do without the aid of this "luxurious rite," as essential to the unfolding of his story as are the morning visits and country balls for Jane Austen? Well, in the sixties and seventies there seems to have been, in Albany and Boston and Northampton, a singular scantiness in the provision of five o'clock tea.

And so the young author, obstinately insisting on patriotic realism, had resort to most heroic means for supplying the want. He will strike through to what lies below convention, and will lay bare the depths of human souls. Perhaps the most constant cause of his failure in these earlier tales is the overweening audacity of this heroism. He is writing clearly in the spirit of George Eliot. He seems to say to himself: go to! let us give an account of human nature, its strength and weakness. Let us take the plainest of types, those that fall most naturally under our observation. That will be a modest under-

---

[5] From "The Bench of Desolation," in "The Finer Grain," p. 274.

taking, he seems to think; but he will shirk none of his responsibilities for the character of his people. The first of his tales, dating from 1865, is "The Story of a Year."[6] It is devoted to the soul of a New England country girl engaged to a soldier at the front. She is a well-meaning creature, but unequal to the strain put on her loyalty by the long absence of her betrothed. She carries on a harmless flirtation with a prepossessing young man from a neighboring town; and to him she falls in the end, with the benison of her soldier-lover brought back from the war mortally wounded. Her lover judges the girl more kindly than does his mother,—a hard, devoted farmer's wife who knows the difference between a steadfast soul and a flirt. . . . It is, you may say, a simple, unambitious theme. . . . Too simple to be unambitious! Such homespun can be given distinction only by the cut. The author has no alternative. He must interest us in the soul of his girl; he must display with convincing truth her processes of thought. The latter obligation he takes most seriously, paying us with paragraphs of grave analysis in the tone of George Eliot. And yet somehow he fails to interest us very deeply in the soul of this most ordinary girl. She is no Maggie Tulliver, no Hetty Sorrel. This is realism of a rigor, as if the author had bound himself by some self-denying ordinance.

In "Master Eustace"[7] the author allows himself more rope, and gives us more for our money. For he provides here the more sensational theme of parentage unknown and revealed at the crisis of the action; and it is a tale of secret sin and loud-voiced passion. In all this one would hardly recognize the James of later years. But the main emphasis is laid on the development of an

[6] In "The Atlantic," March, 1865.

[7] "The Galaxy," October, 1871.

ugly character in a spoiled child. It is that character-development to which the author feels his deepest obligation. And this, in its unmodified banality, is equally out of the familiar range of the master's art.

It is impossible to say why a given character lives. It is often easier to make out why such another fails to come to life,—why such a story remains a shapeless heap of matter without animation. And in these early tales of James we are at once struck, for one thing, with his reckless prodigality of matter. His early tales are generally novels in little, "tabloid" novels. James never indeed conceived the short story in the same rigorous fashion as Kipling or Maupassant or their disciples. And yet, in his later work, the tale—or the *nouvelle,* as he likes to call his favorite length of short story—is distinguished from the novel by the amount and magnitude of what it undertakes. The novel grapples with the central facts of the lives of several persons: it involves a full and rounded development of their characters, a considerable survey of their careers, and a leisurely indication of the accessories in the way of secondary characters and *milieu.* Whether or not covering a long course of years, it takes into account a large number of scenes, each one of which is to be treated at length. The tale is likely to concern itself with less central, less monumental situations,—rather with detachable bits and phases of a life. Few of the characters are to be developed, and these generally only on one or two sides. The action is likely to be confined to a short period, and within this period to a carefully limited number of occasions. James was very proud of his expertness in turning round —as he describes the performance—in so small a space as he allows himself. This he accomplishes by virtue of the most strict economy, by all sorts of tricks of fore-shortening and suggestion.

In the early tales, however, he shows no sign of such expertness. Indeed he seems unaware of the need of it. He conceives a plot big enough for a novel, and disposes of it within the compass of a very short story. He sets out bravely to tell us all about a set of persons; and it must puzzle him to find how soon it is done. Economy is the last thing that seems necessary, especially in the matter of characterization. Every tale begins with a long account of the characters; or if, by happier inspiration, we are treated first to a bit of incident or dialogue, we are soon halted for some lengthy explanation about the participants. Thus in "Poor Richard,"[8] the author permits himself a page or two of conversation near the beginning, only to pull himself up shortly with the following remark: "To appreciate the importance of this conversation, the reader must know that Miss Gertrude Whittaker was a young woman of four-and-twenty, whose father, recently deceased, had left her alone in the world, with a great fortune, accumulated by various enterprises in that part of the State. He had appointed a distant and elderly kinswoman, by name Miss Pendexter [who never again puts her nose into the story], as his daughter's household companion; and an old friend of his own, known to combine shrewdness with integrity [a person equally alien to the story], as her financial adviser. Motherless, country-bred and homely featured, Gertrude on arriving at maturity had neither the tastes nor the manners of a fine lady. Of robust and active make, with a warm heart, a cool head, and a very pretty talent for affairs, she was, in virtue both of her wealth and her tact, one of the chief figures of the neighbor-

[8] In "The Atlantic," June-August, 1867.

hood." And a long paragraph is devoted to the further account of this lady's character and situation; then several columns to the character and history of the two men who are to be rivals for her affections. We should now be thoroughly documented, thoroughly acquainted with these persons. Instead of that we are just tired. We are oppressed with the mere weight of undigested information. We have been given too much and too little. We have listened to so many general statements unilluminated by reference to any particular occasion that we have quite lost the sense of reading a story or making the acquaintance of interesting people. In the later stories, whether long or short, we make acquaintance by more gradual and more human degrees. We are asked merely to observe people in action; we are not expected to swallow the complete formula of their character. We are left to draw our inferences from the gesture, physical or mental, with which they greet the words and acts of their companions. And so we have the impression of story or drama, and feel ourselves agreeably entertained. And whatever we do learn about these people is well learned, being a part not of our information but of our very *feeling* about them.

A similar pitfall yawns for the young experimenter in the number of scenes treated. Again he is generous in his offering. And again the ungrateful reader complains of there being at once too much and too little. There are far too many scenes, and no one of them is adequately developed. They are not so much actual scenes as notes for scenes, abstracts,—making up together a good preliminary sketch or scenario of play or novel.

Even at this early period James was groping his way towards the sort of themes which occupied him later. But he had not hit upon the technique suited to their development. "My Friend Bingham,"[9] for example, is the story of a man who has accidentally shot the only child of a poor widowed woman. He is filled with remorseful compassion, and she on her side is large minded enough to feel compassion rather than resentment towards him. And out of their mutual pity grow esteem and love. So freakish are the ways of feeling. It is a pretty psychological problem, and in conception not unworthy of its distinguished author. But the story is told in so bald and summary a fashion that he would be the first to say it is practically not told at all. It consists of nine distinct scenes, exclusive of the long introductory account of "my friend Bingham" and of "my" relations with him; and the whole history is disposed of in thirteen pages of the "Atlantic"! The all-important matter in this story is naturally the attitude of Bingham towards Mrs. Hicks and her attitude towards him; and in the later years these attitudes would have been indicated with great fineness and at some length in the course of their several meetings. In this tale, but three of the nine scenes are devoted to these meetings, and they are disposed of with amazing brevity. The final scene records an agreement to marry on the part of these two persons in the presence of the narrator. But most summary is the account of how they looked, what they thought and what they said on this occasion. The author seems indeed to have had an uneasy sense that something is wanting to the success of his story, and he tries to cut the Gordian knot with one slashing stroke. "What honest George Bingham said, what I said, is of little account. The proper conclusion of my story lies in the highly dramatic fact that out of the depths of her bereavement—out of her loneliness and her pity—this richly gifted

[9] "The Atlantic," March, 1867.

woman had emerged, responsive to the passion of him who had wronged her all but as deeply as he loved her."

Which is as much as to say: here is my story in one sentence—what is the use of stringing it out? As if the abstract idea of a story were the story itself, in all its concrete embodiment, all its wealth of convincing circumstance. In later years the author came to realize only too well, some feel, what is involved in the art of *representation*. He is able to judge even so masterly a performance as "The Tragic Muse," and say of certain parts of that story: "The whole of [this], as the book gives it, is too rapid and sudden . . . : processes, periods, intervals, stages, degrees, connexions, may be easily enough and barely enough named, may be unconvincingly stated, in fiction, to the deep discredit of the writer, but it remains the very deuce to *represent* them . . . ; and this even though the novelist who doesn't represent, and represent 'all the time,' is lost."[10] In "My Friend Bingham" and the other early tales, he seldom dreams of representing his periods and stages. He feels it sufficient to tell us, of certain psychological processes: this is what happened; with no effort to indicate, to make palpable, the degrees by which it came about. The difference is not that between the novel and the short story. In extreme contrast to the method of these early tales is that of tales in the latest volumes, such, for example, as "The Bench of Desolation" in "The Finer Grain." In that story we assist at the gradual process by which a man and a woman, long estranged, come at last to a mutual understanding and to the same relationship as that reached by George Bingham and Mrs. Hicks. But there we follow in minute detail the largely wordless tug-of-war between the two parties, the final result of which is

[10] Vol. VII, p. xix.

that each one, while maintaining his own particular dignity and advantage, yet manages to yield to what proves their common interest. The author, in conducting his story to this conclusion, lets us lose no single drop of the feeling—at least of the man, from whose point of view the narrative is given—with which these manœuvres are accompanied.

Not all readers are equally fond of this manner of story-telling; and some will simply scorn this art as an art not worth mastering. They must at least grant that in such work the author does not fail for want of developing the latent possibilities of the scene on the side of psychology. They will not deny its distinctive quality. And that is more than can be predicated of the flavorless tales of the prentice period. One source of weakness in the early tales closely related to that we have been discussing is the want of attention to the point of view. In the first ten of these tales (with one exception), the author had no better inspiration than to offer us his own omniscient survey of the action. This means there is *no* point of view at all steadily maintained. In the later years of this period, he was making some feeble experiments towards a more effective method, often employing the device of an interested observer who tells the story in the first person. But in all these prentice years little is gained by this device, owing to the author's want of realization of what should or might come within the field of observation of his chosen story-teller. Sometimes, as in "My Friend Bingham," he fails to choose the person best fitted to follow the action, or he fails to select and develop those scenes in which his observation might serve best to illuminate it. Sometimes, as in "Master Eustace," he simply transfers to the person who tells the story his own editorial omniscience, thus by one stroke sacrificing the technical advantages of his method. In one tale, "A Light Man," he tried the interesting experiment of having a person of mean and frivolous character betray himself in the confidence of his diary. So desperate a venture he never made a second time, so far as I can remember, even at the height of his cunning.

In none of the earlier tales, again, is the limited point of view made use of for developing the sort of suspense that makes the great charm of the later narratives as stories. Even where the narrative is given by an observer in the first person, he begins by telling you more than anyone ought to know at the start. The result is a complete absence of that mystery, that teasing bewilderment, with which he baits his readers in his later work.

And as a corollary to this, we observe the comparative commonplaceness of the characters themselves. As we have seen, the great aim of Henry James came to be the treatment of subjects off the beaten track of observation, subjects vitally dependent for effectiveness upon interpretation. The obvious, the ordinary in character and situation was what he must at all costs avoid. However crude the material, it must be given some particular turn, some special refinement; it must be viewed in some important but neglected aspect. In the light of his later work, one may indeed detect in the earliest some reaching out for this kind of subject. But never does the young author wholly succeed in avoiding the effect of the ordinary. His experience of life is too limited, his observation too little cultivated, his imagination too timid and unresourceful. His subjects are largely young people, their tentative and generic loves. Of the complexities of the social order, of the manifold shapes assumed by character in its adaptation to circumstance, of the ingenious shifts by which thwarted men and women endeavor to give their lives some special distinction, the youthful James has little knowledge. And by the same token he has little acquaintance with the artful tricks of speech by which clever people display and conceal their feelings, and with the help of which they grope their way to an understanding of where they are. He has not learned, for himself, that lightness of touch which invariably characterizes his later style. He has not learned to convey his meaning by allusive indirection. It goes without saying that his earliest style has no hint of that beautiful texture, that suffused glow and shimmer of figurative language, which makes so much of the charm of books like "The Princess Casamassima" and "The Wings of the Dove." He has a copious vocabulary, the young author; but of the suppleness, the grasp of the minor relationships of ideas, the faculties for intimation and qualification of the later James, scarcely a hint. The dialogue in particular impresses one as bald and plain to the point of boredom. All this I must ask the reader to take for granted, especially in reference to the realistic tales, of which thus far I have been speaking more particularly.

It is all equally true of his first little experiment in the longer form of story, "Watch and Ward," which appeared in the "Atlantic" in 1871, and was later accorded the dignity of a volume to itself. In this book we have to do with most ordinary people involved in a most ordinary plot. It is about a nice young man of means who, having adopted an orphan girl, proceeds to fall in love with his ward while she is yet very young. There can be little question that in the end she will become his wife; but a story is rigged up by the usual expedient of devising various obstacles to that desired consummation. These

obstacles take the form of several women and several
men. The women make a very weak trial of the constancy of our hero; the men, who are disposed of with
greater difficulty, serve as steps in the education of our
heroine to the point where she can choose her guardian
with a full understanding of his merits. There are four
or five major characters, and many others of minor importance. The incidents include a suicide, a voyage to
South America, another to Rome, and what practically
constitutes the abduction and forcible confinement of the
heroine; as well as several "scenes" of considerable excitement in which emphatic words are spoken. And it
is all disposed of in eleven short chapters. Something
important happens in each chapter. And yet the effect
is of matter spread out thin, since no scene is developed
according to its possibilities. The people are introduced
to us in extended passages of set description, and yet we
have no feeling of intimate acquaintance with any of
them. They include a corrupt and plausible Episcopal
minister of high fashion, whose more distinguished kin
we seem to have met in the pages of Thackeray and
Trollope; a flashy young man from St. Louis; a slovenly
and ignorant Peruvian beauty; and several colorless
though nominally attractive women of our own clime.
Among the incidental figures are several suggestive of
those tobacco-spitting Americans encountered by Martin
Chuzzlewit on his trip to Eden.

Both persons and places offered frequent occasion for
testifying to a realistic faith in which by some miracle
Dickens and Balzac might be reconciled. We read of a
certain Mr. Franks, that he "was a small meagre man,
with a whitish coloring, weak blue eyes and thin yellow
whiskers, suffering apparently from some nervous
malady. He nodded, he stumbled, he jerked his arms

and legs about with pitiful comicality. He had a large protuberant forehead, such a forehead as would have done honor to a Goethe or a Newton."[11] The personality of Mr. Franks, we may note in passing, has but the remotest bearing on the story, and he makes his appearance only in this one brief scene.

The dialogue is crude and bald without intending to be so. The following is the style of the accomplished clerical Lothario on being reproached by a lady with his double-dealing. He "remained silent a moment, shaking a scornful finger at her. 'For shame, Madam,' he cried. 'That's in shocking taste! You might have been generous; it seems to me I deserve it.' And with a summary bow he departed."[12] Imagine a character of Henry James shaking a scornful finger and crying "For shame, Madam"! Hardly more recognizable is the style when the young author introduces some original reflection of his own. "So she played Weber for more than an hour," runs the account in one moving passage; "and I doubt whether, among the singers who filled the theatre with their melody, the master found that evening a truer interpreter than the young girl playing in the lamplit parlor to the man she loved."[13] In 1871 prevailed, we remember, the undegenerate style of our grandmothers.

But this is like watching someone in the act of dressing. We have stayed our glance too long on a work which the author would doubtless have blotted out of existence had that been possible.

A considerable advance in expertness is to be observed in the romantic tales. This may be to some extent the result of their later date. It was charily and with seem-

[11] P. 178.    [12] P. 156.    [13] P. 144.

ing reluctance that James ventured upon this dubious ground, as if he felt it not to be *his* realm, and was yet unwilling to leave any possibility untried. And there were but two of this miscellaneous group of tales written before 1875 that he saw fit to revive in later years. The reasons are not generally far to seek.

He first tried his hand at the supernatural, and most amateurish is his handling of this weird element. Of "The Romance of Certain Old Clothes"[14] the inspiration is clearly Hawthorne. The occurrences are referred to eighteenth-century New England. But the strictly romantic element is confined to the last paragraph, where the red marks of the ghostly fingers are not more surprising than they are out of place artistically. The story was written for the sake of the conclusion, but the conclusion gives the impression of not belonging to the story. "DeGrey: A Romance,"[15] while it devotes itself more at length to the creation of effects of mystery and terror, shows yet an uncertainty on the author's part as to whether these thrills are to be his main concern, or whether it is not to be rather the psychological processes of the characters. As for the thrills themselves, they are created rather cheaply with a plot involving a family in which invariably the mistress or wife comes to a quick and terrible end. And the author makes use also of the familiar devices of melodramatic phrase and circumstance. There must needs be a Catholic priest with a mysterious past to reveal the fearful secrets of the family to the heroine in the midst of a thunderstorm. "The room grew dark with the gathering storm, and the distant thunder muttered." Feeling and expression are always in the superlative degree. The hero "cries out in an

14 "The Atlantic," February, 1868.
15 "The Atlantic," July, 1868.

ecstasy of belief and joy." The heroine "turns deadly pale." People rush madly, precipitately—and more than once. Piercing shrieks resound through the house. A face "gleams through the darkness like a mask of reproach, white with the phosphorescent dews of death."

Neither of these tales of the uncanny, nor for that matter the much better story of "The Ghostly Rental," dating from as late as 1876,[16] bears the faintest resemblance to those remarkable tales of the later time, "The Friends of the Friends," "The Real Right Thing," and "The Turn of the Screw." The last-named is almost unparalleled in its effects of supernatural terror secured without any resort to the devices of twilight fears and bugbear phrases. But true to the genius of Henry James, it is a moral terror as well as a thrill of the nerves.

And now we take a long step forward. We turn our backs on the American scene. And the romantic glamour of Europe must count for something in all the rest of the experiments. Some of them, however, owe their romantic character not so much to that circumstance as to the remarkable part played in the action by co-incidence or parallelism of incidents. The author was now trying his hand at curious plot-patterns. A young man carefully guarded by his widowed father and brought up in America to be a gentleman of rare quality; a girl similarly tended by her father in a walled garden of Smyrna. They are engaged to each other by their fathers without ever having met. Each rebels against this arbitrary disposition of hand and heart, and in the end they find each other quite to one another's taste. Such is a part of the plot of "Eugene Pickering," dating from 1874.[17] Equally remarkable for correspondences

---

[16] "Scribner's," September.
[17] "The Atlantic," October-November.

of incident are certain tales published within the next few years.

A special essay in romance is "Gabrielle de Bergerac,"[18] so far as I know the single case (apart from "The Romance of Certain Old Clothes") in which James goes back of 1800 for the date of his story. It is a deliberate study in historical romance, and not without its charm—though all the materials are unique in the work of James. It is a kind of *pastiche* of Scarron, Watteau, Rousseau, Walter Scott, with a spice of Hawthorne and other American writers. The influence of Hawthorne is particularly noticeable in "Benvolio,"[19] a story absolutely lacking in dialogue, in which most of the characters are known by function (Countess, Professor) instead of name, and in which the scene is not more localized than is implied by the presence of theatres and castles. This tale is a product of the same year as "Roderick Hudson."

Meantime James's experiments in assorted romance had culminated in a set of tales more interesting than any I have discussed, and heralding his arrival at the state of mastership. The tales of this group derive their interest from the spirit of place,—from the glamour of foreign scenes and crowding old-world associations. Of these he judged worthy of inclusion in his collected works "A Passionate Pilgrim" and "The Madonna of the Future."[20] The first presents through the vision of a half-crazed American the heady charm of the English country, of English houses, English colleges, English

[18] "The Atlantic," July-September, 1869.
[19] "The Galaxy," August, 1875.
[20] Both first published in "The Atlantic," the one in March-April, 1871, the other in March, 1873.

inns and English ghosts. It is written in the youthful glow of first discovery, and cannot fail to captivate any reader who is still capable of enthusiasm. It has a good, if somewhat fantastic, old-fashioned story. "The Madonna of the Future" has less story, but is an agreeable evocation of the atmosphere of Florence and the passion of the artist. Three less favored studies in European glamour are "The Sweetheart of Monsieur Briseux" (an episode in the lives of an American woman and a French painter), "The Last of the Valerii" and "Travelling Companions."[21]

It is sufficiently obvious why the author has repudiated the very early "Travelling Companions,"—the first of his fictions laid in Europe excepting the historical romance of "Gabrielle de Bergerac." It is the story of a young American couple who were drawn together by the sentiments they shared for Italy. The text is made up of alternating blocks of narrative proper and effusions on art and history. This work of fiction, which appeared in the "Atlantic" in the year 1870, might have served for a complete travelers' guide to Milan, Venice and Rome. The readers were given full directions as to what they should see and feel in Milan cathedral, upon the Lido, in the Borghese Gallery and at the Villa Pamfili-Doria. And they were further elevated with the thought of all the personal experiences which might be associated with these sublime artistic impressions. The heroine proves herself "worthy to know Venice," as the hero puts it, by breaking into sobs over Tintoretto's Crucifixion. The author shows himself a man of feeling and taste in his own right in many purple patches of fervid sentiment

[21] First appearing, respectively, in "The Galaxy," June, 1873, and "The Atlantic," January, 1874, and November-December, 1870.

and description. I will underline a few of the emphatic
words in the description of Leonardo's Last Supper;
though that would scarce be necessary to make the reader
feel the exalted tone of the young enthusiast:

> The most strictly impressive picture in Italy is *incontestably* the Last Supper of Leonardo at Milan . . . its
> *immense* solemnity. . . . The mind finds a *rare* delight
> in filling each of its vacant spaces, effacing its *rank* defilement, and repairing, as far as possible, its *sad disorder.*
> . . . An *unquenchable* elegance lingers in those vague
> outlines and *incurable* scars; enough remains to place
> you in sympathy with the *unfathomable* wisdom of the
> painter.

The following description of the Venetian basilica is, I
believe, unique in the work of Henry James for its
orotund arrangements of cadenced repetition. He must
have been reading Ruskin.

> It was that enchanting Venetian hour when the ocean-touching sun sits melting to death, and the whole still air
> seems to glow with the soft effusion of his golden substance. Within the church, the deep brown shadow-masses, the heavy thick-tinted air, the gorgeous composite darkness, reigned in richer, quainter, more fantastic
> gloom than my feeble pen can reproduce the likeness of.
> From those rude concavities of dome and semi-dome,
> where the multitudinous facets of pictorial mosaic shimmer and twinkle in their own dull brightness; from the
> vast antiquity of innumerable marbles, incrusting the
> walls in roughly-mated slabs, cracked and polished and
> triple-tinted with eternal service; from the wavy carpet
> of compacted stone, where a thousand once-bright fragments glimmer through the long attrition of idle feet
> and devoted knees; from sombre gold and mellow alabaster, from porphyry and malachite, from long dead
> crystal and the sparkle of undying lamps,—there proceeds
> a dense rich atmosphere of splendor and sanctity which
> transports the half stupefied traveller to the age of a

simpler and more awful faith. I wandered for half an hour beneath those reverted cups of scintillating darkness, stumbling on the great stony swells of the pavement as I gazed upward at the long mosaic saints who curve gigantically with the curves of dome and ceiling. I had left Europe; I was in the East. An overwhelming sense of the sadness of man's spiritual history took possession of my heart. The clustering picturesque shadows about me seemed to represent the darkness of a past from which he had slowly and painfully struggled." Etc., etc.

How gratifying this passage must have been to the souls of those starved New England spinsters set before us in some of the later stories of James! How fondly they must have read it out to one another!

Of all this group of tales, the most expert, the most consistent in tone, the most successful in its evocation of the spirit of the past and the brooding loveliness of the present in the foreign scene is "The Last of the Valerii." To my taste it is a better story than either of those picked by Mr. James for preservation. The action is laid in Rome, and almost exclusively in the garden of an ancient villa, with its ilex walks, its lingering golden afternoon light, its picturesque decay and its buried statuary. Perhaps it was judged by the author too fantastic in its *donnée*. For it has to do with a Roman nobleman of our days capable of worshipping and doing sacrifice to a Grecian goddess. But this is scarcely less credible than the story of an American cousin so highly distinguished by the visitation of an English ghost. Perhaps the determining fact for James was a sense of having opened for us the intimate consciousness of the passionate Pilgrim as he could not do that of the less self-conscious Roman. Perhaps he wished to avoid being accused of following too closely in the footsteps of Hawthorne. Or did he fear the charge of plagiarism in view of the similarity of his theme to that of Prosper Mérimée in his "Venus d'Ille"? Whatever his motive, it is doubtful whether the public will accept his verdict in this case and leave to oblivion so charming an introduction to "Roderick Hudson" and "The Portrait of a Lady."

And thus Henry James had found himself, and had emerged from the period of helpless groping. It is true these tales may be classed unhesitatingly as romance, while the best work of James would probably be labelled realism. "The Last of the Valerii" dates from 1874, and of the same year is "Madame de Mauves,"—a story of domestic relations, of spiritual adjustments, of the hard conditions and restraints of the common lot. In the following year comes "Roderick Hudson," a study in social contrasts; and so begins the long series of psychological novels and briefer sketches of social action and reaction. But it would be perversity to ignore the strain of fine romance that runs through the whole series. Mr. James himself has acknowledged the obviously romantic background of "The American." And everyone knows how large a part is played in all his great stories by the glamour of the old world,—by its *Weltansicht,* its clustering associations, and its sheer physical charm. In "The American" and "The Ambassadors," is not Paris a prime source of interest? In "Roderick Hudson," is it not the Rome of "The Marble Faun"; in "The Princess Casamassima" and "The Wings of the Dove," the London of Dickens and Whistler; in "The Aspern Papers" and "The Wings of the Dove" again, is it not the Venice of Byron and Ruskin? There was still in 1874 much to learn in the matter of technique and of life. But these things would follow soon enough once the author had discovered his "Europe." "Seek ye first the kingdom of God, and all these things shall be added unto you"!

## II

## EARLY PRIME

The first main period of production, covering a decade and a half, was signalized by five novels of great power and charm. Through these years James was feeling his way towards that method which was to characterize all the work of the later period. It will be interesting to trace his progress through the series, not wholly ignoring the individual quality of the novels in our primary concern with evolving technique.

### (a) *Roderick Hudson*

The first one of James's fictions of really monumental proportions was "Roderick Hudson," produced in 1875. This strong and engaging story is marked in a dozen ways as the production of his youth. Some of these I have already dwelt upon: notably the variegated picturesqueness of the characters, and the use of the dialogue for the display of their humors rather than for the unfolding of the idea. Equally remarkable is the generosity and promptitude with which the author presents us with our information. Before he has given us a dozen pages of the story proper, he takes nearly that number to tell us all he knows of Rowland Mallet and his antecedents—all he knows, and much more than we care to know at the time or shall ever have a need for knowing. When we have arrived at Rome and are present at Rowland's studio tea, we receive an extended conscientious account of the interesting artistic people we are to meet there. Each one has a paragraph to himself, and as some of them are of a certain quaintness of character, we have the feeling that we may be reading a paper by some new Dick Steele giving account of a new Spectator club. There is for example Sam Singleton, whose portrait I shall venture to introduce entire.

Rowland's second guest was also an artist, but of a very different type. His friends called him Sam Singleton; he was an American, and he had been in Rome a couple of years. He painted small landscapes, chiefly in water-colour; Rowland had seen one of them in a shop window, had liked it extremely and, ascertaining his address, had gone to see him and found him established in a very humble studio near the Piazza Barberini, where apparently fame and fortune had not yet come his way. Rowland, treating him as a discovery, had bought several of his pictures; Singleton made few speeches, but was intensely grateful. Rowland heard afterwards that when he first came to Rome he painted worthless daubs and gave no promise of talent. Improvement had come, however, hand in hand with patient industry, and his talent, though of a slender and delicate order, was now incontestable. It was as yet but scantily recognised and he had hard work to hold out. Rowland hung his little water-colours on the library wall, and found that as he lived with them he grew very fond of them. Singleton, short and spare, was made as if for sitting on very small camp-stools and eating the tiniest luncheons. He had a transparent brown regard, a perpetual smile, an extraordinary expression of modesty and patience. He listened much more willingly than he talked, with a little fixed grateful grin; he blushed when he spoke, and always offered his ideas as if he were handing you useful objects of your own that you had unconsciously dropped; so that his credit could be at most for honesty. He was so perfect an example of the little noiseless devoted worker whom chance, in the person of a moneyed patron, has never taken by the hand, that Rowland would have liked to befriend him by stealth.[1]

This is all, it will be observed, a perfectly *general* account of the little painter; it is given *en bloc* on the authority of the novelist. The later method may be illustrated by the description of Little Bilham, a character in "The Ambassadors" somewhat akin to Sam Singleton. We have our introduction to Little Bilham in the account given by Strether to Waymarsh of his visit to Chad's apartments. Strether did not go there to make the acquaintance of any "little artist-man," but to learn something of the situation of Chad. He has now the knowledge that he doesn't know anything. So much he learned from Little Bilham.

"That's what I found out from the young man."
"But I thought you said you found out nothing."
"Nothing but that—that I don't know anything."
"And what good does that do you?"
"It's just," said Strether, "what I've come to you to help me to discover. I mean anything about anything over here. I *felt* that, up there. It regularly rose before me in its might. The young man moreover—Chad's friend—as good as told me so."
"As good as told you you know nothing about anything?" Waymarsh appeared to look at some one who might have as good as told *him.* "How old is he?"
"Well, I guess not thirty."
"Yet you had to take that from him?"
"Oh, I took a good deal more—since, as I tell you, I took an invitation to déjeuner."
"And are you *going* to that unholy meal?"
"If you'll come with me. He wants you too, you know. I told him about you. He gave me his card," Strether pursued, "and his name's rather funny. It's John

[1] Vol. I, pp. 108-109.

Little Bilham, and he says his two surnames are, on account of his being small, inevitably used together."

"Well," Waymarsh asked with due detachment from these details, "what's he doing up there?"

"His account of himself is that he's 'only a little artist-man.' That seemed to me perfectly to describe him. But he's yet in the phase of study; this, you know, is the great art-school—to pass a certain number of years in which he came over. And he's a great friend of Chad's, and occupying Chad's rooms just now because they're so pleasant. *He's* very pleasant and curious too," Strether added—"though he's not from Boston."

Waymarsh looked already rather sick of him. "Where *is* he from?"

Strether thought. "I don't know that, either. But he's 'notoriously,' as he put it himself, not from Boston."

"Well," Waymarsh moralised from dry depths, "every one can't notoriously *be* from Boston. Why," he continued, "is he curious?"

"Perhaps just for *that*—for one thing! But really," Strether added, "for everything. When you meet him you'll see."

"Oh, I don't want to meet him," Waymarsh impatiently growled. "Why don't he go home?"

Strether hesitated. "Well, because he likes it over here."

This appeared in particular more than Waymarsh could bear. "He ought then to be ashamed of himself, and, as you admit you think so too, why drag him in?"[2]

But the last question carries them beyond Little Bilham. We may have, as the result of this dialogue, a small provision of fact about him. But we have, what is more to the purpose, a most vivid impression of what he stands for; and, what is still more to the purpose, we have the states of mind of Strether and Waymarsh in regard to this curious and significant person.

[2] Vol. XXI, pp. 106-108.

Sometimes in "Roderick Hudson" James has one of his characters relate the facts to another in conversation. Thus Madame Grandoni gives Rowland an account of Christina Light and her mother. But she does it in one (very long) breath. It takes an almost uninterrupted speech of five pages. James seems a bit conscious himself of the formidableness of such a block of information, and he makes a kind of acknowledgment of guilt. "Your report's as solid," Rowland said to Madame Grandoni, thanking her, "as if it had been drawn up for the Academy of Sciences."[3]

It is in the same deliberate fashion that the author describes the dwellings of his characters and the scenes they visit. And the narrative itself is largely conducted by passages of generalization. Dialogues are summarized in crowded paragraphs of exposition. The author feels responsible for every moment of his characters' time. But when he gives us an account of their occupations, it is at long range and in shorthand, as one writes up one's diary for the past month without attention to the particular dates. The young author is very bold in the summary account of character and of states of mind. And not content with giving the general facts about such and such a person, he must needs soar still higher to the facts of human nature at large. "Very odd, you may say, that at this time of day Rowland should still be brooding over a girl of no brilliancy, of whom he had had a bare glimpse two years before; very odd that an impression should have fixed itself so sharply under so few applications of the die. It is of the very nature of such impressions, however, to show a total never represented by the mere sum of their constituent parts."[4] Thus he calls

[3] Vol. I, p. 166.
[4] Id., p. 313.

our attention to the fineness and the high comprehensiveness of his psychology,—merits which the maturer artist would have left us to find out for ourselves.

So much for technique in the narrower sense. In the larger view the novel is perhaps equally far from the distinctive manner of James. It has an idea, and a very interesting one: that, to put it briefly, of genius and its frequent tendency to claim exemptions not accorded to ordinary humanity: genius and its sometimes appalling *"nostalgie de la boue."* This idea is scarcely however conceived pictorially. The story is just the chronological account of the degeneration of a genius thus claiming unholy license. And we are never really made to understand this process. There is something too mysterious about the ruin that comes upon Roderick; we are never rightly made acquainted with the demon who rides him to destruction.

A main reason for the failure of the book to make its point is the unhappy choice of an interpreter. It may be that Rowland Mallet regards himself as the person in whom we are most interested. But in that case he is quite mistaken. He is an estimable gentleman, with whom we sympathize, and whom we should like to meet in the flesh—he is indeed an immature forerunner of Lambert Strether—but he cannot divert our attention from his more vivid and naughty comrade. And we naturally resent being cheated of the experience of Roderick by having it shown us through the judicial optics of Rowland.

But in spite of all, the book is unmistakably the work of Henry James. I do not wish to burden the reader with a review of the many ways in which it shows his well-known character. I must content myself with noting the strong, distinctive flavor of James in certain passages between Rowland and Christina. Christina is really the best thing in this book. She is not altogether unworthy of herself as she appears in "The Princess Casamassima." She is to Rowland something of the enigma she became later for Hyacinth Robinson. "He felt it a rare and expensive privilege to watch her. . . . The background of her nature had a sort of landscape largeness and was mysterious withal, emitting strange, fantastic gleams and flashes. Waiting for these was better sport than some kinds of fishing. Moreover it was not a disadvantage to talk with a girl who forced one to make sure of the sufficiency of one's wit."[5] Christina had the beauty of having a "system"; and no little part of their dialogue (as in the fourteenth chapter) reflects Rowland's attempt to get a glimpse of this system. There is one interchange in particular, in the twentieth chapter, which might almost have occurred in "The Awkward Age" or "The Golden Bowl," considering the interest shown by Christina in a fine point of Rowland's and the fine point which she produces herself as an outcome of their sharp fencing match. Rowland has challenged her intentions in regard to Roderick and the Prince, now that she has made the acquaintance of Roderick's Mary.

"Would you have done this [throw over the Prince] if you had not seen a certain person?"

"What person?"

"The young lady you so much admire."

She looked at him with quickened attention; then suddenly, "This is really interesting," she exclaimed. "Let us see what's in it." And she flung herself into a chair and pointed to another.

"You don't answer my question," Rowland said.

"You've no right that I know of to ask it. But it's

[5] Vol. I, p. 277.

very intelligent—it puts such a lot into it. Into my having seen her, I mean." She paused a moment; then with her eyes on him, "She helped me certainly," she went on.

"Provoked you, you mean, to hurt her—through Roderick?"

For a moment she deeply coloured, and he had really not intended to force the tears to her eyes. A cold clearness, however, quickly forced them back. "I see your train of reasoning, but it's really all wrong. I meant no harm whatever to Miss Garland; I should be extremely sorry to cause her any distress. Tell me that, since I assure you of that, you believe it."

"How am I to tell you," he asked in a moment, "that I don't?"

"And yet your idea of an inward connexion between our meeting and what has happened since corresponds to something that *has* been, for me, an inward reality. I took into my head, as I told you," Christina continued, "to be greatly struck with Miss Garland (since that's her sweet name!) and I frankly confess that I was tormented, that I was moved to envy, call it, if you like, to jealousy, by something I found in her. There came to me there in five minutes the sense of her character. *C'est bien beau,* you know, a character like that, and I got it full in the face. It made me say to myself 'She in my place would never marry Gennaro—no, no, no, never!' I couldn't help coming back to it, and I thought of it so often that I found a kind of inspiration in it. I hated the idea of being worse than she—of doing something that she wouldn't do. . . . The end of it all was that I found it impossible not to tell the Prince that I was his very humble servant, but that decidedly I couldn't take him for mine."

"Are you sure it was only of Miss Garland's character that you were jealous," Rowland asked, "and not of her affection for her cousin?"

"*Sure* is a good deal to say. Still, I think I may do so. There are two reasons; one at least I can tell you. Her

affection has not a shadow's weight with Mr. Hudson!
Why then should one resent it?"

"And what's the other reason?"

"Excuse me; that's my own affair."

Rowland felt himself puzzled, baffled, charmed,
inspired. . . .[6]

This dialogue is most characteristic. But apart from
the question of the characteristic, many readers have
declared themselves held and charmed by the story of
"Roderick Hudson." However obscure the process may
remain, the degeneration of Roderick is undoubtedly an
enthralling spectacle, making its appeal both to the moral
sense and to the deeper fount of sympathy. Not too far
below Roderick and Christina in interest are Mary Garland and Rowland. For even Rowland is a more vividly
realized and a more attractive character than most of
those in the novels discussed in the next chapter. And if
the characters in a novel are real and interesting, we need
not resort to the charm of setting or any other merit to
explain why the novel lives.

### (b) *The American*

"The American" is the first large essay of James in
treatment of the theme that was to occupy so much of
his attention all along,—the contrast of the American and
the European cultures. And it remains to this day an
effective piece of work. The self-made American without antecedents and traditions brought in contrast with a
group of persons for whom these are almost the whole of
life; the man of strong and unlimited self-reliance in
contrast to men and women hedged and thwarted in every
direction by the restraints of family and caste—the

[6] Vol. I, pp. 404-405.

simple, straightforward, easy-going westerner in his dealings with these formal, sophisticated, inordinately polite and treacherous people; it makes a story and a spectacle of endless richness and variety. The idea is clearly conceived, and there is no detail of the story that it does not inform and make relevant. The sub-plot of Valentin de Bellegarde and Noémie Nioche is obviously introduced for the purpose of illustrating certain aspects of the social contrast which do not come out in Newman's own love affair. The friendship of Valentin and Christopher is a delightful case of the mutual attraction of opposites. "No two parties to an alliance could have come to it from a wider separation, but it was what each brought out of the queer dim distance that formed the odd attraction for the other."[7]

The social contrast comes out most strikingly, however, and certainly to our greatest amusement, in the series of scenes in which the blunt and humorous westerner is opposed to the frigid courtliness of the elder Bellegardes, above all on those occasions when, having accepted him as a suitor for the hand of Claire, they yet endeavor, largely without success, to make him understand the enormous condescension in their friendly treatment of a "commercial" person. The American millionaire, conscious of his own power and his own good character, can be made to appreciate but dimly the social inferiority imputed to him. He does feel keenly, however, if somewhat obscurely, the quality of culture displayed in the manners of his French friends. He feels it naturally most of all in the style of the woman he loves. "She gave him, the charming woman, the sense of an elaborate education, of her having passed through mysterious ceremonies and processes of culture, of her having been

7 Vol. II, p. 139.

fashioned and made flexible to certain deep social needs. All this . . . made her seem rare and precious—a very expensive article."[8]  Her rank made of Claire de Cintré "a kind of historical formation."  Rank was something which heretofore he had heard attributed only to military personages.  He now appreciated the attribution of rank to women.  "The designations representing it in France struck him as ever so pretty and becoming, with a property in the bearer, this particular one, that might match them and make a sense—something fair and softly bright, that had motions of extraordinary lightness and indeed a whole new and unfamiliar play of emphasis and pressure, a new way, that is, of not insisting and not even, as one might think, wanting or knowing, yet all to the effect of attracting and pleasing."[9]  But even the odious relatives of Claire and the gentry gathered together by them at their ball share this quality of rank, and something of the finish and beauty of style entailed in their being likewise "historical formations."  And we may say in passing that the American himself does not come out at all badly in the comparison.  His manners, while not the least bit historical, have a freedom and candor, a largeness and natural breeding, which make you prefer them to the article more expensively produced.

It is an effective piece of work. . . . And it is very much in the early manner.  I will not dwell on the superficial points of technique in which it resembles "Roderick Hudson."  The dialogue is often very good; but not at all in the way the dialogue is good in "The Awkward Age." It is refreshing to have the hero "bet his life on" something, or to have him urge an amused Parisian to "give" somebody "one in the eye."  There are passages of talk,

[8] Vol. II, p. 165.

[9] Id., p. 122.

however, which have somewhat lost their savor. We
cannot help feeling at times that Valentin and even his
sister are permitted to show themselves younger and less
practiced hands than the author intended. And we are
conscious of a certain perfunctory character in most of
Newman's exemplary love-making.

But the early manner is exhibited in ways more important than these. It resides essentially in what we may
call the greater objectivity of the work. The chief concern of the author seems to be for the scenical effectiveness of what is said and done. In the later work the
scene is used chiefly in order to objectify the idea. Here
the idea is the opportunity for scene. The characters
express themselves more violently here, in word and
gesture. This emotional emphasis reaches its culmination
in the chapter in which Claire announces her intention of
becoming a nun. In this one chapter[10] we read that
"Newman gave a great rap on the floor with his stick
and a long grim laugh"; that "he struck his heart and
became more eloquent than he knew"; that he "almost
shouted"; "he glared as if at her drowning beyond help,
then he broke out"; "he clasped his hands and began
to tremble visibly"; "he dropped into a chair and sat
looking at her with a long inarticulate wail"; "he sprang
to his feet in loud derision." Nowhere else in James,
I think, is there such a lavish use of irony as that indulged in by Newman and the grim Marquise. Their
remarks are as good as lines in a smart play. And that
is the point. These scenes in which new world and old
world are pitted against one another are introduced for
their theatrical effectiveness, like certain brilliant scenes
in Thackeray or in Dumas *père*. Such is the scene in
which the Marquis is obliged to introduce to all his

[10] Chap. xx.

*monde* the "commercial" person who is going to marry
his sister. Such is the scene in the Parc Monceau in
which Newman announces to the Marquis and the old
Marquise his possession of the incriminating paper. It
makes a fine show, the bravery with which his adversaries, deep-stricken as they are, bear up in the face of
the world,—their display of that "very superior style of
brazen assurance, of what M. Nioche called *l'usage du
monde* and Mrs. Tristram called the grand manner."[11]
This is not incompatible with a suppressed but terrible
exhibition of passion. Upon one of Newman's ironic
sallies on this occasion, "the Marquis gave a hiss that
fairly evoked for our friend some vision of a hunched
back, an erect tail and a pair of shining evil eyes. 'I
demand of you to step out of our path!' "[12] That is good
"business," and a good line. But the best line of all is that
of the Marquis in the scene where Newman has informed
him and his mother of Valentin's death-bed apology for
their conduct. He had apologized for the conduct of
his own mother! "For a moment the effect of these
words was as if he had struck a physical blow. A quick
flush leaped into the charged faces before him—it was
like a jolt of full glasses, making them spill their wine.
Urbain uttered two words which Newman but half
heard, but of which the aftersense came to him in the
reverberation of the sound. *'Le misérable!'* "[13]

The point of view is throughout chiefly that of Newman. But not the same use is made of this as would
have been made in a later book. We see what Newman
sees, but he does not interpret it to us. The author interprets it, and he is sometimes obliged—in order to get

[11] P. 496.
[12] P. 489.
[13] P. 431.

Newman into the picture—to give us a glimpse or two beyond what Newman sees. "We have noted him as observant," says James in the scene when the Marquise is forced to invite Newman to a ball at *her* house; "yet on this occasion he failed to catch a thin sharp eyebeam, as cold as a flash of steel, which passed between Madame de Bellegarde and the Marquis, and which we may presume to have been a commentary on the innocence displayed in that latter clause of this speech."[14] That latter clause had been a statement that "it mattered very little whether he met his friends at her house or his own." This showed how little he understood of the ways of thought of those with whom he was dealing. All along he showed surprising unconsciousness of the pitfalls amid which he was walking. All along he was very largely unaware of the comedy in which he was playing his part. It was in vain, for example, that Valentin tried to make him understand what was involved in the condescension of Urbain and his mother. And when he refrained from explanations, Christopher had no idea what that cost him. "I know not," says the author, "whether in renouncing the mysterious opportunity to which he alluded Valentin felt himself do something very generous. If so he was not rewarded; his generosity was not appreciated. Newman failed to recognize any power to disconcert or to wound him, and he had now no sense of coming off easily."[15]

A story in which the main actor is so uninitiated can bear no very close resemblance to the story of Isabel Archer or Fleda Vetch or Lambert Strether. There is here no revelation of anything through Newman's consciousness—nothing that depends on his *understanding*.

[14] P. 285.
[15] P. 160.

There is in fact no spiritual dilemma. That is why the book is not among the greatest of its author's. There is a gallant fight for a woman. There is an amusing and finally tragic social contrast in which the American hero is one of the terms. And that is the main point in which this is recognizable as a novel of Henry James.

## (c)  *The Portrait of a Lady*

Most joyous of dates in all our chronicle is the year 1880. It is in contemplation of that year that the lover of James feels his blood run warmest. The footlights flash on, the fiddles begin, and faces brighten in anticipation of the three knocks and the parted curtain. It is not that "Scribner's" was concluding in January of that year the publication of "Confidence," nor that "Harper's" from July to December was setting forth the charming study of "Washington Square." It is that the "Atlantic" this side the water and "Macmillan's" in London were showing each month in successive tableaux the entralling "Portrait of a Lady." This was the first masterpiece of Henry James.

He was still far from his technical goal. In mechanical ways the work is still very different from that, for example, of "The Golden Bowl," to which it bears a considerable likeness in theme. "The Portrait" is a novel like other novels, taking us through successive stages in the history of its characters. It is the biography of Isabel Archer, and has the general character of a chronicle. It covers a number of years, and includes a number of substantial events. Nearly the whole first volume is taken up with material which would have been excluded from the more distinctive work of the later years. The episode of Lord Warburton and his proposal, the death of Mr. Touchett and his bequest to Isabel are two major blocks of material which would have been treated briefly and referentially as a part of the antecedent facts of the story. "The Golden Bowl" begins at a point corresponding to a point somewhat beyond the opening of the second volume of the earlier novel,—just before the marriage of the heroine, which ushers in (for Isabel as for Maggie) the main dramatic complication. Not merely does the author of "The Portrait" give a whole volume to Isabel's earlier history as a grown woman. When he has once got her launched in this earlier career, he stops for the length of more than two chapters to bring up to date her history as a girl and that of her cousin Ralph. And this is not done, as it would have been done after 1896, by reminiscence and dialogue as an integral part of the narrative of present experience.

Again the earlier technique appears in the large number of characters of considerable importance. As in "The Golden Bowl," there are but four major characters,— Isabel, Osmond, Madame Merle and Warburton. But over against the chorus-figure of Mrs. Assingham stand, in "The Portrait," Ralph Touchett and Goodwood, Henrietta Stackpole and Pansy, even if we leave out of account Mr. and Mrs. Touchett, Mr. Rosier and Mr. Bantling, and the Countess Gemini. And we can hardly leave even them out of account, considering how much attention is given to the character and personal history of each one of them.

Mrs. Assingham, it will be remembered, is given no personal history, and no character except that of a woman exceedingly ingenious in the interpretation of human nature. She is necessary for the dialogue. The minor characters of "The Portrait" have a similar function; but they do not fulfil it to anything like the same extent,

since the dialogue has taken on very little of its later
character. It serves chiefly to display the various breeding and humors of the persons taking part. The author
has not yet so completely neutralized his characters as to
social tone. They still exhibit some of the variety and
picturesqueness proper to characters in a Victorian novel.
Vividest in this respect is Henrietta Stackpole, with her
militant Americanism, her militant independence, her
journalistic preoccupations, and her intense earnestness.
But even Madame Merle is occasionally given a touch
that suggests Thackeray more than James. She is perhaps the most perfect creation of the book, and her line
is by no means any sort of vividness. Her line is the
most perfect suavity of manner, the most impeccable of
self-effacing good taste. But there is at least one occasion on which she is treated for a moment or two like a
person in a novel (or comedy) of "manners." Mrs.
Touchett is discussing the comparatively liberal treatment accorded her by her husband in his will.

"He chose, I presume, to recognise the fact that though
I lived much abroad and mingled—you may say freely—
in foreign life, I never exhibited the smallest preference
for anyone else."

"For anyone but yourself," Madame Merle mentally
observed; but the reflection was perfectly inaudible.

"I never sacrificed my husband to another," Mrs.
Touchett continued with her stout curtness.

"Oh, no," thought Madame Merle; "you never did
anything for another!"[16]

The author now goes on to explain the "cynicism in these
mute comments." Madame Merle had not of course
expected any bequest to herself. But—

[16] Vol. III, pp. 295-296.

The idea of a distribution of property—she would almost have said of spoils—just now pressed upon her senses and irritated her with a sense of exclusion. I am far from wishing to picture her as one of the hungry mouths or envious hearts of the general herd, but we have already learned of her having desires that had never been satisfied. If she had been questioned, she would of course have admitted—with a fine proud smile—that she had not the faintest claim to a share in Mr. Touchett's relics. "There was never anything in the world between us," she would have said. "There was never that, poor man!"—with a fillip of her thumb and her third finger.[17]

Perhaps something of this kind is necessary at this point to give the reader a bit of a "tip" on what lies below the surface of Madame Merle's exquisite manner. But in the later work James would have managed to convey a sense of these depths without the false note of vulgarity. Or else, to the reader's confusion, he would have left him to find out for himself without the aid of tips.

But the early manner is found in points more technical and superficial than essential and organic. Essentially "The Portrait" is the development of an idea by the method of "revelation" described in our first part. The adventures of Isabel Archer are more spiritual than material. The stages of her chronicle are the stages by which the painter fills out her portrait. Even in the preliminary period of her English sojourn, we are occupied with the discovery of a woman intensely concerned to make her life fine, hoping "to find herself in a difficult position, so that she should have the pleasure of being as heroic as the occasion demanded." The proposal of Lord Warburton is admitted merely in order that she may assert in striking fashion her "enlightened prejudice in favour

[17] Vol. III, pp. 296-297.

of the free exploration of life." [18]   It is not ease and
security that are desired by this adventurous American
soul.   She explains to her reproachful suitor that she
cannot hope to escape her fate, cannot avoid unhappiness
by separating herself from life—"from the usual chances
and dangers, from what most people know and suffer." [19]

With the entry of Madame Merle towards the end
of the first volume, the painter attacks the real background of his picture.   A few chapters later his task
begins in earnest with the appearance of the Florentine
gentleman who is to become the most prominent feature
in the heroine's experience.   From this point on, the work
is a masterpiece of revelation; and if the details brought
out are chiefly details of "background"—having to do
with the characters of Osmond and Madame Merle—
that is essentially the case in the later books.   The background circumstances are revealed through the consciousness of the heroine who is the foreground figure; and
they tend to bring out in brighter relief the beauty of this
figure.   Every trait of vanity and selfishness in Osmond
gives play to the corresponding traits of generous large-
mindedness in Isabel, as well as giving her occasion for
the display of resourcefulness in difficult social relations.
The coldness of his nature serves as foil to the flame-like
warmth of hers.   And the earlier stages of their acquaintance bring out sufficiently the large ground of taste and
sensibility which they have in common.   I must deny myself the agreeable task of tracing from scene to scene the
nicely graduated steps by which this "sterile dilettante"
is betrayed to us first and then to Isabel, and the steps
by which there dawn upon her consciousness the more

[18] P. 155.
[19] P. 187.

and more bewildering, the more and more heroic features of her great adventure.

Nowhere is the concern of the story more beautifully than in "The Portrait" the *quality* of experience. It is not the bare facts of Gilbert's relation to Madame Merle and Pansy, revealed at the climax of the story by the Countess Gemini, that are of importance. It is the values of life as conceived by Gilbert and by Madame Merle upon which these facts throw their final interpretative light. Nowhere is there a finer indication of those social and esthetic values to which all the leading characters of James are devoted than in the scenes of Isabel's growing admiration for Osmond. Nowhere short of "Poynton" and "The Golden Bowl" is there a finer display of the spiritual values that transcend the others than in the scenes of Isabel's growing horror of her husband. "The Portrait of a Lady" has thus the distinction of being the first novel in which the "figure in the carpet" stands out in distinct and glowing beauty.

But no mere indication of the order of this novel in the author's development will explain the many graces and charms it possesses in its own right. There is something about the personality and situation of Isabel that gives her a place unique in the whole gallery. It is a place no man can occupy. A man may have the advantage when it comes to the freedom of adventure of a Pendennis or a Tom Jones. But the very limitations upon her freedom, the delicacy of her position, give to the adventures of a brave woman an attaching pathos, and even a spiritual richness, which a man's can seldom have. The limits of her experience outwardly compel her to cultivate it intensively.

Of course it may be urged that Ralph Touchett shares this advantage in disadvantage. And I am willing to grant him a very large measure of the attractiveness of the generous fettered woman. He is a figure beautifully conceived and executed. And indeed there is no novel of James in which we find so many characters of a warm and simple humanity. Something of a like appeal is made by Mr. Touchett, by Pansy. We are fond even of Henrietta, and we have a measure of charity for Mrs. Touchett and the Countess Gemini.

In fineness of execution, Gilbert Osmond and Madame Merle take their place beside Isabel herself. Madame Merle is a figure of even rarer conception,—having no counterpart, as Isabel may be thought to have, among the famous creations of Meredith and George Eliot. And she is herself so much of a victim, and a person of so much *savoir vivre* withal, and of so graceful and touching a manner of exit, that we cannot forbear to open our hearts even to her.

There is again a peculiar charm about the *mise en scène* of this drama. None of the English country-places that figure so largely in James is more lovely than that of the American banker on the Thames. Have we perhaps its model, by the way, in that other banker's home alluded to by Mr. James in his life of Story? Surely at least the golden air so often referred to in that reconstruction of the earlier time is what envelops the Florentine villa of Gilbert Osmond in the days before his true character has been revealed.

The lover of James will ever cherish this work as the prime example of his early manner. It has the open face of youth. There is a lightness and freshness of tone about it that never recurs in the more labored work of later years. It is the first of his compositions entirely free from crudity and the last to show the unalloyed charm of ingenuousness.

### (d)   *The Princess Casamassima*

Five years after "The Portrait of a Lady" appeared another masterpiece, and this too, though very different in quality, was an example of the early manner at its best.

In some ways "The Princess Casamassima" shows an advance in technique. It is true that the history of Hyacinth Robinson is taken up at an even earlier point than that of Isabel Archer, so that the opening chapters have even more the biographical aspect. But the Princess, who represents in the experience of Hyacinth something like what Gilbert Osmond represents in that of Isabel Archer, makes her appearance much earlier in the book. There are decidedly fewer substantial happenings in the later story, and a decidedly more limited cast of characters. There are but two principals; and among the minor characters—Miss Pynsent, Mr. Vetch, Paul Muniment, Lady Aurora, M. Poupin, Millicent Henning —none are made so prominent as several of the minor characters in "The Portrait." They may be as important functionally, but they are not so importunate on their own behalf. They are drawn on a reduced scale, so as to be kept in proper subordination to the "leads."

And if the characters and incidents as such are less in evidence they are more strictly held to accountability for their part in the "revelation." This story is another beautiful instance of an "idea conceived as picture." It is an idea such as Mr. Galsworthy gave so fine a treatment in "Fraternity,"—that of the privileged and the submerged classes stretching out to one another vain hands across the social gulf. But while in Mr. Galsworthy's story the situation is viewed chiefly from the side of the privileged, in "The Princess Casamassima" it is the man born to the shabby life of poverty who seems from his side to see a door opening into the life of large freedom and cultivated leisure. In the consciousness of Hyacinth, the foreground is occupied by the dark and painful spectacle of his fellow victims of the social order, those less fortunate even than himself. And his heart is filled with bitterness and the need for action against the order that admits of so much ugliness and misery. But his encounter with the radiant creature of privilege, his discovery of the possibilities of refined social intercourse, his survey in Paris and Venice of the treasures of art and the accumulated beauty of historical tradition, sap the strength of his conviction until he becomes incapable of revolutionary action. The conflicting forces of his inheritance symbolize and to some extent create the insoluble problem that drives him to suicide.

But I should not use the word problem. This novel has not the slightest political intention. It is not even meant to have historical and documentary value like the Russian series of Turgenieff. Mr. James does not pretend to any exact knowledge of socialism. And I fear that—at least in this connection—he had no practical interest in it. His interest was entirely that of an artist wishing to convey certain impressions. In this case it was the long-accumulated impressions of London life that besought him for artistic liberation. Again we are made aware how little he is concerned with the bare facts of experience. It was the color and feel of Hyacinth Robinson's experience of life that he wished to render. And poverty and mutter of revolution, beautiful clever women and hard resolute men, were—like Rose Muniment and Millicent Henning—but strands in the varicolored web of this experience. As for the revolutionary movement, the very vagueness of its presentation was a part of James's scheme. "My scheme," he says "called for the suggested nearness (to all our apparently ordered life) of some sinister anarchic underworld, heaving in its pain, its power and its hate; a presentation not of sharp particulars, but of loose appearances, vague motions and sounds and symptoms, just perceptible presences and general looming possibilities."[20]

This story can never have quite the intensity of appeal of "The Portrait." It has not the same element of drama. And while the experience of the hero may be poignant enough in its effect upon his feelings, it is not a domestic experience, it is not definitely formulated as a sentimental tragedy. And it is for the domestic and the sentimental drama that we reserve our most intense concern.

For all that, it is a masterpiece, "The Princess Casamassima." It is a work of great and finished beauty. If "The Portrait" glows in our imagination with blue and gold, with rich brown and crimson, "The Princess Casamassima" shines with a subdued pearly lustre that is a greater triumph of devoted skill. There is a velvety smoothness in its movements and transitions. It is a miracle of pitch and tone. The author has at last achieved a perfect command of the mechanics of touch. Character and scene, event and mystery are alike rendered with due emphasis, and kept in their right place in the total scale of values.

This does not mean that any of these elements is subdued to the point of extinction. The minor characters of this story have their special attractiveness. Here for once James has given us his own peculiar variety of what a grateful world agrees to call the Dickens type. To this

[20] Vol. V, p. xxi.

class of quaint and lovable characters belong Aunt Pinnie and Rose Muniment, M. Poupin and the Lady Aurora. And while none of these has the vivid salience of Dickens figures, they are none the less real and endearing on that account. The London of this story is likewise the entire possession of James,—not the terrible black city of "Oliver Twist" nor the burlesque London of the White Horse Tavern; but for that very reason a city more familiar to many a reader who has taken it in in the same somewhat vague and disinterested way as the American author.

But most prominent element of all in the experience of Hyacinth is the mysterious and beautiful Princess, recalled by the author to the stage for his special benefit. She is for Hyacinth what so many of James's characters crave as the breath of life, a "social relation."[21] But she is also, for Hyacinth and for us, the mystery of a character not thoroughly understood. We are soon made acquainted with two of her leading traits,—her world-weariness and her hatred of the banal—which together send her forth on her bizarre adventure in the underworld. But what we are never sure of is how far she is human, how far she is capable of gratifying that desire for a social, a human relation. This doubt becomes the great secondary *motif* of the composition. And the gradual emergence of certainty upon this question takes its place with the gradual aggravation of Hyacinth's larger problem as a perfect instance of the story-telling method of James.

[21] The reader may remember the pathetic figure of Herbert Dodd, keeper of a bookstore, in "The Bench of Desolation," and the surprised delight with which he finally discovers himself to be in a social relation with Kate Cookham.

### (e)   *The Tragic Muse*

It is often assumed, perhaps because of its date, that
"The Tragic Muse" is a transitional work, marking a
great advance towards the technique of the later period.
This seems to me a mistaken assumption.   Both in reference to the course of James's technical evolution, and
in point of intrinsic worth, "The Tragic Muse" shows
a recession from the point reached in "The Portrait" and
"The Princess Casamassima."

It is, to be sure, a very fine novel.   And in certain
obvious ways it is more advanced in technique than the
earlier masterpieces.   It has not the biographical structure, concerned as it is with a company of people all
grouped together at the start in what may be compared
to the first act of a play.   In this respect it gives the sense
of being more compact.   And while there are passages
of generalizing psychology[22] and considerable "blocks of
referential narrative"[23] in "The Tragic Muse," perhaps
upon inspection the earlier novels would show a larger
number of these telltale spots.

It is in the larger view that "The Tragic Muse" shows
the retrograde progress.   I have noted before the effect
of the double plot for dissipating the intensity of interest.
There are just twice as many major characters in "The
Tragic Muse" as in "The Princess Casamassima."   And
if we count as many major characters in "The Portrait"
as in "The Tragic Muse," there is the difference of their
all being actors in one identical drama.   The best that can
be said for "The Tragic Muse" is that the two separate
dramas are related and ingeniously woven together, and
that the idea developed is practically the same in each

[22] See, for example, Vol. VII, pp. 148 and 185.
[23] For example, pp. 81-88.

case. But they remain two stories for all that; and while the idea may gain in comprehensiveness, it must lose in continuity, intensity, and logical neatness of evolution. And so the work is wanting in compactness, and above all in leisureliness. In reference to certain parts of the story of Miriam, James has himself acknowledged the unduly rapid rate of progress, which has made impossible any true representation of the circumstances. And we feel the same want of leisurely development in the whole of the first and last books. The first book is too full of the bustle and commotion of marshalling his numerous cohorts to admit the kind of exposition in which James excels. It is all taken up with stage "business." As for the last book, it makes almost the typical conclusion of an old-fashioned novel, showing the benevolent author's disposition of his puppets (what happened and who got whom). It is very unlike the winding up of a story of Henry James.

And this brings us to a realization that in essentials the book is even less distinctive of James's matured method than in the superficial aspects of technique. It has an idea conceived as picture: so much is true. But it is an inferior idea for the purposes of James. Inferior, as we have seen, because so obvious, offering so little for interpretation. I suppose one would hardly have been able to predicate this in advance, especially considering that James seems not to have done so himself. The case of the artistic as against the practical temperament, exemplified first in the relation of Nick Dormer to Julia Dallow and secondly in that of Miriam to Peter Sherringham, seemed to him to bristle with nice points for elucidation. And it did make handsomely for complication and excitement. It is exciting to read of the triumphs of Miriam, of Nick Dormer's sacrifice of a career, of the confrontation of Julia and Miriam in Nick's studio, of the breathless return of Peter from the Indies. But for the idea proper the material simply didn't "pan out." It panned out best in two directions,—in connection with Miriam and with the minor and altogether incidental figure of Gabriel Nash. The latter is scarcely more than a living type of our "figure in the carpet"; and the degree of Nick Dormer's understanding of him is the degree of his devotion to the life of the artist. So that the scenes in which Gabriel Nash makes his apologia are for Nick Dormer the scenes of "revelation." What Nick Dormer wanted to make out was whether Gabriel Nash could really be considered a gentleman, or whether his theory and practice of "working in life" as an art did actually make an ass of him. Peter Sherringham has a similar perplexity in reference to Miriam. He is forever trying to make out whether she has any "private life," to use the phrase from another story of James. The revelation of the artist-life to him is the revelation of her complete absorption in artistic self-expression. But in the case both of Nick's Gabriel and of Peter's Miriam, the possibilities for revelation are soon exhausted,—certainly before the end of the first volume. After that it is an old story, with new items perhaps, but no extension of light. Here we feel the contrast to "The Portrait of a Lady" and "The Princess Casamassima," where the revelation is only just beginning with the opening of the second volume and where it goes on with growing intensity to the end.

"The Tragic Muse" may very well be one of the most popular of James's novels, especially for readers who are not over fond of *James*. It has many material features of interest. It has to do with the studio and the stage; and we are all crazy about the stage in particular,—or, as James himself makes the distinction, about actors and all the personal and outward side of stage affairs. We like moreover to have the connection made between the more Bohemian occupations and the important figures of the political and the diplomatic world. The people of "The Muse" are all such well-favored imposing characters, playing their parts in the bright light of general interest,—figures to arouse our envy and admiration. It is nothing against them from this point of view that they are *ordinary* figures. But the forte of Henry James is another sort of figure,—the rare, the retiring character, very fine if you can see the fineness, but always in need of interpretation. Hyacinth Robinson is such a rare one, and Ralph Touchett, Fleda Vetch and Maggie Verver. But hardly Peter Sherringham or Miriam Rooth or Julia Dallow. Gabriel Nash may be a rare bird, but he is a bird of too strange a feather for this category. I have spoken of Mr. Galsworthy's "Fraternity" as being called to mind by "The Princess Casamassima." "The Tragic Muse" has more likeness to Mr. Galsworthy's "Patricians," which I presume to be a more popular, as it is a much less beautiful, work than "Fraternity." "The Patricians" and "The Tragic Muse" remind me of particularly splendid oil paintings, sumptuous Lawrences or Gainsboroughs, such as one finds in collections that include only the soundest specimens of certified value. They are guilty of no defect or shortcoming. They are well varnished and magnificently framed. They are guaranteed to hold their colors. They are distinctly important. But they are more handsome than beautiful, more striking than rare. I am speaking only *comparatively,* of course. The work of Mr. Galsworthy as well as the work of James, is never wholly wanting in rarity. But it is our business and our sport to make distinctions. Mr. James speaks with great satisfaction of the sustained "tone" of "The Tragic Muse," and he is no doubt right about it. Only one has to record one's impression that it is—comparatively, of course—a vulgar, or at any rate a common, tone.

## III

## NON-CANONICAL

The work of James, like that of Mr. Hardy, showed, almost to the end of his career, a most surprising unevenness. Novels of great power were regularly accompanied or succeeded by others distinctly inferior. It is as if the stronger works had sapped the strength of those that grew beside them, rising to a greater height and depriving them of sunlight. Once or twice one is inclined to wonder whether this fastidious artist, under pressure, was driven to defend the integrity of his cherished works by a frank sacrifice to the gods of the market of others less happily born. But we are not forced to this hypothesis. It may be sufficient to assume that, up to so late a period, the restless spirit of the artist insisted on trying curious experiments. And this is the more reasonable supposition, inasmuch as James had not thoroughly and successfully tried out his distinctive method in a long novel till very near the end of all his writing. At any rate we must record the fact that, in the course of the early period, while he was producing the five superior novels discussed in the last chapter, he was turning out no less than four others for which he later found no place in his collected works.

It has seemed more worth while to center attention upon the superior works. And I shall not feel bound to go over in perfunctory detail the many and obvious points in which the rejected stories fall short of the ideal of James. There is no one of them, whatever its date, which does not suffer greatly by contrast with "The Portrait" or even with "Roderick Hudson," in point of technique. Everywhere in these experiments triumphs the bald and direct manner of narration, to the great distress of any reader who has learned from James the pleasure of making things out for himself from the data furnished. Such a reader is not flattered to be informed in the first chapter of "The Europeans" that when Madame Münster came to Boston it was to seek her fortune; and he is likely to be bored with the preliminary assurances in regard to Doctor Sloper in "Washington Square" that he was very witty and thoroughly honest, not to speak of what further is vouchsafed in regard to the person and character of the late Mrs. Sloper. But it is in "The Bostonians" that the reader is called upon for the greatest display of patience. For example, he is invited to make the acquaintance of Miss Birdseye. Miss Birdseye is an estimable woman, and her appearance and movements are described with some suggestion of the humor of Dickens where he introduces us to the lady so deeply interested in Borrioboola-Gha. But we cannot imagine Dickens so far forgetting the showman's art as to let us know, of anyone, that she was "a confused, entangled, inconsequent, discursive old woman, whose charity began at home and ended nowhere, whose credulity kept pace with it, and who knew less about her fellow-creatures, if possible, after fifty years of humanitary zeal, than on the day she had gone into the field to testify against the iniquity of most arrangements."[1]

Of the four stories in this group, all but one are laid entirely in America; and in that one, all the main characters are American tourists whose contact with the old

[1] P. 27.

world is of the most superficial sort. I will leave it to the reader to draw a connection between these facts and the other circumstance that, in all of these novels, the people are rather dull and commonplace on the whole. This was not from any unpatriotic intention on the part of the author. In several cases, like those of Robert Acton in "The Europeans" and Angela Vivian in "Confidence," he wished us to think of his creature as clever and interesting. And we know that he regarded the Doctor in "Washington Square" as "very witty." Only he failed to provide for these characters substantial enough materials for them to exercise their wits upon. There is no "idea" in any of these stories, with one possible exception. There is nothing in the situation worthy of the fine interpretation or subtle strategy which these characters are prepared to devote to it. Robert Acton has simply to make out, as we are told in so many words, whether the Baroness is a liar. Doctor Sloper has no more delicate task than that of bullying his daughter. Under these circumstances it is no wonder that the author is constantly moving his post of observation as if the impressions of the several characters were all of equal importance. But it follows from this want of steadiness in the point of view that there is no growth of interest as the story goes on. In every case the interest flags toward the middle; and only in "Washington Square" does the story come out strong and effective at the end.

### (a)  *Confidence, The Bostonians, The Europeans*

Least successful of all these stories is "Confidence." This work saw the light almost at the same time as "The Portrait," but no one will quarrel with Mr. James over his failure to preserve it. It is a mild and rather flavorless tale of misunderstandings between young lovers. Bernard Longueville, having been set by a friend the task of reporting on the character of Angela Vivian, upon whom his friend has sentimental designs, mistakes for coquetry what is really a modest woman's inclination to himself. His friend marries another shallower girl; and when later Bernard discovers his own love for Angela, he feels bound to disguise it. The story is largely worked up out of the ensuing conflict between love and honor, and has about as much relation to real life as those romantic conflicts recorded in old French plays and novels. The strength and quality of the sentiment, as well as the character of the complications, suggest the light comedies of Marivaux, although it must be confessed there is little suggestion of the delicate grace and ingenuity of the French comedy. The dialogue is often juvenile in effect, and well adapted to the taste of very young readers . . . in the years 1879 and '80!

Much more serious, as well as more pretentious, work is that in "The Bostonians," a contemporary of "The Princess Casamassima." But again Mr. James must be applauded for his adverse judgment upon this novel. This story might he said to have a theme. It seems to have been meant for an ironical picture, at the same time, of feminism and of the Boston temper of mind. Earnest-minded Beacon Street is typified by Olive Chancellor, of the high-strung nerves, whose imagination is all taken up with the immemorial sufferings and wrongs of women. Boston as the begetter of fads and freaks is represented, among others, by the humanitarian Miss Birdseye, the professional Doctor Prance (of the same sex), the spiritualist Tarrants. The antithesis to the Boston temper is furnished by Basil Ransome, the Mississippi cousin of Olive,—anti-feminist and champion of nature and common sense. The bone of contention between the two parties is Verena Tarrant, *ingénue* and "inspirational" speaker on the wrongs and the merits of women. In spite of the atmosphere of charlatanry in which she has been bred, she is a girl of simple, sincere nature, well worthy of the devotion of Olive and Basil. Olive longs with all her heart to dedicate Verena to the cause, and to prevent the catastrophe of love and marriage; whereas Basil sees in her only the possibilities for personal and domestic happiness. Basil wins out; and in his triumph, I suppose, we are shown the triumph of common sense, or of natural law.

The demonstration is not very convincing. And the process is often dull.

The first part of the story is fairly interesting, though decidedly crude in comparison with the better work of James. Satire is not his forte, nor humorous portraiture of the Dickens order. The account of the South Boston conventicle is full and conscientious, but rather heavy. The same may be said of several descriptions in the course of the book, in which the disciple of Balzac undertakes to render in some detail the effect of American architecture and urban vistas, giving "a collective impression of boards and tin and frozen earth, sheds and rotting piles . . . loose fences, vacant lots, mounds of refuse."[2]

After the satirical and expository part begins the story proper. It is not very exciting, consisting largely in a perfunctory complication by means of clandestine meetings, rival lovers, scheming widows. Still less interesting is the concluding third of the book, in which we are

[2] Pp. 174-175.

simply waiting for a definite announcement of the outcome. We cannot be greatly in doubt as to what the
outcome is going to be. There are no perplexities of
psychology or situation to be resolved. The delay is occasioned only, it seems, by the author's feeling that the
story should be prolonged on general principles, or—to
do him better justice—by a feeling on his part that he
must give us somehow a due sense of the lapse of time.
The concluding scene at the Music Hall is exciting enough
in conception, and might have been melodramatic in effect
if James had been capable of letting himself go. But that
is not conceivable; and a potentially melodramatic conclusion does not drown the memory of a story dragged
out to a tiresome length.

Much more entertaining is "The Europeans," which
makes no pretensions to a substantial treatment of its
subject. There are in this book several scenes of deli-
cious light comedy, arising from the opposing points of
view of the visitors and their American kin. The comedy
centers in the seventh chapter, in which the somewhat
light-minded young painter, Felix, exchanges views with
his grave and conscientious uncle, while the latter is sitting reluctantly for his portrait. Most amusing is the
perplexity of Felix over the relations of his cousin, young
Clifford, and Lizzie Acton. Clifford, it will be recalled,
had been suspended from Harvard College for undue
indulgence in liquor. He is presumably a "dangerous"
young man. And Felix cannot understand how he can
be allowed such intimacy with the *jeune fille* unless they
are engaged. He is obviously Lizzie's beau, and Felix
is unwilling to assume the existence of anything so im-
proper as a "clandestine engagement." The worldly
young man might be supposed to be gently lecturing his

senior on the proprieties of the situation. The comedy reaches its height when Felix innocently proposes that Clifford be put under the civilizing influence of his sister, Madame Münster. Mr. Wentworth is greatly puzzled and embarrassed by this suggestion, as he takes it, that his son shall make love to a married woman—even though her marriage may be only "morganatic"! "Ah," said Felix, smiling, "of course she can't marry him. But she will do what she can." "Doubtless he supposes," he said to himself after this conversation, "that I desire, out of fraternal benevolence, to procure for Eugenia the amusement of a flirtation—or, as he probably calls it, an intrigue —with the too susceptible Clifford. It must be admitted —and I have noticed it before—that nothing exceeds the license occasionally taken by the imagination of very rigid people."[3]

James is quite happy throughout in his way of hitting off the rigidities of these people. And he succeeds in enlisting our sympathies in the effort of Gertrude Wentworth to throw off the burden of an over-serious view of life. There is here a pleasing study for the social contrast suggested by the title. But there is little more than this. Life is touched only in those tentative preliminary stages where its problems do not become pressing. A typical James situation would arise only after the marriage and migration of Gertrude, when her aspiration towards happiness and gayety might be brought to the test of experience. So that, while these pages undoubtedly contain much that is worth attention, we shall probably agree with the author that the novel as a whole is scarcely worth the double star signified by admittance to the New York edition.

[3] P. 149.

## (b) *Washington Square*

The one instance in which we feel bound to demur from the author's verdict is "Washington Square." And this is the one case in which we have to distinguish sharply between the distinctive and the successful. "Washington Square" is anything but a typical work of James. While we recognize the flavor of his writing in individual passages, the technique on the whole is much more suggestive of Mr. Howells than of the author of "The Portrait" and "The Ambassadors." There is scarcely one of the articles in our definition of the James method which could here be applied without great modification. "Washington Square" is a very simple account of the love affair of a very simple woman. It is indeed an essential factor in the story of Catherine Sloper that she had an exceptionally dull mind and a most limited imagination; and one realizes at once how incompatible that is with the kind of story-telling proper to the case of Hyacinth Robinson or Fleda Vetch. Catherine is anything but lacking in character and sensibility; but she has no active mental reaction to her situation. Her strength is of the passive order,—a strength of resistance, a capacity for suffering and silence. And it is no small credit to the creator of Nanda Brookenham that he has resisted all temptation to state the facts of Catherine's story in any but the plainest of terms. Everything is as simple, as bald if you like, as Catherine's own statement to her lover on his return to her after many years. "You treated me badly," said Catherine.

Catherine is in the beginning a very young girl, utterly without social practice or competence; and the reader is at first impressed with the thinness, almost the insipidity, of the record of her reactions,—her agitation on being introduced to the handsome young man, her naïve affirmation as to his tremendous refinement, her awkward and unnecessary false declaration to her father that she doesn't know the name of the person in question. We are perhaps at first a little impatient. We feel cheated at being paid in coin of such juvenile currency. Before we have proceeded very far, however, we realize that there is more than the usual measure of humanity in the baldnesses and embarrassments of Catherine Sloper. Long before the conclusion lends its sculpturesque roundness and "plasticity" to her figure, we have become conscious of something as peculiar and as piquant about this personality as the citrus flavor in orange or grapefruit. Such a piquancy seasons in particular the awkward interviews of Catherine with her formidable father,—that, for example, in which he asks her ironically whether Morris has proposed to her today.

This was just what she had been afraid he would say; and yet she had no answer ready. Of course she would have liked to take it as a joke—as her father must have meant it; and yet she would have liked also, in denying it, to be a little positive, a little sharp, so that he would perhaps not ask the question again. She didn't like it— it made her unhappy. But Catherine could never be sharp; and for a moment she only stood, with her hand on the door-knob, looking at her satiric parent, and giving a little laugh.

"Decidedly," said the Doctor to himself, "my daughter is not brilliant!"

But he had no sooner made this reflection than Catherine found something; she had decided, on the whole, to take the thing as a joke.

"Perhaps he will do it the next time," she exclaimed, with a repetition of her laugh; and she quickly got out of the room.[4]

[4] Pp. 46-47.

If we are in any doubt as to the exquisite humor and pathos of this passage, our doubt is dispelled by the simple beauty of the pictures with which the story closes. Catherine's lover has proved the mercenary character of his feeling by his retirement in the face òf her father's opposition. She has no illusions with regard to him; but she has the integrity of her own sentiment, and she steadfastly declines all opportunities of consoling herself for her great disappointment. "From her own point of view the facts of her career were that Morris Townsend had trifled with her affection, and that her father had broken its spring. Nothing could ever alter these facts; they were always there, like her name, her age, her plain face. . . . There was something dead in her life, and her duty was to try to fill the void."[5] And so we trace the course of her growth into a quaint and likable "maiden-aunt to the younger portion of society." It is chiefly in her quiet domestic setting that we see her in the end,— seated night after night with her Aunt Lavinia in the Washington Square parlor, the windows open to the balcony, and the lamps lighted or dark according to the state of the mercury. It is here that she had the last meeting with her returned lover, when she declined to see him any more since there was "no propriety in it— no reason for it." It was here that, after his departure, "picking up her morsel of fancy-work, she . . . seated herself with it again—for life, as it were."

By the time we reach this point, the character of Catherine has taken on substance out of all proportion to the length of the narrative. And this is true to a less degree of Washington Square itself. Of all the novels in which James endeavors to fix some aspect of "the American

[5] P. 244.

scene," this is the only one in which he approaches success. And here the success derives not from any completeness or intensity in the representation, but from a certain quiet persuasiveness about the tone of the picture. Perhaps this is largely due to the fond piety of the references to a neighborhood so familiar to the author's childhood, a piety expressed in passages suggesting the manner of earlier Victorian romancers or of Georgian essayists.

I know not whether it is owing to the tenderness of early associations, but this portion of New York appears to many persons the most delectable. It has a kind of established repose which is not of frequent occurrence in other quarters of the long, shrill city; it has a riper, richer, more honorable look than any of the upper ramifications of the great longitudinal thoroughfare— the look of having had something of a social history. It was here, as you might have been informed on good authority, that you had come into a world which appeared to offer a variety of sources of interest; it was here that your grandmother lived, in venerable solitude, and dispensed a hospitality which commended itself alike to the infant imagination and the infant palate; it was here that you took your first walks abroad, following the nursery-maid with unequal step, and sniffing the strange odor of the ailanthus trees which at that time formed the principal umbrage of the Square, and diffused an aroma that you were not yet critical enough to dislike as it deserved; it was here, finally, that your first school, kept by a broad-bosomed, broad-based old lady with a ferule, who was always having tea in a blue cup, with a saucer that didn't match, enlarged the circle both of your observations and your sensations. It was here, at any rate, that my heroine spent many years of her life; which is my excuse for this topographical parenthesis.[6]

[6] Pp. 23-24.

There will be found readers to prefer this passage of reminiscent sentiment to the more involved and elaborate disquisitions of "A Small Boy and Others." Like the rest of the novel, it has escaped that revision which was the price exacted for admission to the canon. The whole narrative wears the same old-fashioned garb in which it first appeared. And it is for once a piece of good luck not to have had the language brought up to date. There is a certain quaintness of formality about the expression that is entirely in keeping with the general tone of the book. Anyone reading it in the edition of 1881, published by Harpers, and illustrated by George Du Maurier, will take pleasure in the suitability of the drawings to the style of the text. There is a distinction, as well as the quaintness, about them both, which does justice to the subject. I cannot believe that the lovers of James will allow this story to sink into the oblivion to which the author consigned it. It is anything but a good example of the method which he later made so much his own. But it is a charming memento of a phase through which he passed on the way to his more distinctive performance.

## IV

## ACHIEVEMENT: THE SPOILS OF POYNTON

The first absolutely pure example of the James method was "The Spoils of Poynton," published in 1896. This book has all the "marks." And as no novel before it had shown so many of the distinctive traits in such perfection, in none had they been blent so closely, so as to work together and reinforce one another. Nowhere in his earlier writing does the "figure in the carpet" come out so distinct, simple and entire. The "idea" stands without rival as a means of bringing out the varying qualities of subjective experience. In showing the attitudes of different people towards precious "Things," the gamut is run through all degrees from mere undiscerning vulgarity up to the finest spiritual insight. The idea is made admirably concrete, converted beautifully into "picture," in the particular question of the "Spoils," which make here the touchstone of character. But if the central subject of the picture is Poynton and the Spoils, the author realized that he must have for interpreter some being more conscious and articulate; and he chose for this the person most capable of appreciating the idea. Never before had he managed so happily this difficult business; never before had he kept so strictly within the limits of the chosen consciousness. But it is perhaps most of all in the dialogue, linked together by the unfailing participation of Fleda, that one feels the break with the earlier manner: a dialogue so little discursive, confining itself so strictly to the matter in hand, and in regard to this so tirelessly inquisitive, so finespun and close-wrought.

The great point is that, for the first time in a story of this length, James was confining himself rigorously to the matter in hand, content to forego all other sources of entertainment, determined to seek all variety within the theme itself.  For the first time he was breaking completely with the tradition of the English novel, which had been made to relate so much that was irrelevant, to provide so copious and miscellaneous a banquet.

The question naturally arises as to how he came at this particular moment to make the plunge, as to why maturity of method appears so suddenly with "The Spoils of Poynton."  In considering this question we have to take into account the fact that James was a writer of short stories as well as of novels.  Indeed, at the time when he wrote "Poynton," he had produced nothing but short stories for more than half a dozen years.°  "Poynton" is itself, for that matter, a very short novel.  It is not twice as long as "The Turn of the Screw."  It is only about half the length of "Roderick Hudson" and one-third that of "The Tragic Muse."

Now it is obvious that the short story is nothing without the benefit of concentration and elimination.  There is no room for copiousness and variety.  There is no room for a shifting point of view, for discursive dialogue, for the elaboration of anything but the matter in hand. And so it is natural that James should have arrived first in the short story at the economy and intensiveness of treatment which became his ideals for the novel as well. This was actually the case; and short stories like "The Altar of the the Dead" (1895), "The Pupil" and "The Chaperon" (both 1891), we may regard in the light of

°See *Supplementary Notes* 1954, page 289

exercises in preparation for "The Awkward Age" and "The Golden Bowl."

All the more so as the short stories of James, like his novels, even more than the earlier novels, tend to subordinate narrative proper to human portraiture. As he puts it himself in one of his prefaces, "A short story, to my sense and as the term is used in magazines, has to choose between being either an anecdote or a picture and can play its part strictly according to its kind. I rejoice in the anecdote, but I revel in the picture." And then he goes on to explain the points of a good picture in terms strongly suggesting the technique of the later novels, dwelling on that "true grave close consistency in which parts hang together even as the interweavings of a tapestry."[1] While the earlier novels tend likewise to show as pictures, it is pictures with a larger, looser composition than the short story can ever allow itself.

If then we suppose that the author of "Poynton" began with the intention of writing a short story, and that it simply expanded beyond the compass of that form, we understand how he first came to realize fully in the longer form the "true grave close consistency" natural to the briefer. And this supposition we find confirmed when we turn to the preface and read that "Poynton" was intended to complete a trio of short stories of which two members had already appeared in the "Atlantic." Mr. James is rather amusing in his account of the "editorial ruefulness" over the embarrassing amplitude taken on by a story confidently expected to be short.[2] This subject simply proved to be larger than it first appeared. It declined to be treated as a hint, an aspect, an episode. However limited the number of characters, it insisted on being

[1] Vol. X, p. xxiv.
[2] Id., p. x.

treated as the record of a life, the history of a soul.  It
was no doubt the mental capacity of Fleda Vetch that was
responsible for this expansion.  Without her interpretation the circumstances might have done well for a short
story; without this, the thing would be an anecdote.  But
without her interpretation we can hardly conceive it as
a James story of any length.

If it was by accident, as it were, that James came to
extend to the novel certain articles of method already
applied in the short story, there is little doubt that he
realized at once what had happened and how much it
made for his "game."  It is certain that he never yielded
an inch of the ground he had gained.[8]  In the following
years the same method was applied in the still longer
stories of "What Maisie Knew" and "The Awkward
Age," and so without a break in the full-length two-vol-
ume novels of his final period.  And thus it was the short
story helped him to full possession and mastery of his
method in the novel.

[8] We have to make an exception of "The Other House," written immediately after "Poynton" in 1896.  This, as we have seen
in the chapter on "Drama," is a very special case.  James refers
slightingly to it in the preface to Vol. X, p. xi, giving the impression that it was written hurriedly and without enthusiasm.

## V

### TECHNICAL EXERCISES

So far from being unaware of what he had done in "The Spoils of Poynton," one may observe in James, in the half dozen years that followed, a rather acute consciousness of his momentous discovery. He shows a disposition to make the most of it, to push to its furthest limits the technique he had acquired by dint of such long-continued practice and exploration. The novels of this period, taken as a whole, give the impression of being, to a considerable extent, technical exercises. They are not experiments towards a method, like the works discussed in Chapter III, like, for that matter, all the novels turned out before "Poynton." The several points of the method are now well understood and established as definite rules of procedure. These books, written at the height of the author's self-consciousness, are rather *experiments with* a method. He wants to put it through its paces, to draw out all its latent possibilities, to make application of it in ways the most curious and *recherché*. It is accordingly not surprising that he impresses one as taken up with his technique almost more than with his subject, and that some at least of the novels of this period strike the reader—that one of them apparently struck James himself—as technical *excesses*.

The works in question are "What Maisie Knew," "The Awkward Age" and "The Sacred Fount," the first making its appearance in 1897, the last in 1901. In connection with "The Awkward Age," we can most conveniently discuss "The Outcry," the last of all the novels of James,[1] much later in date but showing a second application of the same technical device.

### (a)   *What Maisie Knew*

"What Maisie Knew" is most remarkable technically, as we have seen, for the consistency with which the point of view is limited to the consciousness of a young girl without preventing us from following a story full of incident and human nature far beyond the comprehension of a child.   There is no doubt of the success with which James carries out the difficult program he sets himself in this book.   We have no trouble following the story of Maisie's perverse parents and her misguided step-parents.   We never call in question the truth of Maisie's experience, either as to the facts or as to her rather uncanny understanding of them.   The whole situation is reproduced by the author's imagination with a fidelity to life and a vividness of realization possible only to high poetic genius.

And yet we cannot feel that this is one of the most *important* humanly of the novels of James.   And when we seek for the grounds of this persuasion, we find them in the very limitations entailed by this technically so fascinating program.   The choice of Maisie for the "register" of these occurrences makes impossible the rendering of their real significance,—their significance either for the grown-up persons taking part, or their significance (if this might be distinguished from the other) for an author more coolly aware of the broad

---

[1] That is, the last complete novel, and the last to be published during his lifetime.

moral bearings of what is done and suffered. Only in the concluding scenes do we have any approach to an adequately interpretative record of events as they affect the principal—the grown-up—participants. And do we, on the other hand, have the story of Maisie herself? Maisie herself has really no story. She is hardly more than an observer eagerly following from her side-box the enthralling spectacle of the stage. And while, like any precocious child, she takes in much more of the spectacle than her elders had reckoned on, she really does not understand what she sees, in at all the sense in which it is meant by the grown-ups. She takes great pride in letting it be seen how much she "knows," and Mrs. Wix and Sir Claude are actually "taken in" by what seems to be her eventual development of a "moral sense" like their own. But *we* are not taken in: we realize that, so far as the moral sense they have in mind is concerned, she has not the elementary knowledge on which it must be grounded; and if she says the right words at the right time, that is because she is the cleverest of little parrots, much concerned to maintain her professional reputation for knowingness. Her mental process, thanks to the author's conscientious regard for truth, remains that of a child; and for that very reason the book cannot carry the weight carried by those in which we are invited to follow the mental process of a Fleda Vetch or an Isabel Archer. So that we have adequately rendered in "Maisie" neither a story nor a serious subjective experience.

What is rendered, and with the surest art, is always the irony and the pathos of Maisie's connection with the ugly circumstances of the history. Maisie's extreme knowingness is never so great as to prevent her from passing comments that show her profound ignorance

of the troublesome ways of sex and of the rules laid
down by grown-ups for the better regulation of the game.
Nothing is more touching than her eagerness to claim
responsibility for the vulgar relation of her step-parents.
She is always reminding Sir Claude and Mrs. Beale that
it was Maisie who brought them together.[2]  By this means
she is underlining for the author the inherent irony of
the whole situation, and adding one more irony, that of
her own naïve joy in the loves of the two step-parents
for whom she has so much affection.  The very summit
of heaped-up ironies is reached in the attempt of the
childish Mrs. Wix to inoculate the poor little creature
with a "moral sense."  Like everybody else, she wishes
Maisie to know as little as possible of men and women
and the social laws governing their relations, and at the
same time expects her instinctively to condemn any in-
fringement of the said conventions.  What renders most
amusing the long arguments with Mrs. Wix as to the
"freedom" of Sir Claude and Mrs. Beale to live together
is Maisie's anxiety not to appear "simple."[3]  As for
pathos, everything conspires to make touching the situation of little orphaned, bewildered Maisie, called upon
so early, and with such entire want of proper instruction,
to grapple with problems much too hard even for her
elders.  She cannot understand why Mrs. Beale must be
branded as bad.  "She's beautiful and I love her!  I
love her and she's beautiful!"  Mrs. Wix cannot make
her see how the relation is made more vulgar when one
of the persons involved gives money to the other.  That
would seem to her to indicate simply the generosity of
the one who pays.  And then if Sir Claude does pay

[2] See, for example, p. 64 (Vol. XI).
[3] P. 287.

Mrs. Beale as the Countess pays her father, isn't it equally true that Mrs. Wix herself receives her wages from Sir Claude?

"Then doesn't he pay *you* too?" her unhappy charge demanded. At this she bounded in her place. "Oh you incredible little waif!" She brought it out with a wail of violence; after which, with another convulsion, she marched straight away.

Maisie dropped back on the bench and burst into sobs.[4]

If we need any further assurance that Maisie is actually a little girl it is in the proof she offers, the very next day, of her rightness of feeling. If she thought Mrs. Beale was unkind to Sir Claude, she could think of one thing she would do in the premises. She'd *kill* her, says Maisie. "That at least, she hoped, would guarantee her moral sense."[5]

Apart from this tangled web of perplexities, the story of Maisie is crowded with appeal the most simply human. Maisie is a little girl no less charming than she is real, beautiful in the desperation with which her affection clings to a father and mother whom everybody agrees to condemn, as well as in her loyalty to those who have shown themselves more worthy of her love. It is clear that the author has a regular *tendre* for this daughter of his fancy. It is a feeling strong enough to shake him out of his editorial reserve for once and bring him right up with the first person singular and the sign of exclamation. "Oh, decidedly," he exclaims at a certain juncture, "I shall never get you to believe the number of things she

[4] P. 277.
[5] P. 288.

saw and the number of secrets she discovered!"[6]    James
has so thoroughly identified himself with the little lady—
for she is a lady!—that he reproduces for us the very
air of wonder with which all persons and things are
invested by the large round eyes of childhood.    We
lose with him and Maisie the sense of proportion that
for grown people makes distinction between the big and
the little, and everything seen is seen in all the importance
and intensity, all the thrilling immediacy, of a child's
vision.    It would take us much too far if I should yield
to my desire to review the good things in the history of
Maisie.    I must be content to remind the reader of but
one occasion, that on which she and Sir Claude were taking tea and buns at "a place in Baker Street," when,
at the time of reckoning, Sir Claude too thoughtlessly
assumed, and aloud so as to be overheard by the waitress,
that Maisie had been capable of consuming no less than
five buns.    Sir Claude was evidently unaware of the
proprieties in these things, but Maisie was only too
acutely aware of them.    " 'How *can* you?' Maisie demanded, crimson under the eye of the young woman who
had stepped to their board. 'I've had three.' "[7]

But however many good things there may be in
"Maisie," and however true to life, the leading impression made by the book is still that of the author's cleverness in the working out of his scheme.    Every time
Maisie comes up with another of her blessed naïve remarks, every time her inevitable incredible simplicity sets
off like red fire the irony of the situation in its newest
turn, we feel—well, we *feel* like spectators present at the
setting off of some ingenious *feu d'artifice*.

[6] P. 205.
[7] P. 116.

## (b) *The Awkward Age*

Still more formidable an undertaking, technically, was "The Awkward Age,"—a kind of triple exercise, one gathers, in idea, dialogue and point of view. The theme of the book was "the difference made in certain friendly houses and for certain flourishing mothers by the . . . coming to the forefront of some vague slip of a daughter,"[8] the difference, namely, in the character of the fireside talk, which had been more free in its range than is compatible with the presence of the *jeune fille*. Of course this abstract theme must be dramatized; there must be characters, a plot, and above all dialogue. Mr. James explains the design upon which he worked in this matter, taking for his model the clever dialogues of "Gyp," reducing explanations to the minimum, and undertaking to produce a novel nearly as objective as a play. This proved to be something of a mistake. The American author overlooked the enormous difference between his material and that of his French model, who is a mere witty parrot of external "manners." These are indeed capable of being rendered in simple dialogue; which is obviously not true of the intricate human relations involved in a story like "The Awkward Age."

We have glanced in an earlier chapter at the objectivity of view here cultivated by James. He had confined himself, for the fun of it, to the "scene" pure and simple. He would never undertake to give us any information even as to the present scene other than what the participants shared or what might have been gathered by a "supposititious spectator," "an observer disposed to inter-

pret the scene."[9]  If he has frequent resort to such a
spectator, by this very confession of weakness, as he
might put it, he is calling attention to the rigor of his
self-restraint.  The point is that, while he is willing to
let us know everything that actually becomes apparent
during a particular scene, he is steadfastly refusing to
"go behind" the appearances.  His self-denial is sometimes set in higher relief by his putting his reading of
appearances in the interrogative form, as not wishing to
take responsibility for anything beyond the scope of the
eyes.  "Mr. Longdon looked the noble lady . . . straight
in the face, and who can tell whether or no she acutely
guessed from his expression that he recognised this particular junction as written on the page of his doom?"[10]

That these devices are deliberate and that the author
takes pride in the technical ingenuity thus displayed is
evident at every turn.  It will suffice to repeat his boast
on one occasion—for it amounts to a boast—that "as Mr.
Van himself couldn't have expressed at any subsequent
time to any interested friend the particular effect upon
him of the tone of these words his chronicler takes
advantage of the fact not to pretend to a greater intelligence—to limit himself on the contrary to the simple
statement that they produced in Mr. Van's cheek a flush
just discernible."[11]

As a matter of fact, the narrative, as James intended,
is pretty closely confined to what is said, and indications
of the manner in which remarks are delivered and
received are not so much more frequent than in the

[9] Pp. 323 and 130, respectively.  The word spectator recurs on
pp. 149, 215, 229, 317, 319, 400, 424, 449; the word observer, or
something to the same effect, on 142, 238, 269, 310, 319, 344.
[10] P. 234.
[11] Pp. 211-212.

characteristic play of the present time. Among the many other suggestions of dramatic technique is the care with which the author designates the positions of his actors on the stage. This is most called for of course in scenes taking in a considerable number of characters, like the critical scene at Mrs. Grendon's. There we read at one point that "the new recruits to the circle, Tishy and Nanda and Mr. Cashmore, Lady Fanny and Harold . . . ended by enlarging it, with mutual accommodation and aid, to a pleasant talkative ring. . . . Tishy was nearest Mr. Longdon, and Nanda, still flanked by Mr. Cashmore, between that gentleman and his wife, who had Harold on her other side. Edward Brookenham was neighboured by his son and by Vanderbank. . . ."[12]

By such means James has provided well for the objectivity, the plastic realism of the scene. But anyone familiar with the kind of ideas which it is his wont to convey, with the intense *subjectivity* of his present theme, will realize the enormous effrontery of his undertaking to convey it in a vehicle so limited. All the more so as James did not call to his help certain of the devices still open to him, such as that of the confidante. There is here no Maria Gostrey, no Mrs. Assingham, to add her outside interpretation of the situation to that vouchsafed in the talk of the characters most involved. It is true that the later scenes, in the usual manner of James, throw light at last upon the earlier ones. But it is a long wait from the sixth book to the ninth—so long one must stay for an explanation of the policy, and so of the character, of Mrs. Brook.

We are dealing here with people whose motives are, if possible, still further removed from the ordinary

[12] Pp. 423-424.

than is usual in James, and who are at any rate still more sensitive than usual to the imputation of vulgarity. There is one anxious moment in which Mrs. Brook, whose own temptation is the strongest of any of them, exclaims to Vanderbank, "Let us not, for God's sake, be vulgar—we haven't yet, bad as it is, come to *that*."[13] And there are perhaps a dozen places in which the various members of her circle show their horror of this contingency.[14] Vanderbank assures her that she is quite free from vulgarity. "Oh, I know that there are things you don't put to me!" If not putting things to one another is what constitutes refinement, it is obvious how little light there can be for the reader in the talk of people who are never vulgar. If it were not for the occasional running amuck of the Duchess—a foreign Duchess, *bien entendu*—we should be left indeed in darkness.

But not merely are the motives of a strangeness, and strangely veiled by the requirements of good taste, they are, when we take into account the whole story, combined in a pattern whose complexity contributes greatly to our bewilderment. It is not only Mrs. Brook who can boast a strategy, in her admirable cause of keeping together her "saloon," maintaining her "intellectual habits," and at the same time providing for her difficult daughter and so confounding the theories of the Duchess. It turns out the difficult daughter has a strategy, if you please, as fine and as complicated as her mother's and not overlooking the disposition of her mother, either, after she has duly disposed of Mitchy and Aggie, of the Grendons and the Cashmores, and of Mr. Longdon. It is like one

[13] P. 446.
[14] For example, pp. 323, 329, 339, 430, 460.

of·those games with blocks so appealing to youngsters, in which, piece by piece, one structure is taken down and a new structure set up accounting exactly for every block taken from the first. If Nanda takes Mitchy from her mother's coterie, she makes it up by restoring "Aggie," who is a still better subject for her mother's genius. If she deprives Mitchy of the hope of having herself for wife, she makes it up to him by establishing herself in the still more interesting relation of counsellor and friend. If she proves totally unable to sustain comparison with her admired grandmother, that turns out to be the very tie that attaches most closely to her the grandmother's worshipper and his fortune. And it is beautiful to see how in these evolutions, and in others too numerous to mention, Nanda and her mother seem to work together, without communication, to an end equally satisfactory to both. It is true that Nanda cannot have the man she loves. But that somehow seems to have been ruled out from the start; Nanda declares herself to be one of those strange creatures who "positively *like* to love in vain."[15] The great thing appears to be, not to have everyone happy—that is perhaps too absurdly vulgar—but to have every one "squared."[16] But it might give an idea rather of simplicity than of complexity if I dwelt too heavily upon this reversed pattern of the plot and the relations of Nanda and Mrs. Brook. These are great strategists; but the reader has to reckon also with the Duchess, and with the unknown quantities represented by Mitchy and Vanderbank and Mr. Longdon.

And the worst of it is that, among all these competitors, the reader is at a loss to know where to invest his sympa-

[15] P. 359.
[16] For example, pp. 523, 525.

thies.  This is an almost fatal oversight in a novel, not to give the reader better direction.  It arises here, I think, from the author's preoccupation with technique.  He is so largely absorbed in his game of illuminating that central idea by means of those "lamps" that form a ring about it.[17]  How is he to show us which of these lamps to take for our guiding star?  He has cut himself off from his usual means of indicating his bias by the choice of a personal point of view.  As a matter of fact, the work outgrew his original intention, as he tells in the preface.  From a series of illustrative dialogues, it grew into a story.  But the author seems not sufficiently to have realized this while the story was in progress.  The subject was being treated minutely and to his satisfaction; and the subject did not require the particular salience of one or a small number of characters.  But the *story* does require the dominance of special characters who engage our interest.  And in "The Awkward Age" the story hardly gets itself started in this sense before the seventh book.  Not till then are we confident that the heroine is Nanda Brookenham.  And even then she does not continue steadily to hold the center of the stage.  And so the story forfeits that intensity of appeal which goes with our special concern for some particular person or group.  It fails to take hold of us emotionally.  We are deeply interested through our intelligence, our curiosity.  But we do not really take stock in these people as human beings laboring under the strain of life.  We are not made to feel how much they *care*.  We are more impressed with their self-consciousness,—the pride they take in being "wonderful."

Mr. James was very well satisfied, on review, with

[17] See chapter on "Idea."

his work in this book,—with its "exemplary closeness," with "the quantity of meaning and the number of intentions, the extent of *ground for interest,* as I may call it, that I have succeeded in working scenically, yet without loss of sharpness, clearness or 'atmosphere,' into each of my illuminating Occasions."[18] And he was quite right. There is perhaps no novel that offers greater store of satisfactions to any reader who will dig for them. But we cannot regard any novel as supremely good in which one has to dig so for what one gets, and where one's satisfactions are so often in the recognition of the author's cleverness. James takes pride in the fact that one cannot distinguish, in this book, form and substance: it is impossible to say "where one of these elements ends and the other begins."[19] This may be so: but with the reader, at any rate, the impression that remains is very largely that of form; not form without substance, but form dominating or even bullying its inseparable twin.

### (c)  *The Outcry*

It is interesting to note that once again before he laid down his pen James tried his hand at a novel written on the lines of a play.[p] The dramatic form is even more marked in "The Outcry" than in "The Awkward Age." The three parts correspond exactly to the three acts of a modern play. Each part rises invariably to a good theatrical climax for the curtain. The scenes, or numbered sections, are distinguished by a mere variation of *dramatis personæ* within an identical setting, certain characters giving place to others on a stage that is never left vacant. And objectivity of treatment is as carefully

[18] P. xxii.
[19] P. xxii.
[p] See *Supplementary Notes* 1954, page 289

maintained as in "The Awkward Age," and by the same devices. In this case, however, the dramatic treatment is perfectly suited to the subject-matter, and whether as novel or play, the story is "got across" with entire success. In each act there is something at issue sufficiently objective and material for easy presentation on the stage. In both the first two, indeed, the climax consists in nothing less stagey than a quarrel between the heroine and her father—in one case, her suitor too—in which she flings defiance at her formidable parent. There is, to be sure, an interesting and characteristic theme, relating to the honorable obligation of noble families who possess great art treasures not to let them be lost to their country. And the changes are rung in a manner worthy of James on the freakish varieties assumed by the sense of honor. But there is nothing about the idea requiring development; there is no occasion for a close following of the mental evolutions of the heroine. As a consequence, the story is at once much more successful and much less important than "The Awkward Age." And while it is a book that would easily get itself readers among the less discerning, its interest for students and devotees of James is almost wholly technical.

### (d)  *The Sacred Fount*

We cannot be sure what disposition Mr. James would have made of "The Outcry" had it been in print at the time he brought his stories together. "The Sacred Fount" we know he rejected, and so presumably branded as not one of his first-class productions. It seems not unlikely that this judgment was based on some feeling that the book was rather too simply what I have called a technical exercise. It is much more simply and obviously that than any of the other novels I have discussed.

It is an extremely interesting idea from which he takes his start, and one that no doubt corresponds to something profoundly true in human nature,—the idea that, between man and woman, one party to the relation is liable to pay for the happiness, the vitality, the efflorescence, of the other. Every human relation, it may be, has somewhat the character of a struggle for life, in which one gains at the expense of the other. This would be a fact most rich in material for drama, for tragedy indeed; and it is strange that not more has been made of it in the type of fiction represented by the novels of James. But true and serious as was his subject-matter, James seems for once to have but superficially conceived its possibilities.

Mr. James may well have felt that he was here betrayed by that excessive love of symmetrical patterns in the disposition of his human units that is so constantly cropping out, especially in his later period. It was this same love of patterns which determined the complicated symmetries and coincidences of the plot of "Maisie"; the remarriage of both unparental parents, the love-affair between the step-parents thus introduced, the repeated infidelity of the original guardians of Maisie, leaving "free" the adoptive guardians to pursue their own relation. Maisie's passion for "squaring" everybody— that is, for disposing happily of everybody in some relation that restores the balance of love and self-respect— corresponds to the similar sense for decent equilibrium which forms the excuse of Charlotte and Amerigo in "The Golden Bowl." We have seen what a genius for such arrangements was Nanda Brookenham's. The same instinct for patterns—and for shifting patterns—is shown in the reversal of the rôles of Chad and Strether in "The Ambassadors," which is so neatly and thoroughly worked out. And other instances may occur to a reader sufficiently familiar with the stories of James.

In the case of "The Sacred Fount" it is easy to follow the process of growth of the amazing figure from the original germ-idea. We are present at a week-end party where, by assumption, all persons concerned in the psychological problem are in evidence. We have had enunciated the principle of "the sacred fount," and one instance is given us at the start, involving the persons A and B. If the principle holds for one couple, why not for another? X is to Y as A is to B. We observe a third person D who exhibits the same symptoms as B. Only, to make the pattern more interesting, D is a woman where B is a man. It is naturally a principle that works without prejudice of sex. We have then the equation

$$X : D :: A : B$$

A, B and D being known quantities, what is X? or, in this particular equation, who is X? There chance to be more than one person present who fill the conditions, or at least two opinions prevail as to which person fills them best; and a debate ensues. "I" hold a brief for C, and my perfect equation reads

$$C : D :: A : B$$

There arise several minor considerations of great fascination. We cannot go into more than one of these. It appears that B and D are involved in a special relation distinct from the main relation of each. What can it be but that of two persons suffering from the same malady—two persons equally drained of their vitality by the partner who draws life from the common waters of the sacred fount? They come together for mutual comfort. Would it not be natural, then, to look for a similar connection between A and C? The beneficiaries of the relations so damaging to B and D may be expected to make common cause for the defense and disguisement of their own position. And such an entente seems to "me" to be actually in existence. So that I have the interesting secondary equation,

$$A : C :: B : D$$

And according to my psychologic algebra, the demonstration of the second equation is a further confirmation of the first.

But I have not been allowed to carry out these demonstrations without vigorous dispute. For there has been present from the beginning a most troublesome complicating factor. One of the persons to the debate is one of the "quantities" of my equations; and this person has excellent reasons for denying the truth of my contentions as soon as she realizes where they are leading us. So that she soon begins a campaign for demolishing the facts on which I base my contentions. All the latter part of the discussion is taken up with the presentation of evidence on one side or the other for supporting the two rival hypotheses. A bewildering display of ingenuity accompanies the completion of the two perfect and corresponding structures reared by the two debaters.

Not less remarkable than the fascination of this game is its artificiality. The original idea has been entirely lost sight of save as the chess-board on which Mrs. Briss and "I" play our game. There has been no real study of the problem in human relations save from the outside, as regards its susceptibility to mathematical manipulation. Of course it is inevitable that in any dialogue of James there should be no end of light thrown on various aspects of human nature. But it must have been as clear to him as it is to his readers how totally, in this book, he failed to develop the idea of the "sacred fount."

It is no wonder that readers of "The Portrait" and "The Tragic Muse," let alone "Daisy Miller" and "The American," should have been somewhat taken aback by these exhibitions of virtuosity with which James introduced his latest phase. Many would have found fault, no doubt, even had it been "The Ambassadors" and "The Golden Bowl" instead of "The Awkward Age" and "The Sacred Fount." But their objection would then have been the result of that conservatism which demands that an artist continue to perform the tricks to which he has accustomed the public. As it is, they had some grounds for their feeling that their author was growing perverse "in his old age." And there were many who never outgrew the prejudice thus aroused, in spite of the beautiful work he was yet to offer.

## VI

## FULL PRIME

It is characteristic of James that his best work of all should have come at the end of his career. His was an art that had to be learned. It is in the first decade of the present century that we reach the period of his richest self-expression. Having mastered his technique, having done with experiments, he launches at last upon that series of novels which are but the natural and seemingly unstudied application of his method, and the best demonstration of its possibilities for art.

We need not go over again the several points and show how they are applied in these novels. What does invite us is the opportunity of remarking on the beautiful fruits of this method. It is in "The Dove," "The Ambassadors" and "The Golden Bowl" that we taste most those esthetic gratifications which only such a system can procure us. These are all structures of generous dimensions; and they are in no case overcrowded with tenants, who have thus ample room to turn around and ample leisure to make themselves at home. In other words, the process of selection and elimination makes possible the fullest and most faithful treatment of what is included. The central idea is allowed to grow as steady and unhampered as some great elm in New England fields, reaching out on all sides to the sun, and showing at last dense-foliaged and round, broad and symmetrical in its green acre. Each particular situation, or historical passage, which is deemed worthy of treatment at all, receives the same full-rounded development; each process in the consciousness of the characters, chosen for illustration or for intrinsic interest, is followed closely from step to step through all its course without abruptness, haste or violence. This smooth progress, free from jolts and jars, is a marked feature of the work of James in general, distinguishing it from the type of fiction that ministers to our love of rapid movement, variety and change. James has naturally a predilection for slow movement, inappreciable change, for neat articulation and orderly evolution. He prefers likeness to difference, the familiar to the novel, since in each case the former has actually more to yield to the understanding, is more readily assimilated and made a part of one's total impression.

The amplitude of the record gives room for the carrying out of those large operations, or manœuvres, which amount to nothing less than a revolution in someone's life. Such an operation is not an affair like going to bed or taking breakfast, and is not to be disposed of in any light and cavalier fashion. It is a matter of long preparation, of many stages both in conception and execution. It has a logic and a sequence, which have to be followed throughout. In no part of James's work are there such fine examples of these operations extensively carried out as in these three late novels.

There is, for example, that of Maggie Verver in "The Golden Bowl." The first half of that novel sets forth the circumstances by which is built up the strange and wicked balance of relations which groups together Maggie's husband and her father's wife. The second half is devoted to the long process by which Maggie, becoming aware of the situation, restores the proper and original balance, and so wins back her husband, making him hers for good. The earliest hint of any uneasiness on Maggie's part is given just before the beginning of the second part of the story in Mrs. Assingham's talk with her husband. Mrs. Assingham's understanding of the situation runs far ahead of Maggie's, and so when we come to Maggie's, we have to start further back and follow from their obscurest beginnings the double process of her growing realization and her groping strategy. In Maggie's case the realization of evil requires a large allowance of time and endless rumination before it can grow complete and assured. For it was just the trait in Maggie that she could not and would not conceive of evil that provoked the situation in which she had to deal with it. So that with her the light breaks very slowly; she will not let it come by more than gradual degrees.

And her strategy is complicated and made difficult by the character of her adversaries and allies. Amerigo and Charlotte are, like Maggie herself, persons who cannot tolerate violence and vulgarity. And the last thing she wishes is to humiliate either of them. What she wishes is to give them full opportunity to beat an honorable retreat. There can accordingly be none of those explosions that clear the air and advance matters by overleaping stages. No one gives away his hand, and in every contact through a series of weeks, each party is feeling his way with the greatest caution. It is some time before Maggie comes to understand what it is that her husband is "growing under cover of" his princely reserve. What he is growing is evidently his policy of joining forces with his wife by keeping Charlotte in the dark as to Maggie's discovery. And we all have to wait for Charlotte to see the light. It is long before she does see that the game is up and reconciles herself to the necessity for exile. It needs first those tense scenes of confrontation with Maggie, in which the latter, all generous in her position of vantage, gives her opponent no hold or opening for attack.

As for Mr. Verver, Maggie has at first no idea what he knows. Her first instinct of all is to shield him from this knowledge. His marriage was undertaken with the idea of leaving his daughter freer to enjoy her husband; and Maggie wouldn't for the world have him realize the ironic issue of this undertaking. It turns out that Mr. Verver's chief solicitude is similarly to shield Maggie from the knowledge of his suffering. And when they are both morally sure of the full enlightenment of one another, their delicacy and consideration for one another's dignity lead them to continue to the end their difficult policy of bluff.

Meantime, obscurely, under all these moves and counter-moves, is growing Amerigo's appreciation of Maggie. And this is given ample room to spread and reach the stature it shows at the final curtain.

Such a large slow evolution again is, in "The Dove," the process by which Merton Densher gives himself up to the designs of Kate upon Milly, wandering farther and farther from the straight way, until the last momentous visit to the dying woman, where comes to a head the slow spirit of rebellion against a sinister manipulation, and he takes the sharp, decisive turn back to truth and decency. We need not trace out the course of this operation nor of that other performed by Strether in "The Ambassadors." The point is that only on this method, in this kind of novel, is it possible to conceive the execution of any such broad continuous figure. It is one thing to say, of such and such a change in a character's outlook, that it came about; it is another thing to give the reader the impression of its coming about. Every movement of the plot cries out for elbow-room. Each plot as a whole is like a fleet of warships demanding large waters in which to form and reform and go through their wide-sweeping manœuvres.

It is a double undertaking. The situations must be worked out completely in relation to the idea they make palpable; and they must be completely realized in scenes felt as real and particular human experience. Here again the leisurely fulness of treatment makes for our satisfaction. The situations grow upon us. Familiarity itself takes hold of us; and we are further convinced by the many little faithful touches, which are introduced as quietly as in life itself.

We have time to get acquainted, for example, with the special predicament of Maggie Verver. We have time to sit with her before the drawing-room fire on that crucial evening when she waited there for her husband's return from Matcham. By her coming home for dinner she had intimated—oh, so gently!—that the shadow of a change had touched her spirit, and that she was turning over a new leaf in their domestic chronicle. In relations so delicately balanced as theirs, even so slight a hint was fraught with significance and peril; and we are made to feel the varying shades of trepidation with which she watches the slow hands of the clock. We share her sense of the momentous nature of the "small shades of decision" involved in her having left no message for Amerigo in Eaton Square, her having dressed for dinner on coming in. Most convincing is the touch of Maggie's anxiety over the style of her gown, and her somewhat extended reflections upon her inability really to satisfy the taste of Charlotte in these matters of dress. "Yes, it was one of the things she should go down to her grave without having known—how Charlotte, after all had been said, *really* thought her step-daughter looked under any supposedly ingenious personal experiment. She had always been lovely about the step-daughter's material braveries— had done for her the very best with them; but there had ever fitfully danced at the back of Maggie's head the suspicion that these expressions were mercies, not judgments, embodying no absolute but only a relative frankness."[1] Of course we need no reminder that this critic before whom she stands in awe is none other than the woman whom she is beginning to suspect of having appropriated the love of her husband; and we realize accordingly the high importance of these sartorial considerations.

Another such occasion, to cite an example from "The Ambassadors," is that in which Strether, in his river-side pavilion, becomes aware of the presence of Chad and Madame de Vionnet in a row-boat, and of being himself discovered by the watchful eye of Madame de Vionnet. It takes indeed but two paragraphs to give an account of the moment that follows, but there is so much excitement crowded into this one moment of hesitation and suspense and the circumstances are so vividly imagined that we realize it as a complete little drama. We see the figures clearly in their physical relation and aspect,—Madame de Vionnet with her pink parasol shifted as if to hide her face, Chad in his shirt-sleeves and with his face turned

[1] Vol. XXIV, pp. 13-14.

away, having let his paddles go on receiving the mute warning of his companion, and poor Strether staring petrified in his pavilion. And we *feel* the tense indecision of the two in the boat, the horror of the gentleman on shore. It is of course the sensations of Strether that make the scene *live*.

It was a sharp fantastic crisis that had popped up as if in a dream, and it had had only to last the few seconds to make him feel it as quite horrible. They were thus, on either side, *trying* the other side, and all for some reason that broke the stillness like some unprovoked harsh note. It seemed to him again, within the limit, that he had but one thing to do—to settle their common question by some sign of surprise and joy. He hereupon gave large play to these things, agitating his hat and his stick and loudly calling out—a demonstration that brought him relief as soon as he had seen it answered. The boat, in mid-stream, still went a little wild—which seemed natural, however, while Chad turned round, half springing up; and his good friend, after blankness and wonder, began gaily to wave her parasol. Chad dropped afresh to his paddles and the boat headed round, amazement and pleasantry filling the air meanwhile, and relief, as Strether continued to fancy, superseding mere violence.[2]

In comparison with such work the narrative method of much of our most-admired fiction seems conventional and superficial. The characters are but lay-figures, hastily furnished with cloaks and swords, with legs and noses, from some theatrical wardrobe, and made to go through certain movements which, by a pious convention and the indulgence of the reader, are taken to mean action and emotion. Each situation is presented in merest outline, with no attempt at filling in those intimate

[2] Vol. XXII, pp. 257-258.

touches that give reality to any situation and differentiate one situation from another. In James, we have the pleasure of seeing the figures grow and fill until they reach the rounded proportions of living beings. We watch the situation opening up, depth behind depth, with calculated distances and objects so placed as to give a sense of perspective. Whatever is undertaken is done, and we are satisfied.

But if James does impress us, in this ultimate work, with his adequacy of treatment, that goes, as I have said, with the rigor of his elimination; and the very omissions contribute their element of beauty to the general effect. Certain surfaces are closely and finely covered, while others are left altogether blank, with the effect of wide significant margins. Their white spaces are something to rest and please the eye on their own account, as well as to give an accent to the shaded greys and blacks of the portions treated. There is given a pleasing sense of reserve-power, of fertile unbroken ground, particularly desirable for work that might otherwise incur the reproach of an excess of cultivation.

## (a) *The Wings of the Dove* [k]

Naturally there are, even here, varying degrees of effectiveness. The first of the three novels is distinctly less satisfying than the others. The comparative want of lucidity of "The Dove" has already been referred to the less happy management of the point of view. But that somewhat technical circumstance must be referred back still further to a fault in conception. "The Dove" seems not to have been so steadily and singly conceived as its companion works. Hence the several "blocks" of narrative,—those dealing primarily with Kate, those with

[k] See *Supplementary Notes* 1954, page 288

Milly, those with Merton, and those of which one cannot so readily declare with whom they deal primarily. These give somewhat the impression of plates separately engraved, and while concerned with related subjects, engraved each in its own style, thus leaving room for uncertainty as to their being of the same set. They have their carefully devised relation to each other, their reference back and forth; and yet when one attempts a clear statement of the general design running through the series, one is somewhat at a loss. One is at a loss whether to make the statement in terms of Kate's experience or Milly's or Merton's; and if the key lies in the community or correspondence of experience of the three characters, it is a key hard to turn in this lock. For the stubborn fact remains that at times it is one, at times it is another that is our main concern. The first book, dealing with Kate's family background, the third book, showing us Milly in the Alps, are both considerably out of focus; and in the Venetian part of the story, Milly is not sufficiently present in person, she has too passive a rôle, for a fully satisfactory development of the contrast between her and Kate which accounts for the final conversion of Merton. The account we get of his final visit at the palace is too roundabout to appease our legitimate appetite for explanations. It may appeal more to our imagination, with its mystery so maintained, but our intelligence remains unsatisfied. We make out in retrospect the process by which Merton's heart and conscience were alienated from his beloved; we make out at last the set of the main tide. But the surface is too much broken up with choppy waves and cross-currents, for us to make this out without more study than the artist can properly demand.

## (b)  *The Golden Bowl*

There is no hint of confusion or unsteadiness about the conception or execution of "The Golden Bowl."  If the two parts do show us two different faces of the medal, they are two faces that exactly correspond.  And the story could hardly have been told in any other way.  It *was* in the first part the story of the Prince, Maggie being, by the very conditions of the plot, so innocently unconscious of the situation that was growing up about her devotion to her father.  And, since the author did choose to show us the second part through the eyes of Maggie, we realize how much richer were the possibilities of that alternative.  *She* has now become the center of the web.  *She* is now the principal actor, since it has been so clearly put up to her to bring them out of the labyrinth into which she has led them.  And it is the magnificent generosity of her reactions, best exhibited from her own side, that brings about the conversion of Amerigo.

Besides, and this is perhaps the great point, the change of center from Amerigo to Maggie enables the author to show us the situation dawning slowly on the mind first of one then of another of the principal actors.  This is not a reduplication, since the position and the outlook of the two are so different that it is, subjectively, a different situation.  But it makes possible that cumulative effect that is so precious a result of this method,—that reinforcement by gradual accretion, by repeated insistence. It is like the effect of a solemn theme in music, growing in effectiveness through repetition in different keys. With the deepening of our concern, the situation grows at once more real and more urgent.  It wraps us about more and more voluminously.  It looms ever more solid and portentous.  It weighs upon us with ever increasing weight. It is here the method shows its possibilities for drama. The peculiar strength of this book lies in the long strain almost to agony of a struggle largely beneath the surface and all the more terrible for the suppression of word and gesture. This and the darkness and ugliness investing the mind of Charlotte give its sombre tone, its deep rich coloring to the work.

There is nothing sensational about this drama, since, for one thing, Maggie does not allow it to become for her an affair of the nerves. There is nothing Poësque about its sinister and mysterious notes. And yet there is some suggestion of the earlier American writer in the strange figures of speech and the romantic accessories that raise the whole to a high imaginative level. It might be the fantasy of Poe that conceived the images with which Maggie represented to herself the domestic situation she confronted.

This situation had been occupying for months and months the very center of the garden of her life, but it had reared itself there like some strange tall tower of ivory, or perhaps rather some wonderful beautiful but outlandish pagoda, a structure plated with hard bright porcelain, coloured and figured and adorned at the over-hanging eaves with silver bells that tinkled ever so charmingly when stirred by chance airs. . . . The thing might have been, by the distance at which it kept her, a Mahometan mosque, with which no base heretic could take a liberty; there so hung about it the vision of one's putting off one's shoes to enter and even verily of one's paying with one's life if found there as an interloper. . . . She had knocked . . . though she could scarce have said whether for admission or for what; she had applied her hand to a cool smooth spot and had waited to see what would happen. Something *had* happened; it was as if a sound, at her touch, after a little, had come back to her from within; a sound sufficiently suggesting that her approach had been noted.[3]

Somewhat in the Oriental vein again is the image in which Maggie, on the night of their great encounter at Fawns, pictures Charlotte hunting her as a splendid animal which has broken its bars and is dangerously at large. Throughout this scene the imagination of the author seems tuned up to the pitch of excitement of the drama. It is here we have the figure which may serve as the note for the whole second part, where Maggie realizes "the horror of finding evil seated all at its ease where she had only dreamed of good; the horror of the thing hideously *behind,* behind so much trusted, so much pretended, nobleness, cleverness, tenderness."[4]

This richness of imagery matches that of the title, and reinforces the effect made by the repeated appearance of the golden bowl, with its insistent symbolism. And these join with the special sumptuousness of the setting to heighten the total effect of richness. So that if we feel the color scheme of "The Golden Bowl" to be a sombre one, it is as the pictures of Rembrandt or Velasquez are sombre. It has a dark and lustrous splendor.

### (c)   *The Ambassadors*

"The Ambassadors" has the distinction of being at once the simplest and the most complex in design of all the studies of James. It is simple in being an uninterrupted record of the intellectual adventure of one man in the exploration of one simple human situation. The problem of Strether draws its beautiful continuous line

[3] Vol. XXIV, pp. 3-4.
[4] Id., p. 237.

through the whole series of twelve books, a line gently and at last decidedly curving, yet never broken or obscured. But the study is at the same time complex or multiple in the number of aspects under which the subject may be viewed and named.

There is most obviously the particular problem of Chad Newsome, which forms the subject upon which the intelligence of Strether is perpetually exercised, and which determines the direction of all his "adventure." Yet I should hardly call this the subject of the book: it is too particular, too limited in its *portée*. The subject proper is something more abstract: it is the matter of free intellectual exploration in general, of the open mind in contrast to the mind closed and swaddled in prejudice and narrow views. Under another aspect this is seen to be again the inveterate contrast between the cosmopolitan and the provincial, between the European and the American outlook. Strether's discovery of the open mind is his discovery of Europe. It is Europe that teaches him how many and how delicate considerations are involved in the solution of his problem,—how much depends on facts and "values" not to be lightly determined in advance. And if it is Europe that stands here for the open mind, this Europe is more specifically embodied in the most cosmopolitan of cities.

Which makes it possible to say that the subject of this study is Paris. It is Paris that gives its particular tone and color to this work. It is hard to determine the respective parts in producing this effect of Paris material and Paris spiritual. If the predominance of white in this picture and the special quality of the white always bring to mind the color of Manet, it may well be our own impressions of the physical city upon which the author draws largely for his effect. His descriptions are no more extended, I think, than is usual in the later novels, but we cannot escape the insistent note of this background, which is always so vividly and yet discreetly present. The high balconies over animated streets, the cheerful interiors of restaurant and café, domestic interiors in varied but ever exquisite taste, the more stagey *décor* of church and theatre, the light open spaces of *place* and *quai,* all keep us reminded of the physical brightness and amenity of Paris.

But one can hardly distinguish background and foreground. There is not the least suggestion—such as one may sometimes detect in the earlier novels laid in Paris—of an artificial bringing together of characters and setting, of the scenery's being let down behind the figures. It is one result of the method of James that his people seem to belong in their setting. It has had time to grow up about them; they have had time to take on the coloration of their environment. Chad and Maria Gostrey and Little Bilham, as well as Gloriani and Madame de Vionnet, have quite the air of natives; and we are invited to behold the entire process of acclimatization of Lambert Strether.

The characters are Paris spiritual. And as the physical atmosphere is one of suffused and tempered light, so the spiritual atmosphere is one of intelligence tempered with imagination. When Strether looks back so wistfully on his earlier visit to Paris, when he regrets the subsequent employments which have cheated him of "life," it is the life of the intelligence that he has in mind. He thinks of all the "movements" he has missed through his absence from the capital of the world. He thinks of all the *talk,* —talk freely and genially ranging without vulgar hin-

drance over the fields of life and art, which in such a
view are not to be divorced. He has done the best he
could for himself in Woollett. He has attached himself
to the woman of highest intelligence and most imposing
character in the place. He has published a magazine
with a green cover. But he has not enjoyed there the
intellectual amenities for which he has himself such an
unusual aptitude. He has never found intelligence
tempered with imagination, intelligence made sociable.
The errand that takes him abroad proves to be his great
occasion for making up arrears. The fortunate encounter
with Maria Gostrey opens his eyes to the possibilities of
discriminating thought on many subjects. Europe, on
her showing, appears to be an institution offering special
facilities for play of mind and imagination. The problem
confronting him is not so bald and simple as he had
been led to believe. It is a subject calling for planned
and gradual stages of approach. It has as many aspects
as a problem in metaphysics, and must be considered
again and again from one side and another. It is a
fortress of many circumvallations, or a Jericho that must
be seven times encircled before its walls will tumble to the
blowing of his trumpet. He must not let himself be
bullied or hurried into a decision by his own interest or
by any moral prejudice or anxiety. He may allow himself—what is, we feel, the luxury he most craves—that
clear impartiality of consideration which is so congenial
to the Gallic spirit.

If there is one of his characters whom we are tempted
to identify with Henry James himself, it is Lambert
Strether. His rôle calls more than any other for this
brooding exercise of a mind detached upon the human
spectacle. His maturity and independence, his sympa-

thetic and discriminating quality of mind, his patience and the unfailing satisfaction he takes in the interpretation of his subject, all make us think again and again of the author of these novels and the man who sat for Mr. Sargent's portrait. And in this story, so given shape by the intelligence of this character, James fashioned for himself the most perfect vehicle for his own habit of reflection. He is himself, like Strether, profoundly moral in his sentiment. But he and his creature both seem to feel that, if the intelligence is to be used for the eventual benefit of the moral passion, it must not be warped by any moral pressure; it must be left absolutely free to reach its own conclusions. And for both of them the greatest of pleasures is that extended rumination over life by which its true values may come to be appreciated. The tone of "The Ambassadors" is accordingly the nearest we ever come to the very tone of Henry James. It is the tone of large and sociable speculation upon human nature, a tone at once grave and easy, light and yet deep, earnest and yet free from anxiety. It is the tone, most of all, of the leisurely thinker, well-assured that maturity can be the product only of time. And what he offers us are fruits well ripened in the sun of his thought.

# CHARACTERS

Certain characters are referred to, some of them rather frequently, without naming the stories in which they appear. The following partial list may be helpful to readers who are not familiar with all the stories:

Isabel Archer, "The Portrait of a Lady."
Mrs. Assingham, "The Golden Bowl."
Nanda Brookenham, "The Awkward Age."
Kate Croy, "The Wings of the Dove."
Merton Densher, "The Wings of the Dove."
Mrs. Gereth, "The Spoils of Poynton."
Maria Gostrey, "The Ambassadors."
Rowland Mallett, "Roderick Hudson."
Mitchy, "The Awkward Age."
Gabriel Nash, "The Tragic Muse."
Christopher Newman, "The American."
Hyacinth Robinson, "The Princess Casamassima."
Charlotte Stant, "The Golden Bowl."
Lambert Strether, "The Ambassadors."
Milly Theale, "The Wings of the Dove."
Maggie Verver, "The Golden Bowl."
Fleda Vetch, "The Spoils of Poynton."

## BIBLIOGRAPHICAL NOTE

A comprehensive bibliography of James is not called for within the scope of this work. There are already in print two satisfactory bibliographies, up to and including the year 1905: one, compiled by Mr. Frederick Allen King, included as an appendix in Miss Elizabeth Luther Cary's "The Novels of Henry James" (Putnam, 1905); the other, by Mr. Le Roy Phillips, more complete and making up an entire volume, published in 1906 by Houghton, Mifflin in this country and by Constable in England. There is also a list of the first editions of publications in book form, both English and American, appended to the volume on Henry James in the "Writers of the Day" series (Holt, 1916) written by Miss Rebecca West. It is sufficient for the purpose of this study to include a list of books by Henry James which have appeared since 1905, not including reprints, together with a chronological list of all the novels, indicating their first appearance in magazines and in book form, both in America and in England. This latter will be of assistance to the reader in tracing the progress of James in working out his "method." In both lists I include certain books not yet published in America at the time of printing. I have had frequent occasion to mention the New York Edition of the Novels and Tales published during 1907-1909 by Scribner in this country and by Macmillan in England. Besides the studies of James by Miss Cary and Miss West already mentioned, there is one by Mr. Ford Madox Hueffer, Secker, 1914, and Dodd, 1916. "French Poets and Novelists" and "Partial Portraits," volumes of critical essays by James, were first published by Macmillan in, respectively, 1878 and 1888.

## List of Books by James Published since 1905

The American Scene. 1907. Harper, New York; Chapman and Hall, London.

Views and Reviews. Introduction by Le Roy Phillips. 1908. Ball Publishing Co., Boston.

Italian Hours. Illustrated by Joseph Pennell. 1909. Houghton, Mifflin, Boston and New York; Heinemann, London.

The Finer Grain. 1910. Scribner, New York; Methuen, London. This volume includes the following tales: The Velvet Glove, Mora Montravers, A Round of Visits, Crapy Cornelia, The Bench of Desolation.

The Outcry. 1911. Scribner, New York; Methuen, London.

The Henry James Year Book. Selected and arranged by Evelyn Garnaut Smalley. 1911, R. G. Badger, Boston; 1912, Dent, London.

A Small Boy and Others. 1913. Scribner, New York; Macmillan, London.

Notes of a Son and Brother. 1914. Scribner, New York; Macmillan, London.

Notes on Novelists: with some other notes. 1914. Scribner, New York; Dent, London.

Pictures and other Passages from Henry James. Selected by Ruth Head. 1916. Chatto and Windus.

The Ivory Tower. 1917. Collins, London; Scribner, New York.

The Sense of the Past. 1917. Collins, London; Scribner, New York.

The Middle Years. 1917. Collins, London; Scribner,
New York.


CHRONOLOGICAL LIST OF THE NOVELS OF JAMES.

(Stars are attached to the titles of novels not included
in the New York Edition. The last three appeared too
late for inclusion; in the case of all the others, exclusion
from the canon must have been deliberate.)

1871.     *Watch and Ward. Atlantic Monthly, August
              to December.
                —1878, Houghton, Osgood (present pub-
              lisher Houghton, Mifflin).
1875.     Roderick Hudson. Atlantic Monthly, January
              to December.
                —1876, James R. Osgood (present publisher
              Houghton, Mifflin), Boston; 1879, Macmil-
              lan, London.
1876–77.  The American. Atlantic Monthly, June, 1876,
              to May, 1877.
                —1877, James R. Osgood (present publisher
              Houghton, Mifflin), Boston; Ward, Lock,
              London.
1878.     *The Europeans. Atlantic Monthly, July to
              October.
                —1878, Houghton, Osgood (present pub-
              lisher Houghton, Mifflin), Boston; Macmil-
              lan, London.
1879–80.  *Confidence. Scribner's Monthly, August, 1879,
              to January, 1880.
                —1880, Houghton, Osgood (present pub-
              lisher Houghton, Mifflin), Boston; Chatto
              and Windus, London.

1880.　　*Washington Square. Cornhill Magazine, June to November, and Harper's Monthly, July to December.

　　　　—1881, Harper, New York; the same, together with The Pension Beaurepas and A Bundle of Letters, two volumes, Macmillan, London.

1880–81.　The Portrait of a Lady. Macmillan's Magazine, October, 1880, to November, 1881, and Atlantic Monthly, November, 1880, to December, 1881.

　　　　—1881, three volumes, Macmillan, London; one volume, Houghton, Mifflin, Boston and New York.

1885–86. *The Bostonians. Century Magazine, February, 1885, to February, 1886.

　　　　—1886, three volumes, Macmillan, London and New York.

1885–86.　The Princess Casamassima. Atlantic Monthly, September, 1885, to October, 1886.

　　　　—1886, three volumes, Macmillan, London and New York.

1889–90.　The Tragic Muse. Atlantic Monthly, January, 1889, to May, 1890.

　　　　—1890, two volumes, Houghton, Mifflin, Boston and New York; three volumes, Macmillan, London.

1896.　　The Spoils of Poynton. This novel appeared under the title of "The Old Things" in the Atlantic Monthly, April to October.

　　　　—1897, Houghton, Mifflin, Boston and New York; Heinemann, London.

1896.      *The Other House. One volume, Macmillan,
           New York; two volumes, Heinemann, Lon-
           don.

1897.      What Maisie Knew. The Chap Book, Jan-
           uary 15 to August 1, and The New Review,
           February to July.
           —1897, Herbert S. Stone, Chicago and New
           York; Heinemann, London.

1898–99.   The Awkward Age. Harper's Weekly, Octo-
           ber 1, 1898, to January 7, 1899.
           —1899, Harper, New York; Heinemann,
           London.

1901.      *The Sacred Fount. Scribner, New York;
           Methuen, London.

1902.      The Wings of the Dove. Two volumes, Scrib-
           ner, New York; one volume, Constable,
           London.

1903.      The Ambassadors. North American Review,
           January to December.
           —1903, Harper, New York; Methuen, Lon-
           don.

1904.      The Golden Bowl. Two volumes, Scribner,
           New York; one volume, Methuen, London.

1911.      *The Outcry. Scribner, New York; Methuen,
           London.

1917.      *The Ivory Tower. Collins, London; Scribner,
           New York.

1917.      *The Sense of the Past. Collins, London;
           Scribner, New York.

# INDEX

Novels, tales, books of criticism and reminiscence, referred to, alluded to, or quoted. Figures in italics refer to passages in which the story is taken up for particular consideration.

# SUPPLEMENT TO BIBLIOGRAPHICAL NOTE
## 1954

The Le Roy Phillips bibliography referred to in the original note was republished in extended and elaborated form in 1930 by Coward: McCann, in New York.

Lyon N. Richardson, in his "Henry James: Representative Selections," in the American Writers Series, American Book Company, c.1941, has two highly useful bibliographical tables. The one is a Chronological Table and Selected Bibliography of the Works of James, coming down to 1934. The other is a Bibliography, consisting of (I) Selected Bibliographies, (II) Selected Biographical Works, and (III) Biographical and Critical Studies. This third table, comprising nearly three hundred items, is reprinted in F. W. Dupee's "The Question of Henry James," Holt, New York, 1945.

Two volumes of James's plays, "Theatricals," were published in 1894-95, in London and New York. In 1949 appeared "The Complete Plays of Henry James," edited by Leon Edel, with an introductory study of "Henry James: The Dramatic Years," Lippincott, Philadelphia and New York.

As for the short stories, the "Uniform Edition of the Tales of Henry James," in 14 vols., was published by Martin Secker, London, 1915-19. Separate collections of selected short stories have appeared between 1918 and 1940, including "The Turn of the Screw and the Lesson of the Master," with an introduction by Heywood Broun, New York, Modern Library, 1930.

The most comprehensive collection of all his fiction is "The Novels and Stories of Henry James, New and Complete Edition," 35 vols., Macmillan, London, 1921-23.

During the period of the great revival of Henry James, in the 1940's, a considerable number of the novels have been reprinted separately, or together with certain of the longer tales. Among these are the following:

The Great Short Novels, ed. with introduction by Philip Rahv, Dial Press, New York, 1944.

The Bostonians, Dial Press, New York; Sidgwick and Jackson, London, c.1945.

Selected Novels, Caxton House, New York, c.1946 (includes The American, The European, and two shorter stories).

The Other House, with introduction by Leon Edel, New Directions, Norfolk, Conn., 1947.

Roderick Hudson, J. Lehmann, London, 1947.

The Princess Casamassima, with introduction by Lionel Trilling, Macmillan, New York, 1948.

The Tragic Muse, R. Hart-Davis, London, 1948.

The Ambassadors, Hamish Hamilton, London, 1948.

The American, with introduction by Joseph Warren Beach, Rinehart, New York, c.1950.

Certain others of the novels have long been separately available in low-priced editions, mainly for college use.

During the same period, many selections of James's tales have appeared, including the following:

Ten Short Stories, selected with introduction by Michael Swan, J. Lehmann, London, 1941.

Stories of Writers and Artists, ed. with introduction by
    F. O. Matthiessen, New Directions, New York, 1944.
The Short Stories, ed. with introduction by Clifton Fadi-
    man, Random House, New York, c.1945.
Fourteen Stories, ed. David Garnett, R. Hart-Davis, Lon-
    don, 1947.
Selected Tales, Richards Press, London, c.1947.
The Lesson of the Master and Other Stories, J. Lehmann,
    London, 1948.
The Ghostly Tales of Henry James, ed. with introduction
    by Leon Edel, Rutgers University Press, New Bruns-
    wick, N. J., 1948.
The Reverberator, with a critical note by Simon Nowell-
    Smith, R. Hart-Davis, London, 1949.
Eight Uncollected Tales, ed. with introduction by Edna
    Kenton, Rutgers University Press, New Brunswick,
    N. J., 1950.

# SUPPLEMENTARY NOTES 1954

(a)   In accordance with my decision not to *revise* the text of this book, I have here and elsewhere retained the polite "Mr." in referring to Henry James, as I have in referring to John Galsworthy, Thomas Hardy, George Moore, and other contemporary writers.   I comfort myself with the thought that this will not merely lighten the task of the type-setter, but will preserve a certain quaint formalism of tone suited to the original date of publication.   For similar reasons I have left "an historical subject" on page 11, though my present taste, with the support of Fowler, inclines me to "a historical subject."

(b)   These prefaces were reproduced in "The Novels and Stories of Henry James, New and Complete Edition," 35 vols., Macmillan, London, 1921-23.   They are also accessible to the reader, still more conveniently, in a single volume, "The Art of the Novel," edited by R. P. Blackmur, Scribner's, New York, 1934..

(c)   This is, I now realize, a highly personal judgment. Perhaps it may be allowed to pass as a convenient assumption for a critic whose lifelong interest has been greater in the novel as a form than in the short story, and who would like to set some limits to his undertaking.   Since the notable revival of interest in James beginning about 1940, many collections of his short stories have appeared, and it is not improbable that he is more widely known through them than through his longer stories. In my present Introduction, I have taken occasion to illustrate certain features of his art by reference to his tales as well as to the novels.

(d) This was the period in which James was busy writing plays, of which he published two volumes in 1894-1895, and vainly hoping for the stage success of the dramatized "American" and his original play, "Guy Domville." I refer in my Introduction to Leon Edel's very thorough account of this phase of James's career, and to the lessons for the writing of fiction that James derived from his practice in writing plays.

(e) It appears that there were other than artistic reasons for not including "The Bostonians" in the New York Edition. They had reference perhaps to the unpopularity of that book because of its supposed anti-feminism and satirical treatment of well-known Boston figures. Mr. Dupee says: *"The Bostonians was left out less by James's wish than by that of the publisher, and with the understanding that it might come in later if the success of the Edition warranted its expansion."* (p.278)

(f) Studies of revisions made by James for the New York Edition have been published, among others, by Helene Harvitt, "How Henry James revised *Roderick Hudson,*" PMLA, March, 1924; by Raymond D. Havens, "The Revision of *Roderick Hudson,*" PMLA, June, 1925; by F. O. Matthiessen in his "Henry James: the Major Phase," 1944 (revision of "The Portrait of a Lady"); and by C. Royal Gettmann, "Henry James's Revision of

*The American,"* in American Literature, January, 1945.
Mr. Richardson, in his table of Biographical and Critical
Studies refers to articles by Robert Herrick which contain "important references to the changes in James's style
when he began dictation."

(g)   The Prefaces are very illuminating on this subject.  But great floods of further light have been turned
upon it by the publication, in 1947, under the editorship
of F. O. Matthiessen and Kenneth B. Murdock, of "The
Notebooks of Henry James."  See my Introduction.

(h)   It is now taken for granted by James's biographers that the dear friend whose image was his main suggestion for Milly Theale was his cousin Minny Temple.
See, for example, Dupee, pp. 232, 248.

(i)   In his volume, "The Great Tradition," F. R. Leavis prints as an appendix James's "Daniel Deronda: A
Conversation," dating from 1876.  The characters in this
dialogue are neatly and amusingly discriminated, and with
their several contrasting views, produce among them an
acute and balanced criticism of George Eliot's work.  One
realizes that, in a period more favorable to it, James might
have made a very great success of the outmoded genre of
the imaginary conversation.

(j)   The statement is made rather strong here, and
the case somewhat over-simplified, in order to underline
the *peculiarities* of James's method of telling his story.
As the reader goes on, he will understand that I do not
mean we have no sense, in the story, of going somewhere.

We do have that sense strongly, and are much concerned with where it is we are going. In that way there is plenty of "story-interest."

(k) I trust that in my present Introduction I have made due amends for my earlier underestimation of this work.

(l) It now appears that this story was originally intended for a play. The Notebooks show that in 1893 he sketched a play in three acts with a particular actor in mind for the title role. After the project of the play was abandoned, he used the plot for a serial novel published in the popular Illustrated London News. James thought it was sufficiently melodramatic to "capture the public of the *Illustrated News.*" In 1908 James took up his twelve-years-old novel, and dictated the scenario of a play; the following year he wrote the play, but his hopes of having it produced were in the end disappointed. See Edel's Foreword to "The Other House" in "The Complete Plays," pp.677-9.

(m) In my Introduction I have discussed in more detail the elements of the "realistic" and the "romantic" in James.

(n) This does not of course mean that James himself is ethically neutral, or that moral attitudes and valuations do not make themselves felt as an emanation from the whole body of his work, or, for that matter, from each separate story in its final impact. It means that as an artist James does not formulate his moral attitudes, like a

Thackeray or a George Eliot, in specific commentary on the characters and their behavior; that he leaves his characters to work out their ethical problems for themselves; and that the moral of the tale appears only in the total movement and upshot of the dramatic action. It is, I think, a failure to appreciate this artistic principle that often leads brilliant critics like Van Wyck Brooks and F. R. Leavis to find him guilty of inconsistencies or lapses of moral insight where what is really manifest is the simple dramatic objectivity of presentation. But this point I have sufficiently labored in my Introduction.

(o)  Nothing, that is, except *plays*. Since my book was written, Leon Edel and others have opened up to us the long and painful chapter of James's play-writing and made clear how much importance James attributed to his training in stage techniques. This should be taken into account along with what is said here of the influence of the short-story upon the longer form.

(p)  "The Outcry" was written as a play for a repertory company in 1909 on invitation of the American producer, Charles Frohman. The hopes of producing it finally collapsed in 1910. During the following year James turned it into a novel, which ran through several editions. After James's death it was produced by the Incorporated Stage Society, but without *éclat*. See Edel's Foreword to the play, pp.761-5.